Realms of Knowledge: Academic Departments in Secondary Schools

Education Policy Perspectives

Realms of Knowledge: Academic Departments in Secondary Schools

Leslie Santee Siskin

 The Falmer Press

(A Member of the Taylor & Francis Group)

Washington, D.C. • London

UK   The Falmer Press, 4 John St, London, WC1N 2ET
USA   The Falmer Press, Taylor & Francis Inc., 1900 Frost Road, Suite
      101, Bristol, PA 19007

First published 1994

A catalogue record for this book is available from the British Library

Library of Congress Cataloguing in Publication Data are available on request

ISBN 0 7507 0278 8 (Cased)
ISBN 0 7507 0279 6 (Paper)

Jacket design by Caroline Archer
Typeset in 11/12pt Bembo by
Graphicraft Typesetters Ltd, Hong Kong

Printed in Great Britain by Burgess Science Press, Basingstoke on paper which has a specified pH value on final paper manufacture of not less than 7.5 and is therefore 'acid free'.

Contents

Contents

Acknowledgments

Sometimes the light's all shining on me,
Other times I can barely see
Lately it occurs to me
What a long, strange trip it's been. (Garcia, Lesh, Weir, Hunter)

The experience of writing this manuscript has indeed been a long, strange, trip, spanning several years and thousands of miles, two coasts and two careers. It has been a trip that taught me much, not only about departments, teachers, and high schools, but also about the demands of academic research, and the value of colleagues — however they are connected.

Milbrey McLaughlin, as my dissertation advisor and director of the Context Center, has been particularly important to teaching me about both. Her insights about the importance of departments and her conviction that teachers are worth listening to shaped this research from the beginning, while her careful readings and extraordinary support sustained me through the end.

My debt to the other members of my dissertation committee is also substantial. Jim March offered a wealth of expertise on organizational behavior and David Tyack on the history of schools. Extended conversations with both of them consistently provided me with provocative questions, new insights, and a renewed sense of the pleasures of doing research. Larry Cuban also carefully read through the manuscript, challenged assumptions, and provided valuable advice.

The Center for Research on the Context of Secondary School Teaching, through a grant from the Office of Educational Research and Improvement (No. G0087C0235) provided funding for this project, access to the schools, and a rich bank of additional data and analyses to draw upon. Teachers and administrators opened up their schools, classrooms, and lives, and then patiently translated the meanings of their work. And as my father first taught me, you can learn a lot by just hanging around a school and listening. Center researchers enhanced my understanding of how high schools work, and how we can study them, in ways too numerous to adequately acknowledge. I owe particular thanks to Joan Talbert, for her ongoing curiosity about professional communities and her contagious enthusiasm for discovering patterns, and to Marian Eaton, who devised the computer program to create such dramatic representations of departmental networks. Nina Bascia, my traveling companion through much of this trip, shared field-sites and stories, data and friendship.

Friendships formed at Stanford have continued to provide emotional and intellectual sustenance. As an extended support group, Nina Bascia, Beverly Carter, Berta Laden, Pat McDonough, and Marc Ventresca readily offered encouragement and sympathy when they were needed, gave careful criticism to emerging ideas, and rescued me from the computer lab.

Outside the university, this research effort has brought me into contact with a number of people who have been more than helpful. Judith Warren Little not only studies the potential of professional support among colleagues but lives it; she has been a generous critic, colleague, and friend. Stephen Ball, Ivor Goodson, Andy Hargreaves, and Ann Lieberman, whose scholarly work on subjects and teachers opened up new ways of understanding departments, also opened new professional and personal paths, showing me what the notion of 'invisible college' colleagues could really mean.

Closer to home, I am grateful to my family, who maintained their patience and supplied me with music to write by. Clifford Siskin has been a challenging reader throughout, and our debates have led both of us to new ways of understanding the work of writing, and the organization of knowledge — and to discover the economy of words. Finally, I would like to thank Corin, Nathaniel, and Johanna, who put data into the database, numbers onto pages, and writing into perspective.

Leslie Santee Siskin
April 1993

List of Figures and Tables

List of Figures and Tables

The Realm of Knowledge

It is still standing — the little red schoolhouse where I, a little girl barely fourteen, began my career as a teacher; still standing, though with sunken roof and broken windows, a solitary reminder of the days of long ago . . . I did not limit the field of instruction to matters Biblical, attempting rather to cover the entire realm of knowledge in art, science, history, literature, and what you will. (Lucia Downing, teaching in 1885)

They haven't moved my room. I'm not in the English wing. So I'm kind of out of the realm. (Joan Frances, teaching in 1988)

Roughly one hundred years separate the experiences of these two teachers. In that time, the context of teaching has changed dramatically, particularly in the relatively new institution of the American high school. The numbers and characteristics of students who attend school, and for how long, the physical and organizational structures, the activities of district, state, and federal policy makers — all converge to alter the context of teaching in secondary schools. What is it like to teach in a high school today, and how is it different from Lucia Downing's time?

One important difference lies in the emergence and adoption of the departmental structure. For between the statements of the two teachers above, quietly but significantly, the location of the 'realm of knowledge' has shifted, and its meaning has altered, in ways that substantially change what it means to be a teacher.

The purpose of this study was to explore that change, and what it means today to be a teacher inside, or 'kind of outside the realm' of knowledge which constitutes the academic department.

From Downing's Realm to Frances' Realms

It was in 1885 that Lucia Downing began teaching in the 'Keeler Deestrict School' in Vermont. At 14 she was young, even for a time when young females were common in teaching. But she had, along with her older sister, passed the qualifying test: an exam which began with Arithmetic and continued through Grammar, Geography, History and Civil Government, and Physiology (all of which she would be expected to teach), and finally Theory and School Management — which involved control of students, 'ventilation and temperature'. The authority who read her exam and certified her entry into the field was the superintendent: 'In our little town, the duties of the school superintendent were not burdensome, nor the position lucrative, and for many years our superintendent was the village doctor, who was probably the best-educated man in town, not even excepting the minister!' (Downing, 1950, p. 28).

At the end of the year it was this superintendent who came to hear and judge the recitations of her students, on a public occasion where pupils were to provide evidence not only of their learning, but also of her successful teaching, in front of

> a vast and terrifying audience having assembled — entirely out of proportion to the number of pupils. There were fond parents, and grandparents, and aunts and uncles and cousins thrice removed. (p. 35)

To this end Lucia Downing remembers devising

> what I thought was a wonderful set of 'Instructive Questions and Answers' suggested by a *New England Primer* that had come down in our family, but I did not limit the field of instruction to matters Biblical, attempting rather to cover the entire realm of knowledge in art, science, history, literature, and what you will. (p. 33)

The students performed well,

> though if I had made a slip and asked the question out of order, the results might have been disastrous. They might have said that Vermont is the largest state in the union, or that George Washington had sailed the ocean blue in 1492. (p. 35)

While Downing may have had doubts about her students' ability to remember their facts out of sequence, she had little doubt about what it was that she — with only the help of a few textbooks — was expected to do: to 'cover the entire realm of knowledge'.

In 1988, Joan Frances described her experience in teaching in the Burton District in Michigan, to researchers with the CRC project on secondary schools.[1] Like Lucia Downing, Joan Frances began teaching while still in her teens: 'it was about my junior year . . . one of the nuns [was] sick, and they asked me would I take over a classroom. They thought I did such a tremendous job [that] I stayed for the week.' Like Downing, Frances found that, at least at the start of her career, 'I think at that particular time teaching was a good profession for a woman.' Also like Downing, Frances described herself as somewhat of a generalist, a reading teacher prepared to cover a variety of subjects: 'My major is in sociology, minor in political science, and I have a master's degree in counseling and reading.' She operates in a manner that bears some similarity to Downing's one-room school: 'I conduct my class a little bit different than the other ones . . . I have five different groups and they all go on at one time.' In her classroom, students go at different levels, and in different subjects, with some working on 'drawing conclusions' and others diagramming sentences, some reading science textbooks and others novels.

There are remarkable parallels between the stories of the two women, in how they chose, began, and conducted their teaching. And many observers have presented a strong case for the argument that remarkably little has changed in teaching over the past hundred years. Sirotnik (1983), reporting on the Study of Schooling's data from over 1,000 elementary and secondary classrooms, observed that in terms of the process of teaching and learning, classroom practice 'appears to be one of the most consistent and persistent phenomena known in the social and behavioral sciences' (p. 17; see also Boyer, 1983; Cuban, 1984; Sizer, 1984).

Yet while much remains the same, the contexts in which Frances and thousands of other high school teachers work has changed dramatically since Downing's time. The very fact that Frances teaches in a 'high school', for example, was an opportunity rare in Downing's time — and non-existent in her rural area. In the decades which separate their teaching, schools have moved fully to a formalized and graded system, with high schools spinning off into separate buildings and growing to what would have been to Downing unimaginable size and complexity.

Downing's recollections are particularly enlightening because she, as a new teacher, came roughly on the 'cusp' of a changing system — at the beginning of a new era in the organization and staffing of schools as well as at a time of dramatic change in what had been a long-standing configuration of knowledge and subjects. And the changes in both categories combine to radically alter the meaning of the term 'realm of knowledge', as departmentalization reifies and literalizes the realms of academic subjects.

Lucia Downing talks about the 'entire realm of knowledge'. In her use the term is singular: an image of the organization of knowledge as a single continuous entity that students (at least some students) would gradually, and partially, come to know. It echoes the unified, but hierarchically linked, model of the subjects in medieval universities, the 'common course of education' which 'offered a unification of the medieval universe of thought', and through which a single master would lead his students (Perkin, 1984). This common course was a pyramidal ladder with the liberal arts at the bottom, theology at the top. Careers were linked not so much to which field one studied, but to how far one had progressed on the ladder. Teachers had typically stopped on a low rung, ministers at the very top; in describing her superintendent as 'probably the best-educated man in town', Downing makes the point that she was 'not even excepting the minister!' (p. 28).

By Frances' time, the dominant model is quite different: the organization of universities, and increasingly of high schools, reflects modern understandings of knowledge as distinct fields, with, in her usage, discrete and plural 'realms' into which knowledge has been compartmentalized. Students choose among the fields, rather than moving up through them. These are separate and separated bodies of knowledge, each specialized discipline with its own 'territory', and populated by its own 'tribe' (Becher, 1989; also Clark, 1987; Geertz, 1983). For Frances, the desired 'realm' is the knowledge territory of the English department, where she would share subject matter in common with her colleagues.

Second, the 'realm' Frances refers to is also the literal territory of the English department: the set of classrooms clustered together in one wing of her school. This realm is external, physical, spatial — a place she can go (or could if time and distance would allow) to be with the other members of her disciplinary 'tribe' and to share materials, ideas, and support. For Downing, the place where the knowledge is located was largely internal; she would 'cover the entire realm' out of the knowledge she herself possessed; in her school there were few materials, only one room, and no colleagues of any kind.

These differences in the use of the word realm, then, point to substantial and substantive differences in the contexts in which these two teachers teach, differences which alter the meaning even of the parallels between them. Being a reading teacher, and a bit of a generalist, is a similarity which epitomizes difference: it creates problems in 1988 which Lucia Downing could hardly have imagined, for Frances has not only to teach her classes, but to fit into the larger system of the comprehensive high school, and the operations of the school have changed substantially. Her place in that system is unclear, since both her formal and professional identification is as an English teacher but her physical location is not. Highlander, far from being a 'little red school house', is a large urban high school, an imposing three-story building housing 100 teachers in wings designated by academic subject. And when Frances talks about 'realm' of knowledge she refers not only to the kinds of knowledge she hopes to impart, but to what has become the literal territory of those categories — the physical domains of the academic departments. Although she is officially a member of the English department, her classroom is in the Social Studies wing. It is in talking about the difficulties of finding time for access to the English wing, about the physical distance which reduces the collegial support and participation in planning which full membership should provide when she replies 'I'm still in the Social Studies department . . . they haven't moved my room. I'm not in the English wing, so I'm kind of out of the realm.'

Between the careers of these two teachers the realm of knowledge has moved from being a part of Downing — she will 'cover the entire realm' out of the knowledge she herself possesses — to something Frances wants to be part of, something she finds missing because of the location of her classroom. The realm of knowledge, reified in the formation of academic departments, has multiplied in number and created boundaries which divide knowledge into disciplines and schools into subunits, has populated them with specialized teachers, laid claim to territories in particular physical space, and from Frances' perspective, created a 'realm' in which membership is important. What is it she feels is missing? What would full participation afford? What does it mean to be inside a department, to be one of the inhabitants of these realms of knowledge within the modern high school?

The purpose of this study is to explore those changes, to look at the academic department as a context for teaching in three contemporary comprehensive high schools. It is an exploratory study, for while the department has become a familiar feature, it has remained largely an unstudied one. But as the teachers in this study tell and demonstrate, the departmental context is 'very crucial in a high school'.

From their stories, four critical aspects of the department emerge: 1) it represents a strong boundary in dividing the school; 2) it provides a primary site for social interaction, and for professional identity and community; 3) it has, as an administrative unit, considerable discretion over the micro-political decisions affecting what and how teachers teach; and 4) as a knowledge category it influences the decisions and shapes the actions of those who inhabit its realm.

Before turning to these four critical aspects of departments, and the stories teachers tell of what their lives are like inside and on the edges of these realms of knowledge, the first two chapters provide background information on what we know from existing literature about subject departments. Chapter 1 examines both the relative invisibility of the high school department as an object of study in educational research and recent suggestions of why it might be important to now illuminate these contexts. Chapter 2 explores the historical evidence on where, when, and how departments came to quietly constitute realms of knowledge in contemporary high schools.

Notes

1   The Center for Research on the Context of Secondary School Teaching (CRC) has been engaged in a five-year study of American high schools, supported by the US Department of Education. As is discussed more fully in Chapter 3, the research on which this study is based was conducted as part of that larger project, and all sites and participants here are identified by CRC pseudonyms and codes.

Chapter 1

The Invisibility of Departments

The subject department has been strangely ignored as an object of study both from the perspectives of the sociology of the school and the sociology of the curriculum. (Ball and Lacey, 1980)

A lot of people believe that I do nothing. 'You're not in a real department; what do you do?' (ESL (English as a Second Language) resource teacher, 1988)

What is it that we need to know to understand teachers and teaching in high schools today? In 1988 the Center for Research on the Context of Secondary School Teaching, the larger project sponsoring this study, held its first meeting with the teachers who had agreed to sit on an advisory board and to help a team of researchers address that question. In that informal conversation the topic of departments appeared and reappeared with remarkable frequency, for while the subject department may have been 'strangely ignored' from the perspectives of educational researchers, when teachers themselves portray the world of the high school the subject department is a highly visible feature. It appears prominently in their depictions of what matters to teaching, both as subject — it is what they teach — and as organizational setting — it is where and with whom that teaching takes place.

In their first introductions, all of the consulting teachers invariably identified themselves by their subjects: 'I'm an English teacher at x'; 'I teach Social Studies.' They talked of what their schools were like, but qualified their statements as perhaps only true within their own departments, since that was the only part of the school they 'really see'. One teacher, who had recently moved, explained that to choose among several offers he spent enough time visiting each site to give him 'a sense of the department'. For him, it was primarily the department, rather than the school, that he understood to be where — and with whom — he would work.

Departments were also highly visible in discussions of colleagues, and of collegial efforts to improve or sustain practice — support which all of these teachers named as essential to being a good teacher. A Math teacher reported that her school was drawing on community input for improving curriculum, but that 'weak departments are having a horrible time' working together — and departments were the units held responsible for collectively analyzing data and setting goals. An English teacher talked of the collaborative planning of her own 'very close' department, and of the support these colleagues provided for her own efforts. While she noted that it would be a 'mistake to talk about the department as a unified whole', she observed that 'departments have a *gestalt* about the way they operate', in which they can differ markedly, even within the same school. Another veteran, on the other hand, did talk about his Social Studies department as a unified whole, of the deliberate 'team effort' it had taken to build that sense of cohesive community, and of the exciting results. His example was, the English teacher suggested, perhaps exceptional: 'I've heard of it myself; it's a unique and famous department.' Whether understood as close or unified, strong or weak, for all of these teachers the department appeared as a critically important context for their professional identity, collegial relations, and practice. They work in departments.

No statement or description, however, revealed the presence and significance of the department more vividly than the one cited above, from a resource teacher who does not have a 'real' department in which to work, and therefore finds her work open to question. Even among her colleagues, in an urban school where reaching students with limited English has been identified as a major challenge, this ESL teacher reported that 'a lot of people believe that I do nothing.' So inextricably linked are teaching and departments that her high school colleagues have no frame of reference for understanding what teaching is if it is not done in a department: 'You're not in a real department; what do you do?'

From the perspectives of these high school teachers, the department is highly visible, and central to understanding the complex workings of their schools: important to who they are, consequential in affecting what they do, and largely determining how their work is perceived. For them, as the resource teacher's statement illustrates, the puzzle was to understand what high school teaching would mean if it were not done in a real department.

For the researchers in the room, the obverse was true — the puzzle was to understand what it means to teach 'in a real department' at the high school level. In the literature on schools, the subject department has been largely invisible, or, as Ball and Lacey suggest, 'strangely ignored', perhaps because to researchers from universities it is too familiar to warrant much attention. One study of successful schools, for example, sums up the influence of departments in a succinct sentence: 'Department chairs and teachers also played significant leadership roles' (Wilson and Corcoran, 1988, p. 58). After listening to these teachers, it did appear 'strange' that research has largely 'ignored' the issues of how, or when departments play leadership roles, or with what consequences. But from the research perspective, high school teaching has not been framed as being done in departments — real or otherwise. The result is that we know little about what it is that teachers do within a real department, let alone what it means to be without one.

Invisible Divisions

The organization of high schools into the 'realms of knowledge' of subject departments is now a nearly universal feature of the 22,000 secondary schools across the United States. In schools of widely varying location, size, mission, and governance style, highly standardized departmental labels divide teachers and courses along academic lines. So well institutionalized have they become that we think we know them well. A case description for Ernest Boyer's study of high schools, for example, can refer to 'generalized stereotypes about the character of departments' — biology and math being more conservative than English and social studies — 'that seem at least half true' (Lightfoot, 1985, p. 260). The arrangement into departments has been so taken for granted, however, that we know almost nothing about it beyond our 'generalized stereotypes', and even those may be inadequate: in how many high schools, for example, would biology have its own department? The empirical evidence and theoretical models to provide more than half-truths are notably absent from the literature on American high schools. In one of the few studies to directly engage the topic, Susan Moore Johnson (1990a) describes the department as a 'fundamental' part of the school which 'deserve[s] close scrutiny', but which researchers have long disregarded (p. 168).

First appearing at the turn into the twentieth century, primarily as a term for programmatic divisions, departments designating subject content had become a highly standardized arrangement by the 1930s. In sharp contrast to the 'mothering plan' of a single teacher for all subjects in a given elementary class (Kilpatrick, 1905, p. 475), departmentalizing content along disciplinary lines helped to reconfigure secondary schools as 'the people's college' (Tyack, 1974, p. 57). The resulting configuration lies between the model of the elementary school (where teachers are teachers, students are students, and the key identifier is grade), and that of the college (where key identifiers for both faculty and students are subjects); in high school, students are organized by grade across subjects, but teachers by subject across grades.

Educational research, however, rarely acknowledges this hybrid configuration; elementary and secondary schools appear as a single or-ganizational topic and teachers as a single occupational category (quite distinct from colleges and 'faculty'). Research titles reflect the assump-tion of K-12 education as a unitary area of study: we read of 'effective schools' (Edmonds, 1979), of the 'schoolteacher' (Lortie, 1975), of 'teachers at work' (Johnson, 1990b). Only rarely does someone suggest that 'prescriptions for effective elementary schools don't fit secondary schools' (Firestone and Herriott, 1982).

The dominant metaphors are of schools as factories, and teachers as isolated individuals — images both vivid and compelling. Dan Lortie (1975) called them 'egg crate schools', with 'cellular patterns' of sepa-rated classrooms staffed by isolated teachers. Mary Metz (1990) talks of teaching as 'parallel piecework', where teachers work side by side, but alone. Theodore Sizer (1984) provides a more regal but still isolating image of the teacher 'working alone in the castle of one's classroom' (see also Cusick, 1983; Little, 1987; Johnson, 1990a). Even when using the alternative metaphor, developed by March and Olsen (1976) and Weick (1976), of 'organized anarchies' which has been widely used to analyze the workings of 'semi-autonomous departments' within uni-versities, researchers looking at schools retain the notion that 'instruc-tion is usually carried out by single teachers in isolated classrooms' (Firestone and Herriott, 1982, p. 43). Such conceptual images demand studies at the individual or school level; they have largely precluded the questions about internal differentiation or external linkages which might bring departments into focus. High school teachers may identify them-selves, and be identified, as subject specialists (Lortie, 1975; Lieberman and Miller, 1984; McLaughlin, 1987; Smetherham, 1979; Tucker, 1986), yet the organizational *structure* which differentiates them by subject groups within smaller units of colleagues has remained largely invisible.

At this particular time that structure may need to be made visible, not only to gain a better understanding of how teachers themselves see and experience their work, but because as the subjects teachers teach, as the colleagues with whom they work most closely, and as an or-ganizational structure, the department sits squarely at the intersection of three areas of activity in reform and research efforts. And it is only at the point of their intersection, only in looking at the subject depart-ment, that the interactions, and potential conflicts, of these efforts become apparent. Efforts to strengthen subject knowledge, for exam-ple, without considering the organizational realities of departmental-ized schools, risk making some teachers even more 'real' than others; efforts which aim at restructuring, without attending to the firmly entrenched identities of subject specialists, risk unexpected conflict and resistance.

The value placed on subject knowledge, particularly for the aca-demic subjects of 'real departments', grows increasingly important in reforms aimed at teacher preparation. In calling for 'alternate' routes to certification, particularly for those with expertise in math or science, for example, the federal government is privileging disciplinary knowledge over pedagogical training. The enthusiastic response to the 'Teach for America' program, which draws in those with solid backgrounds in liberal arts rather than the arts of teaching, relies on the same assumption, that content is what counts. State certification boards are following a similar logic in requiring a major in an academic discipline: increasingly 'neither the major nor the minor may be in education' (Burks, 1988). The percentage of high school teachers holding at least a college major in their assigned subject rose from approximately 60 percent in 1962 to 80 percent in 1986 (NEA, 1987). The continuing trend in preparation and certification of secondary teachers has been toward subject knowledge and specialization.

The complex interrelations between the subjects in which teachers are trained and the conceptions of teaching which they then take into the classroom has been the focus of a research project led by Lee Shulman (see, for example, Shulman, 1987; Grossman, 1990; Wilson and Wineburg, 1988; Wineburg and Wilson, 1991). In these studies it becomes apparent that disciplines shape not only choices of content but also quite different understandings of what teaching and learning are all about. What happens when those different understandings come out of the classroom and into contact with other teachers and administrators in the high school, however, has yet to be addressed.

Yet this emphasis on academic knowledge does reach not only into teacher preparation, but also inside the school organization to existing modes of practice, where it is likely to reinforce the boundaries, and the status, of 'real' academic departments and subject-specialist teachers. New programs, such as Academic Alliances and the Urban Math Collaborative, bring university faculty together with their disciplinary 'counterparts' at the high school to share time, knowledge, and legitimacy — but such arrangements are available only to some teachers, from particular departments (Tucker, 1986; also Atkin and Atkin, 1989; Little and McLaughlin, 1991). Principals routinely charged with supervising and evaluating a staff generically categorized as 'teachers' are now seeing themselves, and are being seen, as lacking the expertise to direct these 'specialists' (Perrone, 1985; Shulman, in Brandt, 1992). Teaching in more than one subject area, considered necessary and normal in Downing's day, has become the 'problem' of misassignment or out-of-subject teaching. With the growing emphasis on subject matter in preparation, collaboration, evaluation, and assignment, teachers are rewarded intellectually and organizationally for time spent within the boundaries of their own separate departments — a consequence to which those pressing for increasing academic preparation have given little attention.

The department has thus become a crucial part of the context of teaching in high school, for it is the department which organizes teachers spatially, temporally, administratively, and symbolically along those increasingly important subject lines. What does it mean to teach 'in a real department?' How strong have these departmental boundaries become, and what do they contain? How do departments function within the organizational routines of the school? How do subjects matter?

Peripheral Images

Although much of recent educational research has turned from psychology to sociology to 'look at the entire school and how its organization affects the individuals within it' (Coleman, 1988), even studies which specifically address high schools or school organization have remained relatively silent on the structure or dynamics of subject departments. While there has been no major systematic study focused on departments, there are studies of American high schools in which departments appear as peripheral images, and in which they appear to have powerful effects on teachers.

In large scale studies, for example, statistical data are typically analyzed by personal characteristics (e.g., age, sex), or by institutional characteristics (e.g., school size). In a study of organizational climate, using data from a 1984 federal survey of teachers and administrators (High School and Beyond), one research group noted that while analysts have argued over treating this construct as a measure of individual or school variance, few have considered intermediate levels such as departments (Rowan, Raudenbush, and Kang, 1989). In fact, such analysis is largely precluded by the design of the instrument, since the survey included only one variable (subject assigned) and insufficient samples at the department level. Yet this group found that this single variable, when used across the full sample, produced 'results surprisingly robust and consistent' (p. 22). Social Studies teachers, for example, consistently showed higher responses on school climate measures. The lack of detailed or systematic data on departments leaves much unexplained, and analysts are left with unanswerable, but intriguing questions: do Social Studies teachers interpret climate questions differently, or do they, in fact, inhabit different organizational climates?

In recent qualitative studies, analysis also tends to occur at the level of the school — the 'good' (Lightfoot, 1983), the 'shopping mall' (Powell, Farrar and Cohen, 1985), or just the 'high school' (Boyer, 1983) — or the teacher 'Horace's compromise' (Sizer, 1984). Significantly, the word 'department' does not even appear in the index of these major studies of American high schools.

But the department, although not the 'topic of inquiry', has often 'emerged' when teachers tell their stories, creating a series of puzzling fragments (Johnson, 1990a). Researchers for the Boyer study on high schools, for example, provide particularly tantalizing glimpses, as departments repeatedly appear at the peripheral edges of their focus on high school life. In one case study, they note that there is 'very little interaction across disciplinary lines', but report that teachers do find 'friendship and support within their departments' (Lightfoot, 1985, p. 260). In that school, departments have 'clout and status' (p. 261); in another, they are 'running the school' and controlling instructional programs (Perrone, 1985, p. 591). Moreover, although the authors do not make this point, the correlation within their study between schools identified as particularly effective and those with strong departments is nearly perfect. Where friendship and support sustain professional effort, where teachers are highly engaged, where constructive conversations and decisions about teaching occur, strong departments are there in the background.

While the glimpses of departments are generally cast in a positive light in the Boyer study, this characterization is not always the case. Bruckerhoff (1991) provides a rich ethnographic study of teachers in a dysfunctional Social Studies department, where rival cliques wage petty battles in ' "the closest thing to war in the whole central part of the state" ' (p. 107). Because his study takes place entirely within the single department, however, it remains unclear whether this is an embattled school, or whether departmental boundaries in this instance might productively contain a destructive atmosphere. Theodore Sizer (1984; 1992), after studying a wide range of high schools across the country, casts departmentalization itself in a negative light, as a 'villain' in the 'fragmentation' of school faculty and of content, but his study did not examine what it was that departments were actually doing. Cusick (1983), on the other hand, did look directly and deliberately at the role of departments in three 'egalitarian' high schools of the 1970s, seeking a control mechanism for what he found to be curriculum fragmented by the individual interests of individual teachers. Instead, he found departments to be little more than 'labels' attached to highly autonomous teachers: 'I just could not find departments doing much as departments' (p. 88). These peripheral glimpses are intriguing, but they provide little sense of just what it is that departments do when they do 'much as departments', or when that is likely to occur.

As studies have shifted from examining teaching methods in general to exploring teaching in context, the department, although still in peripheral vision, becomes visible as an essential element in understanding the working conditions of high school teachers (McLaughlin, Talbert and Bascia, 1990). Departments emerge in studies whose focus ranges from casual conversation to formal policy: they relate to the frequency of collegial encounters (Charters, 1969; Johnson, 1990a;

Willower and Smith, 1986), opportunities for professional development (Little, 1990a), support for new teachers (Yee, 1990), the distribution of female teachers (Acker, 1983; NEA, 1972, 1987), and differences in policy implementation and effects (Bell, Pennington and Burridge, 1979; Brophy and Good, 1986; Erickson, 1987; McLaughlin, 1987). These analyses, however, typically engage departments as labels for differences in subject matter. While their findings hint at the salience of, and the kinds of variation among, departments, they provide more in the way of incidental observations than framed analyses.

There are research efforts which provide both important exceptions to the general absence of attention to departments, and evidence of the value of attending to these units. At Research for Better Schools, studies of the organizational patterns of — and differences between — elementary and secondary schools (Herriott and Firestone, 1984; Firestone and Herriott, 1982) have led researchers to explore the department as a formal subunit with substantial control over resources, personnel, and communication channels, and the department chair as a critical — if ambiguous — administrative role (Wilson and Herriott, 1990; Adducci *et al.*, 1990). And at the Center for Research on the Context of Secondary School Teaching, of which this project is a part, the department has become a central focus. Here researchers have turned to the 'primacy' of departments in teachers' worklives (Johnson, 1990a), to differences among subject subcultures (Siskin, 1991), to the contrast between work in academic departments and 'work on the margins' in vocational ones (Little and Threatt, 1991), and to departments as 'boundaries of teachers' professional communities' (Talbert, 1991) and providers of professional support (McLaughlin, 1993). A different kind of focus is being brought to bear on the department by a team of researchers in Canada, who, like Sizer, have identified departmentalization with 'balkanization', and departmental boundaries and subcultures as a 'problem' in bringing about school-wide change (Hargreaves and Macmillan, 1992; Fullan, 1992).

These are projects currently underway, with empirical evidence and theoretical arguments just beginning to emerge. But while departments were largely invisible, or relegated to the shadows, in American research on high schools, there were two neighboring areas of educational research where a focus on departments was directly, and avidly, pursued: in the university system, and in the British schools.

Departments in Universities

The absence of studies of high school departments stands in sharp contrast to a rich literature on their counterparts in higher education, where much has been written about the workings of departments and their consequence for the faculties within them. Researchers looking at the organization of the university have repeatedly and consistently documented and explored the importance of the academic department. In the 1960s, one study found departments in control of key decisions, including the selection of faculty and 'the criteria and content of teaching' (Demerath, 1967, p. 182). Ten years later, another claimed departments were 'the central building block — the molecule — of the American University' and, as relatively autonomous organizational units, central to understanding 'the realities of academic life' (Trow, 1976, p. 11).

This continuing focus on the department as a central unit of analysis has led to explorations of academic 'territories', and of turf wars, of departments as political realms competing for power and control over essential resources within the organization (Becher, 1989; Lawrence and Lorsch, 1967; Pfeffer and Salancik, 1980; Trow, 1976). In their study of occupational communities, Van Maanen and Barley found that a department 'tends to develop its own language, norms, time horizons, and perspectives on the organization's mission', and 'when forced to compete for resources or to cooperate on joint ventures, [is] likely to vie for the privilege of defining the situation' (Van Maanen and Barley, 1984, p. 333). Drawn from organizational theory, these studies have tended to portray departments as local political coalitions, competing against each other (Pfeffer and Salancik, 1980), or as administrative units, with policies and procedures distinguished from each other (Olsen, 1979). In either case, the view of departments is basically as internal units of a larger organization, although connected to differentiated external environments and influenced by the subjects they contain.

Other lines of thought, however, suggest that academic departments can be understood in terms of the knowledge paradigms, rather than the universities, which organize them. Kuhn, in his seminal work on the topic, declared that in universities 'the study of paradigms [of a discipline] . . . mainly prepares the student for membership in the particular scientific community with which he will later practice' and that later research 'will usually appear as brief articles addressed only to professional colleagues, the men whose knowledge of a shared paradigm can be assumed and who prove to be the only ones able to read the papers addressed to them' (Kuhn, 1970, pp. 11, 20). Disciplinary colleagues are likely to, and may only be able to, speak with each other.

Here the discipline itself can be seen as the 'system of control in the production of discourse', and in the behaviors of those who produce and profess particular kinds of knowledge (Foucault, 1972, p. 224). Faculty, as inhabitants of disciplinary 'cultures', become

15

understood as 'natives' speaking different languages, and unable to communicate effectively across departmental boundaries (Snow, 1959; Geertz, 1983; also Jacoby, 1987). This focus on the disciplines has led researchers outside the university walls, to explore ways in which geographically distant faculty are interconnected directly, through disciplinary networks (Caplow and McGee, 1958; Crane, 1988; Gouldner, 1957), as well as indirectly, through shared paradigms and disciplinary cultures (Becher, 1989; Geertz, 1983; Snow, 1959; Van Maanen and Barley, 1984). The notion that a department, for example, constitutes a distinct community within a distinctive disciplinary culture is pursued by Burton Clark (1987), who examines how characteristics of the 'bodies of knowledge variously determine the behavior of individuals and departments', in what are seen as 'different worlds'.

In looking for characteristics of the 'bodies of knowledge' which affect behaviors, researchers have turned repeatedly to 'tightness', 'maturity', or 'height' of paradigm: the level of agreement on the 'foundations, laws and methodologies' of a discipline (Tricamo, 1984). Although different authors use slightly different vocabularies, the pattern is consistent. The natural sciences and math are found to be high paradigm fields, the social sciences and English low, and the level of paradigm to be an important predictor of standardization in decision-making processes and outcomes (Lodahl and Gordon, 1972, 1973). High paradigm fields show greater consensus on course content (Lodahl and Gordon, 1972) and greater reliance on rules than negotiation (Pfeffer, Salancik and Leblebici, 1976), and, at least within one university, report significantly more collaboration in teaching activities (Biglan, 1973; Deatrick, 1988). In their study of the college textbook industries in physics and sociology, Levitt and Nass (1989) found 'degree of development of paradigm' a key dimension in predicting homogeneity of both content and sequencing. The seemingly abstract characteristics of knowledge paradigms thus can be seen as playing out in the most concrete aspects of practice.

Further, and more critical, explorations of these bodies of knowledge and the extent of their effects have arisen as philosophers, feminist scholars, social historians, and literary critics have begun to map out interrelations among the position and structure of the disciplines, their demographic make-up, and the kinds of knowledge they produce and preserve (Culler, 1988; Foucault, 1972; Gumport, 1989; Lincoln, 1986; Scott, 1988; Shumway and Messer-Davidow, 1991).

Clearly the 'realities of academic life' differ substantially between universities and high schools, and the degree to which these insights would obtain across the levels remains unclear. Nonetheless, this literature does provide a background for the overall phenomenon of departmentalization, and for ways of thinking about faculty as subject specialists within and across schools.

Departments in the UK

Across the Atlantic, departments have also been highly visible in England, where the design and redesign of high schools has been the recurrent subject of national debate, and whether teachers should be trained and organized as subject specialists a contested issue.

According to one study, even by 1943 British policy makers were concerned that 'subjects seem to have built themselves vested interests and rights of their own' (Norwood, 1943). That often-cited report clearly cast subject departments as a problem:

> Subjects have tended to become preserves belonging to specialist teachers; barriers have been erected between them, and teachers have felt unqualified or not free to trespass upon the dominions of other teachers. The specific values of each subject have been pressed to the neglect of the values common to several or all . . . In the meantime, we feel, the child is apt to be forgotten. (Norwood, 1943, cited in Goodson, 1988a, p. 189)

A partial solution for many years lay in a dual system of high schools: departmentalized grammar schools resembled the universities from which they drew their faculties and for which they prepared their students, while secondary moderns maintained the more generalized pedagogical approach of elementary schools (D. Hargreaves, 1980). The tension between the two approaches remained, however, and both the 'barriers' which divide 'preserves' of knowledge and the 'specific values of each subject' continue to be topics of debate and research.

Studies concerned with the 'barriers' dividing subjects often trace back to the work of Basil Bernstein (1971, 1973) on the boundaries between different categories of knowledge, and the degrees to which those boundaries are maintained. Like much of the research on university disciplines, this line of work has taken a macro-level focus, on the social organization of knowledge, but here attention has been turned more toward the divisions between subjects than the paradigms within them. Some systems (the US, the grammar schools) have stronger barriers than others (the UK, the secondary moderns). The primary issue, as the title of one collection of major papers makes clear, is the relationship between 'knowledge and control' (Young, 1971). Subjects are typically treated as unitary — the knowledge is 'held in common' with other members of the subject community (Esland, 1971, p. 99) — and specialist teachers as passive — 'these traditions initiate the teachers' (Goodson, 1988a, p. 181). It is the classification system of knowledge itself which is the focus, with departments examined only as reflecting stabilized and guarded categories of content.

Further work along this line examines the historical and political patterns of how the 'preserves' of specific subjects are established and preserved, in the contested process of 'becoming a school subject' — a process which not all subjects survive (Goodson, 1988b, p. 160). Departments are here portrayed as the local enactments of a larger war, and teachers play a more active role: subjects themselves are engaged in a continual battle for survival, with specialist positions, required courses, external A- and O-level exams, and ultimately departmental status the territory at stake (Ball, 1983; Ball and Goodson, 1984; Goodson, 1987; 1988b). Personnel are enlisted in, and defined as members of, coalitions largely by virtue of their subject, which supports the formation of 'subject subcultures' within the school.

Following a different line, other researchers have focused on 'values' within the preserves of specific subjects, and how they are revealed in subject-specialist teachers. Disciplinary distinctions are strongly reflected in differences in behaviors and attitudes, and in the choices of friends, of even pre-service teachers (Ball and Lacey, 1980; Goodson, 1988a). A closer look at the 'values' of practicing teachers of English, while acknowledging the sharp differences between subjects, also explored the possibility of differences within them, finding that even within the same department teachers can hold varying, and sometimes conflicting, ideas of what their subject is all about (Ball and Lacey, 1980). The investigation of the 'values' of the specific subject was taken in a slightly different direction, into classroom practice, and how the values and behaviors associated with science match — or do not match — the developing gender identities of adolescent students (Measor, 1983). These last two studies begin to address explicitly the issue of connections between subject paradigms and local organizational practice.

The organizational side of departments, and the dynamics of employing and differentiating teachers along subject lines, comes into focus in studies of organizational change, such as the case study of Phoenix Comprehensive, where grammar and secondary modern staffs were brought together in the new structure of the comprehensive high school (Riseborough, 1981). There the issue is not the values of the different subjects, but the value placed by the organization on subject-specialist knowledge itself. As Riseborough shows, the more university-trained and subject-oriented teachers tend to gain status, the support of administrators, and positions of authority. Like the resource teacher from the CRC advisory board cited at the beginning of this chapter, those whose job descriptions, training, and orientations are aimed at the more 'pastoral' side of teaching find themselves treated as somehow less than real.

These two lines of research — the values of the subjects and the preserves of organizationally sanctioned units — come together in a micro-political theory of schools, which brings departments themselves most sharply into focus — and provides a theoretical framework with which to view them — at the intersection of subject, organizational structure, and teachers. Here Stephen Ball (1987) brings the values and assumptions, the 'technical differences between the subjects', together with the structure of the department, which can 'give organizational teeth to the intellectual ethnocentrism of disciplines' and provide 'the "organizational vehicle" within which subjects play out their characteristic roles, and teachers their careers' (p. 41).

While such work brings the department clearly into focus, it also raises the question of whether the very attributes which help make subject departments so visible in the British system also make them different in form and function than their American counterparts. The unfamiliar terms which abound in these studies mark not only differences in semantics, but also in the histories, structures, and politics of schools which are linked to the workings of their departments. The external A-level and O-level exams which are offered in only some subjects (and only to some students), the career paths of junior and senior teachers, the disparate traditions of grammar, secondary modern, and comprehensive high schools — all come into play in the formation and functioning of these departmental units — and all have no direct counterparts in US schools. In some cases even the subjects (European Studies) or the departments (Geography) themselves are unfamiliar. Such studies, then, can help to shape questions, provide a frame of reference, and offer empirical touchstones for comparison, but they cannot answer the question of what it means to teach in a real department in an American school.

Conclusion

While subject departments have become a nearly universal feature of American secondary schools, they have remained largely invisible to educational research. In studies of other aspects of high schools, departments have emerged as consequential to the structural, social, and professional nature of teachers' work. These studies further suggest that the role of the department varies both by site — in some schools departments control instructional programs (Perrone, 1985) — and by subject — math is more conservative than English (Lightfoot, 1985). But these 'suggestions' emerge from small samples in studies designed for other purposes, and without a theoretical frame. Research on departments in universities and in British schools points to the complex interplay between the organization of knowledge and the organization of schools, and provides convincing evidence that the department is crucial to understanding the 'realities of academic life' in those settings. Such works provide useful background and theoretical lenses for examining the realities of academic life, but how well they apply to US secondary schools is less certain, for high school teachers are not university faculty, and the American educational system is not the same as the British one.

How do these 'realms of knowledge' function in the particular context of the US high school, and how is it that they have become so common without attracting public attention? To begin to address those questions, I turn in the next chapter to the history of departmentalization in American high schools.

Chapter 2

Historical Background: From Realm to Realms

The profession of teaching must grow by each movement which emphasizes the necessity of special preparation on the part of the teacher. Greater differentiation of function has been characteristic of advancement in all ages, and division of labor is a principle which applies to all professions and occupations except the Jack-of-all-trades.

Departmental education, in its future development, promises, above all else, a means, or a stepping stone to real individual education. How to educate children *en masse* and still preserve the strength of each growing individual is a problem of increasing importance.

The grandest promise of all, then, found in departmental education is in the fact that it makes possible the division into 'work-units' of the course in each department . . . When individual education is enhanced, then surely the ascendancy of the departmental plan will be certain. (Van Evrie Kilpatrick, New York City Schools, 1905)

I have a general secondary certificate; you don't see many of those any more. (English teacher, 1988)

When Lucia Downing began teaching in Vermont she was the only teacher in the only school in her community, making organizational issues such as specialized teachers or differentiation of function rather irrelevant. But that model of 'the little red schoolhouse', while 'still standing' in many rural communities, was clearly on its way to becoming a 'reminder of the days of long ago' as the United States moved into an era of urbanization, industrialization, and specialization (Downing, 1950); those changes, as Kilpatrick predicted, brought with them the 'ascendancy of the departmental plan' (p. 485).

This chapter explores the shift between Downing's realm of

knowledge and Frances' realms by examining historical accounts for evidence of the emergence and institutionalization of the academic department. As with the literature on contemporary schools, evidence in these histories is fragmentary, and occurs in glimpses of the feature in discussions of other topics. One admittedly brief examination of the historical literature turned up only two pieces of evidence: Ben Franklin's Academy in Philadelphia had Latin, English, and mathematics 'departments' in 1751; and structural differentiation has long been a common phenomenon in organizations (Wilson and Herriott, 1990).

While there are mentions of the department in the histories of schools (Brown, 1926; Cremin, 1964; Sizer, 1964; Tyack, 1967; 1974), of curriculum (Goodson, 1987; 1988b; Krug, 1960), or of teaching (Cuban, 1984; Elsbree, 1939), these are works which focus their attention on other issues. Even Edward Krug (1964; 1972), who spent 817 pages in two volumes chronicling 'The Shaping of the American High School' provides only occasional, and incidental mentions of the department, and no discussion of its role or implications for teachers. There are no histories of departments *per se*, no 'heroes' of the move to departmentalize high schools, no documented 'legends' of a reform agenda, or constituency clamoring to put this feature in place. No charter or legislation mandates their existence. Instead, the history of the department emerges as a largely unintended and ancillary by-product of other efforts in three related areas.

First, the increasing size and bureaucratization of schools led to organizational differentiation and the institutionalization of the word 'department', but definitions of the term were varied, and the subject department was only one of a number of organizational experiments. Second, as changes in the organization of knowledge from a model of unified whole to branching fields made their way through the educational system, disciplinary modifiers were attached to these divisions. Again, there were a variety of responses as different groups battled over which subjects were appropriate to the changing definitions of the high school student. Finally, and most recently, came changes in the numbers and career patterns of teachers, filling up what had become an already accepted label with groups of specialized and professionalized teachers. As these three components — the administrative division, the subject, and the people — converge, departments emerge as something quite different from what Kilpatrick envisioned: organizational units with consequence for the political, intellectual, and social lives of the teachers who inhabit them.

The Departmental Plan

At the turn of the century, in New York, as in other urban areas, educators such as Kilpatrick were already beginning to wrestle with the issues which would come to characterize modern schools, and out of which would come the 'ascendancy of the departmental plan': specialization and division of labor in the bureaucratic era; the tremendous rise in numbers and kinds of students and teachers who would rapidly redefine the meaning of *en masse* as mass education became a reality; and the appropriate content for these new students in a new era.

When Kilpatrick spoke at Harvard University in 1905, he and his colleagues were presenting a vision of what the departmental plan could, and would provide, once its ascendancy in the public schools was certain. On two points, Kilpatrick's vision accurately forecasted coming events. While one might well take issue with whether 'differentiation of function' applies equally well 'in all ages', there is little question that specialization and division of labor would characterize the coming changes in teaching in general, and in secondary school teaching in particular, over the next eighty years. And while critics have suggested that the departmental plan did anything but provide 'above all else, a means, or a stepping stone to real individual education' (p. 484), the ascendancy of that plan has become a virtual certainty in the modern high school.

Yet in many ways, the papers presented by Kilpatrick and his colleagues provide more in the way of puzzles than of predictions or explanations for the ascendancy of that plan; if his vision matched the future in the two aspects noted above, it is strikingly divergent in others, making Kilpatrick's plan seem almost as far removed from today's arrangements as was Lucia Downing's situation. While Kilpatrick acknowledged that 'it is doubtless too early to say positively what the final outcome of this innovation will be' (p. 468), the differences between what he envisioned and what finally materialized are striking, both in terms of where the departmental plan succeeded, and in the particular organizational arrangements it came to define. Most obviously, and most importantly, the plan and the result differed in three critical aspects: 1) school size; 2) the role of the teacher; and 3) which schools adopted it.

For Kilpatrick, the departmental arrangement promised 'above all else, or a stepping stone to real individual education', but this was a promise which depended heavily on school size. An increase in individual attention would be possible because 'under the departmental plan, a teacher teaches the same pupils for years' (p. 473), and thus would come to know them, and their work well, 'while the single teacher has his child for a brief period only, at the end of which his influence is entirely ruptured' (p. 481). That promise rested upon the assumption that there would be 'a teacher' responsible for each subject: 'teachers of these classes, usually from four to eight in number, distribute the studies of the curriculum so that each shall teach only one study, or a group of related studies' (p. 470). It was an assumption quickly exploded as schools — and faculties — grew to accommodate a rapid influx of new students.

Not only would the numbers of teachers change, but so, too, would their roles. In Kilpatrick's plan teachers would be assigned to their respective subject, or 'group of related studies', *after* they were members of the school staff, and according to school needs. His was an argument for the efficient use of existing staff, one in which 'the teacher can use his time to prepare in a single study or group. He soon becomes highly proficient in the science of his branch' (p. 470). There would be fiscal benefits, too, in this model of efficiency:

> One of the first tendencies noted is that each teacher equips his department. The teacher of history is on the lookout for maps and charts, the teacher of arithmetic is collecting weights, measures, etc., while it is not an exaggeration to state that there is not an efficient science teacher in New York who has not, from his own resources, purchased from $10 to $50 worth of apparatus. (Kilpatrick, 1905, p. 472)

Teachers, for Kilpatrick, were instruments that could be deployed to fit and satisfy school needs.

Finally, the most obvious disparity between this plan and what eventually came to pass lies in the kinds of schools where the departmental arrangement did ascend, and where it did not. Kilpatrick and his colleagues at the Harvard Conference were arguing for the adoption of the departmental plan in elementary schools, where it would replace the 'mothering plan' of the single teacher, a plan he described as resulting in 'the most pernicious system of over-helpfulness' (p. 475). At the time of the conference, Kilpatrick could claim the departmental plan was being tried in 130 elementary schools in New York alone. Surveys of teachers and principals were highly favorable, according to Kilpatrick, but 'no city or state seems yet to have taken up departmental teaching to the extent found in New York' (p. 469). Other urban systems were 'taking up' the idea, although to a lesser extent: similar experiments were tried in Boston (Brooks, 1905), Medford (Morss, 1905), San Francisco (Myers, 1964), Springfield, and Utica (Krug, 1964). But despite the intentions of the reformers, despite repeated experiments in various locations at a variety of times, the departmental plan never reached 'ascendancy' in the elementary schools, and still remains strongly contested in the junior high-middle school debate today. Yet at the high school level the departmental plan was not only taken up, it has taken over.

Moreover, while we can examine the calls for departmentalization and the logic invoked by advocates for its elementary school adoption, the plan appears to have been adopted largely silently in the high schools; neither reformers nor historians provide much evidence of its debate, implementation, or spread. When Krug (1964) discusses the 'problem of organizing the daily schedule and arranging for the use of the teaching staff' which confronted both elementary and secondary schools at the turn of the century, he notes '*but* in elementary schools . . . [this] gave rise to the question whether departmentalization or the single teacher was to be preferred [my italic]' (p. 93). Apparently, for the shaping of the high school, the question did not become an issue. Departmentalization became an example of the disjunction between 'policy talk' and 'institutional practice' (Tyack, 1991): at the elementary level, there was policy talk with little change in institutional practice; at the secondary level, practice changed with little talk. How did something which teachers, administrators, and reformers now see as having profound implications for teaching and learning come into being without becoming an issue? What allowed it to take over the high schools so easily, when it was so readily defeated in the elementary schools?

The New Organization of the High School

Part of the answer to those questions lies in the difference in the ages of the two levels of schooling — not the ages of the students (though one could argue that this, too, had an effect) but the ages of the institutions themselves. When Kilpatrick was arguing for his departmental plan, high schools were still a new, and uncommon, organizational form, and it was unclear what form that new organization would take. Some were extensions downward from the colleges: Charles Eliot, lamenting the 'wide gap' which separated the established institutions of elementary schools and colleges, noted that 'five-sixths of the colleges and universities in the United States maintained preparatory departments' (in Sizer, 1964, p. 522). Many were extensions upward, from the other side of that gap, and were physically and organizationally linked to elementary schools. An 1894 US survey found 3,964 high schools in operation, but these schools had 'twice as many elementary students as they had high school students' (Labaree, 1989, p. 159). In an 1896 accounting of the 258 secondary schools in the state of Illinois, 220 were actually housed in elementary schools (Tyack, 1967).

Just what this new institution should be, whom it would serve, and whether it should more properly be an extension upwards from the elementary school or downward from the college was unsettled, and hotly contested at the turn of the century. People might know what these schools were to be called, but what they would contain was still open to question, and to confusion, as David Tyack (1967) illustrates: ' "The term high school is the vaguest in the school vocabulary", observed a schoolman in 1892. "It covers an endless variety of courses of study, aims, ideals, and methods" ' (p. 352).

The vagueness of the term did little to impede its rapid spread. In 1860 there were only an estimated forty secondary schools in the US; in 1890 the US Commissioner's Report counted 2,526 public high schools; in 1900, there were 6,005, and by 1910 a reported 10,213 (cited in Brown, 1926, p. 35). The actual numbers may not be highly accurate — different reports give different counts, and some of these schools had few or no students, but the trend is extraordinary. Not only were the numbers of high schools exploding; so, too, were the numbers of students who attended them (figures are taken from Krug, 1964; and Tyack, 1967):

Year	Number of Students	% of school-age
1890	200,000	6.7%
1920	2,200,389	28.0%
1930	4,399,422	47.0%
1940	6,399,422	73.3%

As newly formed organizations, and organizationally relatively unformed, the high schools were far more fertile ground than the well-established elementary schools for the plans of a generation of educational reformers concerned with efficiency, rational management, and differentiation.

Departmental Divisions

If the term 'high school' was the vaguest in the school vocabulary, as educators formulated plans to accommodate the rising tide of incoming students, the term 'department' must have been a strong, if overlooked, contender. This was the era of efficiency and of rational design, but in the first decades of the twentieth century, educators were still searching for the 'one best system' among a profusion of organizational forms (Powell, 1980; Tyack, 1974). While it may have been clear that schools were adopting a division of labor model — Kilpatrick (1905) claimed that 'division of labor is the congealed spirit of the age' (p. 471) — it was unclear what these new divisions would divide.

In line with the prototypes of the factories, in the first decades of the century many schools created their departmental divisions along functional lines. They differentiated among inputs, in terms of student characteristics, or outputs, in terms of their projected careers. Thus, in some schools, 'departments' retained the nineteenth-century pattern of dividing students in the 'Girls Department' from the 'Boys Department' (Tyack, 1974, p. 51). In others, they designated the age or preparation of the students: students might be in the '3rd Department' and study history, natural history, arithmetic, French, and composition (Pfeil, 1989, p. 8).

Most common are references to departments which divided programs: divisions based on the expected futures of the students, who, as the high school population expanded, were headed in a variety of directions. The label 'Classical Department', for example, typically designated the most traditional college-preparatory program while the 'Department of Commerce' served 'those not headed for college' but for trades (Labaree, 1988, p. 153, also Krug, 1964; Sizer, 1964). The 'Normal Department', in many city schools, prepared future teachers. Steele High School, in Dayton Ohio, with twenty-six teachers, had four 'courses of study' or 'Departments', in 1896: Classical, Scientific, English, and Commercial (Cuban, 1984). This pattern of functional differentiation, though linked to the increasing size of schools, was more than simply a response to size; it was a symbolic participation in the spirit of the age. Nor was it limited to large urban systems: Mishwaka, Indiana, in 1914 maintained eight different programs; in 1916 Newton, Massachusetts had fourteen (Krug, 1964).

These labels described the expected paths of the students, but they were not divisions of faculty. In a large school, such as Steele, teachers might become subject specialists: 'Mr. Kincaid, in the Classical Department, for example, taught only two subjects, Latin and Greek' (Cuban, 1984, p. 27). But more typically, teachers by necessity taught across subjects, and across departments in schools too small to have specialist teachers: 'the most typical, in the sense of the most frequent, secondary school in the United States [was] a school taught by one teacher', and there were 'more pupils in the two teacher high schools than in any other one group' (Thorndike, 1907, p. 245). Across the country, regardless of departmental labels, typical teachers covered the range of subjects: the only 'assistant teacher' in the North Bend High School found herself teaching 'no fewer than eight subjects during her first term alone' (Labaree, 1989, p. 163); in Missouri a single teacher 'was responsible for teaching botany, zoology, Latin, general history, English, etymology, and arithmetic' (Sizer, 1964, p. 45).

Neither was the departmental label a division of subjects. While the labels of Classical, Scientific, or English might resemble current terms for departmental divisions, the similarity is deceiving. The curriculum of English Departments, according to Charles Eliot's 1892 survey for the Committee of ten, might include 'various sciences, fragments of philosophy, history and political economy, some English literature, and perhaps a modern foreign language', as well as 'subjects representing such fields as astronomy, geology, and logic' (Krug, 1964, p. 198).

That Committee was to provide a 'blueprint . . . to bring order out of the chaos that was the American high school' (Tyack, 1967, p. 356). Although the Committee itself was organized along subject lines (the 'Conference on Mathematics', the 'Latin Conference') its recommended organization for the high schools followed the functional departmental divisions: Classical, Latin-Scientific, Modern Languages, and English. These divisions could coexist 'in a single school; because, with a few inevitable exceptions, the several subjects occur simultaneously in at least three programmes' (Eliot, 1894, cited in Sizer, 1964, p. 258). Across the four divisions, for example, the first year of study would include English, Algebra, History, and Physical Geography; only the Modern Languages department diverged, offering French or German where the other three required Latin.

The early use of the word department thus covered a variety of kinds of internal divisions: some were logically and rationally connected to functional differentiation; some were efficient responses to problems of increasing size; and in some cases they were simply words, dividing little of substance, but making the department label a familiar and expected one. Formulated in response to increasing numbers of students, divergent expectations, and the division of labor as 'the congealed spirit of the age', these early experiments account for the emergence of departmental plans, but not for a plan based on academic divisions.

To account for *academic* departments requires attention to the role played by academics from recently departmentalized universities in the battle over the organizational form of the high school (Tyack, 1974). This connection suggests that the key antecedent conditions for subject departments, as we now know them, involve not only issues of size and bureaucratization, but also issues of institutional isomorphism and of the way knowledge itself was being organized and rationalized along disciplinary lines.

Subject Divisions

As the purpose of the high school was debated, so too was the knowledge it should provide. In the early 1900s the most prominent educational debate centered around the purpose of education, whether schools should offer the broadly defined 'classics' or the 'modern' subjects (Krug, 1964) — the 'symbol of culture' of college preparation or the more 'practical instruction' of fitting students for work (Sizer, 1964, p. 3). The functional divisions of departments, as is apparent from the 'Committee of ten' report, both embodied these diverging goals and functioned to reconcile the two, by doing both. It was a compromise, however, in which preparation for college was clearly privileged, and justified as also preparing the majority of students for the 'duties of life'.

It was not a compromise which would satisfy for long. By 1920 the battle resumed. In this generation the terms and the tenor of the debate shifted, challenging the existence of specific subjects, including the 'modern' subjects for which Eliot had so recently fought. The debate brought in new standards against which content should be judged, and new experts to judge them. It was an academic war fought in the name of the citizenry, with charges toward progressive ideals and the liberation of school control from the tyranny of the university elite, such as Eliot and his Committee, but it was led by the generals of school administration. The group who produced the *Cardinal Principles of Secondary Education*, for example, included four school and state administrators, three education professors, only one university president (a former professor in education), and a representative of the YMCA. As the principal of Philadelphia's Central High School (a former professor at the University of Pennsylvania) recounted, 'the tendency of nearly all these innovations is to exalt the Superintendency as the central and initiative power of the School System and to bring everything else under control' (cited in Labaree, 1988, p. 87).

The most frequent target in these battles was the academic subject, which was now seen not as preparing students for life, but as driving them away from schools, for while more and more students were entering high schools far fewer were graduating. In the rhetoric of this debate the term department appears as a subject-department, and departmental status becomes an important stake in the battle for subject-survival.

The standards by which each subject would be measured moved from an accounting in terms of costs and economic efficiency to one of social efficiency. A 1914 paper by the principal of Girls' High School, in Brooklyn (cited in Krug, 1964) reveals the shift, and illustrates dramatically the flavor of emerging debate:

> The paying public is demanding of us an accounting of our stewardship . . . Every subject must present itself at the bar of competent opinion and plead for itself . . . Latin, justify thy presence in a twentieth century American high school curriculum! What has the prevailing study of physics, of chemistry, of biology to do with a liberal education? These are the days of accounting. High school sciences, what report can you render? History, you too are on the rack . . . Every subject is up for discussion, for examination, for acceptance or rejection.
> (Krug, 1964, pp. 314–15)

In these 'days of accounting' subjects seen as fit for those students who would go on to college were questioned for masses — and high schools increasingly were called upon to educate, and socialize, the masses.

The high schools were at this time drawing fully a third of the eligible adolescents, and becoming a potential vehicle for molding a new citizenry. What reformers sought was 'a more systematic, rationalized, and controlled social process, for the sake of greater social control over the whole of human life' (Charles Ellwood, 1921, cited in Krug, 1972, p. 5). In the process they would also reclaim the territory of the high school, which they saw as too closely linked to, and too strongly influenced by, the colleges.

To the activists in the Progressive Education Association, to the writers of reports such as the *Cardinal Principles of Secondary Education*, schools needed to reclaim their content, to prepare students for universal 'core' experiences of life rather than for universities. It was the academic subjects themselves which were cast as the enemy, and charged with 'vicious' crimes. Academic subjects were 'poorly adapted to the needs of the students' said an administrator in Chicago; a principal in New York declared that one could attribute 'potential criminal behavior' to 'forced subjection to hateful and impossible courses of study' (Krug, 1972, p. 25). Algebra, said another, 'injured the mind, destroyed the health, and wrecked the lives of thousands of children' (Tyack, 1967, p. 359). As late as 1940, in *What the High Schools Ought to Teach*, one section was headed 'Vicious aspects of the ninth grade' (Krug, 1972, p. 314). Among the most 'vicious aspects' were English composition, a foreign language, and what still continued to be a favorite target: the often required and equally often maligned algebra.

While the continuation of the rhetoric in 1940 might suggest that the progressive reformers had gained no ground, curriculum patterns had already begun to shift by 1930 — although it is not clear that the reformers were the cause (Krug, 1972). They could claim to have succeeded in overthrowing some of the targeted subjects, such as Greek, and in reducing the status of others, such as Latin, which lost its departmental status and retreated to the territory of what was becoming the Foreign Language department. German, which was attacked as not only academic but treasonous, largely disappeared in most states. History, assailed for its emphasis on ancient worlds and long-dead people, was modified to include more socially appropriate knowledge, such as political economy or the responsibilities of citizenship. Algebra, however, proved a formidable and largely invulnerable opponent; it was still required in most schools, enrolling, in 1928, almost a third of all high school students (Krug, 1972). Favored subjects attracted new advocates, and new status: Industrial Arts, Home Economics, Agriculture, and Business commonly appeared as school subjects, and occasionally as departments; less common and less lasting were the 'core' or 'life experience' offerings which directly opposed the subject-specific organizational model of the college.

That model of disciplinary classification and departmentalization had fully taken over the university structures only fifty years before, but it was proving a powerful force (Gumport, 1989; Perkin, 1984). David Labaree (1988), in his history of Central High School, provides an example of its strength: in 1894 the school hired a head who had been a university professor

> until he was fired in the wake of Penn's professionalization effort. The primary charge against him was that he was behind the times: in the new specialized and research-oriented university of the 1890s he was conspicuously a generalist and a moralist (teaching a half-dozen subjects while preaching on weekends). (Labaree, 1988, p. 87)

This 'new university' model was clearly a disciplinary one, in both senses of the word. It reorganized faculty and curriculum, and by its entrance requirements, the training of its graduates, and its example, the university continued to shape high schools, despite the efforts of progressive reformers to loosen its 'iron hold'.

This disciplinary model provided a template: a developed, established, and legitimated system of matching the organizational divisions of departments to the knowledge divisions of subjects. Even as the reformers hammered against these categories, they helped forge them into familiar and concrete existence, and bring their high school counterparts into focus. What emerged by the 1930s as an almost universal pattern of required high school courses, now securely housed in departmental homes, were the traditional Math (including algebra), the modern — and now slightly streamlined — Science and English, and the newly created Social Studies.

Specialist Teachers

The battles over subjects were fought neither over, nor by, teachers, for the departmental lines which divided courses had little connection to who taught them. While disciplinary divisions organized universities, and then high school curriculums, they still had little to do with staffing. Slowly, however, changes in the role of the teacher were making their way through the system, in terms of their training, their certification, and their careers.

The calls for specialized training in the subjects teachers would then teach have been repeated, persistent, and, for a long time, ineffective. Labaree (1989), in his study of teaching careers at the turn of the century, notes that

> In their personal accounts, high-school teachers complained frequently about being required to teach subjects in which they

did not feel competent, and of thus being forced into the demeaning position of having to rely heavily on the text. (Labaree, 1989, p. 167)

But since high school teachers often taught the range of subjects, it made little sense to train them as subject specialists. Even Kilpatrick's departmental plan, which would have encouraged teachers to specialize after they were assigned, would have been foiled by the fact that few of them stayed in teaching more than a few years.

Most often teachers were expected to have little education beyond that of their students, and if more was necessary, it could be provided locally, allowing for considerable flexibility. When the state of Mississippi decided to have Greek taught in high schools, but only had a few teachers who could teach it, the problem was easily overcome. In 1896 the University 'offered a summer course in Greek' and, according to the report of this venture, 'sixty teachers returned to their classrooms with a desire to teach Greek, and many with a fair idea of how it should be taught to beginners.' It was pointed out that 'those teachers who had not studied Greek before did not become capable instructors from one course. For these a correspondence course was offered.' That fall eighteen schools were thus able to introduce Greek (Krug, 1964, p. 132).

Certification standards at the time allowed for maximum flexibility. Teachers were often moved from elementary to secondary levels, as well as from subject to subject (Labaree, 1989). In 1906, according to Elwood Cubberley, 'in almost all of our states a teacher's certificate of any grade is good to teach in any part of the school system in which the teacher may be able to secure employment' (cited in Elsbree, 1939, p. 343).

A similar call for specialized training echoes in John Brown's study of high schools in 1926, which again linked subject expertise to quality in teaching: 'wherever it is possible to do so, the prospective high-school teacher should choose early in life the subjects which he wishes to teach, and he should devote the greater part of his time to them throughout his course' (p. 196). He acknowledged that this ideal was hardly practical, since most teachers would have to teach multiple subjects.

It may not have been practical, but it was beginning to be possible, since in that decade the training of high school teachers was moving to the universities where the subject specialists were. In 1920 only ten states required a college diploma for secondary teaching, and most of those allowed numerous exceptions. More common routes into teaching were the two-year normal schools, county schools, or training courses offered in the high schools themselves. In 1918, studies estimated that there were '30,000 teachers with no schooling beyond the eighth grade' and 'one-half of the nation's 600,000 teachers had no more than a high school education' (Sedlak, 1988, p. 30. These figures are for all teachers, not just high school teachers).

At the time when progressive reformers were attacking entrance requirements as the point of entry by which universities gained control of the high schools, the universities were moving in on the territory of teacher training, laying particular claim to the preparation of secondary school teachers (Krug, 1972). By 1930 the number of states requiring a college degree had more than doubled (Sedlak, 1988). As this shift of location of training occurred, disciplinary boundaries were being linked to state certificates: 'certificates have been broken down in some states into licenses to teach science, mathematics, English etc.' (Elsbree, 1939, p. 343). The North Central Association was an advocate of subject-specific certification, proposing that states 'redefine a "qualified" teacher as one who was certified to teach — and who taught — only in the subjects of his or her collegiate major or minor' (Sedlak, 1988, p. 35).

Still, however, advocates for tightening the links between teachers and subjects were confronted by less than ideal practical conditions. State standards were erratic, as were district hiring and staffing policies. From within the educational community came competing demands for more training in pedagogical and psychological skills. Subject matter expertise, while one of the specified areas of the first National Teacher Examination, for example, was only one of a long list including 'reasoning, comprehension, expression, contemporary affairs, social problems . . . education and social policy, child development, and methods' (Sedlak, 1988, p. 46). External conditions, too, such as the teacher shortages in World War II and again during the 'baby boom' years slowed the move toward subject-expertise.

In the 1960s the call continued for increasing preparation in the subjects teachers would teach. California adopted the Fisher Act in 1961, eliminating the General Secondary Certificate, and requiring at least a minor in the subject to be taught. This was strengthened in 1970 in the Ryan Act, which required either the passing of the NTE on content or a university 'program' in the subject (more than a minor, but not quite a major). This act, according to one of the staff at the Commission on Teacher Credentialing, 'centered around the idea that if you wanted to be a good teacher, then what you needed was your academic content — a lot of academic content'.

By 1988, similar standards were in place in most states, but not all: Michigan required both a major and a minor in fields related to the subject — specifically rejecting education as a field; New York required thirty-six credit hours in the subject; Arkansas, however, demanded only six credit hours in the 'subject he/she is assigned to teach' (Burks, 1988).

Such standards, of course, can often be circumvented through 'emergency certificates' and temporary or split assignments, and at best they only affect new teachers. The change in practice occurs far more slowly, particularly in schools which have difficulty attracting teachers. Some desirable public schools, and many private ones, have a long established practice of hiring experts in their subjects, but only very recently has there been both the general expectation that teachers should be trained in, and only teach in, specialized subjects, and the need for a term like 'mis-assignment'.

Paradoxically, when teachers were supposed to acquire their subject expertise through their teaching experience, few stayed in teaching long enough to acquire it: in 1920 one half of US teachers were under 26, and one-fifth under 20 (Sedlak, 1988); as late as 1950 the mean age group of teachers was 25 to 29 (Herbst, 1989). As subject-matter expertise has been located in university training, the demographics have changed markedly: only one-tenth of teachers fall into the 21 to 29 age range, and one-fourth are over 50 (NEA, 1987). Thus, while California moved to subject-specific certificates in 1961, in one of the schools in this study a teacher referred to her own 'general secondary certificate', though she noted that 'you don't see many of those any more.'

What you do see, far more commonly, is the expectation that the teacher, the certificate she holds, the education she has had, the subject she teaches, and the department to which she belongs should all match. At the same time the size of faculties has continued to grow, creating subgroups of considerable size, who can claim expertise over what they teach, and who now stay in teaching long enough to make new claims on the system (Sedlak, 1988). It is not the plan Kilpatrick envisioned. It is a model not quite realized, as familiar calls to strengthen those links in the Holmes Report remind us. However, it is a model which has nearly, and only very recently, reconfigured high school teaching as these three major components have come together producing, bounding, and populating the realms of knowledge of academic departments.

Conclusion

The history of the department is a difficult history to construct, for it must weave together chance mentions and peripheral glances from other histories centered on other topics. Those disconnected fragments, in turn, tend to rely on the views and articulations of those who wrote about schools, who attempted to reform them, or who managed them. Nowhere do we find the experiences or the words of the teachers who comprise and work in academic departments. Nowhere do we get a sense of how these divisions serve, or whether they serve, the interests of teachers, or how the interests of teachers and the practice of teaching may be shaped by them. Those are questions which can only be addressed by turning to the teachers, the inhabitants of these realms of knowledge, themselves.

Chapter 3

The Study

To turn from trying to explain social phenomenon by weaving them into grand textures of cause and effect to trying to explain them by placing them in local frames of awareness is to exchange a set of well-charted difficulties for a set of largely uncharted ones. (Clifford Geertz, 1983)

Teachers feel, and justly, that the rest of the world has no idea how complex, time-consuming, and difficult their work is. (Advisory Board Teacher)

How do departments function now that they constitute groups of specialists within subject-based subdivisions of the school? What do 'real' departments do, and what does membership in one mean for secondary school teachers? What *does* go on inside these realms of knowledge?

The studies examined in Chapter 1, on the roles of departments within other organizational and intellectual systems, provide a background for thinking about how departments might work in US secondary schools. They suggest considering departments as located within both the formal organization of the school and the disciplinary organization of knowledge. Left unanswered, however, are questions of how those organizational and intellectual systems might intersect and interrelate *within the American high school*, and why within that particular setting the subunit has remained a largely invisible phenomenon.

The historical background traces the shift in the meaning of the department from a functional division to one intimately connected to the university system and the organization of knowledge represented there. That historical analysis also provides one answer to the puzzling absence of the department in educational research, particularly in the days when the subgroup was such a major focus of organizational theorists, and organizational theories such a focus of educational research (Scott, 1989). At that time, the typical high school department divided curriculum rather than people: it had no group in its subgroup.

Now, however, a new set of conditions has arisen: the organizational divisions are entrenched, the academic subjects are well-established and firmly divided, and the realms which they create populated by significant numbers of certified and educated specialists — specialists whose career orientation gives them a substantial stake in school operations. These are conditions under which we might well theorize that departments would become visible, and would: 'emerge' as a 'fundamental unit' (Johnson, 1990a); acquire 'clout and status' (Lightfoot, 1985); lay claim to curricular matters (Perrone, 1985); and question the expertise of administrators as evaluators of subject-specific pedagogy (Perrone, 1985; Shulman, in Brandt, 1992).

The analysis of the literatures and historical background, then, enables a theoretical argument for the increasing visibility and potential importance of departments. The question now, for this study, is how those pieces come together in the daily realities of teaching in a modern secondary school. What remain as invisible, and inaudible pieces of the puzzle are the detailed observations of practice, the 'local frames of awareness' which can only come from the perspectives and stories of the teachers themselves. It is those pieces that this study begins to assemble, by examining what teachers say and do inside the realms of academic departments in three high schools. This, then, is an exploratory study of the department as a context for teaching.

Context and Design of the Study

The study itself is one strand of a larger project looking more broadly at the context of teaching in American high schools today: the Center for Research on the Context of Secondary School Teaching. This project provides the context for this 'special study' on departments, and, as the members of that study have found, context matters.

A team of researchers at the Center began, in 1987, a federally funded study to identify and elaborate contextual factors that influence secondary school teachers and teaching. Out of the first year of planning, and three years of field work, the Center generated not only a rich source of interview, observational, and survey data, but also a developing and collective conception of what context means, and how it matters to teachers' understandings and practice of teaching. As departments provide an important context for understanding teaching, the Center project provides an important context for this study conceptually, methodologically, and logistically.

Conceptual Context

Over the three years of Center fieldwork, and out of the collaborative efforts of a team of researchers, an emerging conception of the complexities of teachers' contexts has developed (McLaughlin and Talbert, 1993). In terms of a conceptual base for this study, three features stand out; the workplace of teaching is understood as open, embedded, and socially constructed.

While many have suggested that teaching is an essentially private activity, one conducted behind closed doors, Center research frames classrooms and schools as *open* systems. Classrooms are seen as open to a variety of influences, from a variety of directions and distances; these can affect expectations for students and teachers, the rhythms of the year and day, parameters for what is tolerated and what is desired. Thus we see contextual factors implicated not only in the sharp contrasts between an inner-city public high school and a suburban private school, but also in more subtle contrasts between the Advanced Placement physics class in the six months before the AP exam and the month after, between Brad Carter's 4th period science class and his 5th period one, and between any of his laboratory-oriented classes and a math colleague's blackboard-centered ones.

One important aspect of understanding those variations is to conceptualize classrooms as *embedded* within those larger environments, rather than linked in a linear chain. Actions and attitudes arising from any of these external sources may penetrate and permeate other levels, bypassing intervening bureaucratic levels, moving up or down, affecting some departments or teachers while leaving others unaffected. Thus new state tests, or changes in AP exams can reach one classroom without flowing down through district and school channels, and while remaining unnoticed in others. Teachers who participate in formal or informal networks bring new ideas and influences into the school through side doors, or push them outward to policy makers.

An understanding of contexts as *socially constructed* has two important implications for this study. First, it suggests that the classroom is open not only to explicit strategies such as policies and tests, but to more complex and subtle influences — the implicit ones of shared cultural understandings. The student who dislikes math for its rigid rules but argues that 'there are certain subjects that can be lenient and some that can't; and math has to be taught straight because you have to learn math . . . I just don't think there's any way of changing math' reveals a contextual influence of a different, but no less influential kind (Metz, 1978, p. 76).

Second, to understand workplaces as socially constructed focuses attention on the active side of construction. Context features thus become not determining factors, but rather a set of constraining and enabling conditions within which individuals actively and collectively shape the meaning, and the practice, of teaching. Inner-city schools may be fraught with common constraining conditions, but even in the same objective circumstances some schools forge effective practice; a high school may be overwhelmed by external pressures, but even there one department may construct an environment which stands out for its collegiality, commitment, or performance.

Methodological Context

This conceptual framing of schools has methodological consequences; the project is centrally concerned with a 'bottom-up' perspective of schools. In understanding the policy context, for example, rather than beginning with a specific policy, and tracing its effects down the system to the classroom, the Center effort begins at the 'bottom' level of different classrooms or schools, and looks to see, from this 'teacher's eye' view, which policies appear on the horizon, which have reached inside to become salient issues in particular sites, and how those sites have interpreted and sometimes translated them. Thus, California and its state education system can be a very different policy context for teachers in an urban school with a shrinking fiscal base, than for those in a growing, affluent, suburban one.

This focus has led to a particular 'Center style' of open-ended interview protocols. Core interviews, conducted by a team of researchers, share opening questions and a list of issues to listen for, to probe on, or to follow up, but they also provide an opportunity for teachers to shape the research design. Questions such as 'What things are important for us to understand about this school?' or 'What else should we be asking about?' take advantage of teachers' expertise and reduce the danger of finding only what we set out to look for. For this study, it allowed the department, if it mattered, to make unsolicited appearances in conversations about how teachers understand their workplace and their work. It also generated a data set shared by researchers interested in a number of studies within the larger project. Those core interviews provided crucial background and additional information for this study.[1]

The combination of open-ended interviews and frequent visits over a three-year period led to close relationships with many of the teachers and administrators participating in the Center project. This was especially true for special studies, such as this one, where researchers spent more time in fewer sites. We would often, on arrival, be greeted by teachers or administrators who 'have some stories I was saving for you', and in some instances they would telephone with stories that couldn't wait. In initial meetings many had asked questions about what it was that we would be looking for — and at — partly for their own curiosity and protection, partly to be helpful. Some had had painful experiences with other research projects; many questioned their value. In investing their time with us they wanted to understand, and to in part determine, what value that time would have. Teachers frequently represented stories as ones policy makers needed to hear, and understand — including the story of departments.

For many of these teachers, the lack of researchers' and policy-makers' awareness of, and attention to, departments was frustrating, and produced supposed benefits which were wasted if not harmful: policy requirements that do not acknowledge differential needs or demands; professional development programs which ignore the 'obvious' fact that teaching remedial English is not the same as teaching calculus, and does not require the same skills or resources. The story of departmental difference and influence was a story they judged in need of telling, and it is the story this research project attempts to convey.

Logistical Context

Logistically, the Center provided access to, and a wealth of information on, a sample of sixteen schools in two states. These schools represent a broad variety of teaching contexts: large and small, public and private, with different fiscal and policy settings. From within that sample, this study focused on three schools, which are described more fully in later pages. All three are large, public high schools; all offer comprehensive programs, but send a majority of their students on to higher education. It is a biased sample, then, in the sense that these are the kinds of schools where one would expect academic departments to matter, and to be most visible. Their differences allow for an examination of how departments might matter under varying conditions found in fairly typical American high schools:

> **Oak Valley**, with 3000 students and 130 faculty, is the largest of the Center schools. It is located in an affluent and growing suburb in a highly centralized district and state (California). Survey responses show only 6 per cent of Oak Valley teachers teach in more than one department, and that on the 'departmental identification index' scale, this school's 9.6 is the highest of the Center sample.[2]

> **Rancho** is in the same state, and in an urban district whose desegregation effort has recently pushed them toward highly centralized and standardized policies. Budget constraints and labor disputes are prominent issues here. Within the school

seventy-five faculty members are deliberately grouped into advisory units; one explicit purpose of these units is to break down departmental barriers. Fully one-third of Rancho teachers teach in more than one subject area, and their departmental identification index is 6.7 on the Center scale.

Highlander is also relatively large school, in a urban community in Michigan. State and district policy systems are relatively decentralized, relying on high certification standards and moving increasingly toward state tests; this is a state with a long history and political commitment to local control. Resources here are extremely limited, with state, city, and district all facing economic downturns and high lay-offs. District desegregation efforts include the creation of magnet programs in different high schools, and Highlander has magnet offerings which draw top Math and Science students from the entire district, but only for those courses. Only 16 per cent of Highlander's ninety teachers teach in more than one subject, and their departmental identification is 9.5.

While the full Center project looks at teachers in all departments, the focus of this study is on what one administrator called the 'basic' subjects: Math, English, Science, and Social Studies. Like the schools, these subject areas were chosen for a mix of their similarities and differences. All are fairly standard divisions, and generally secure in their status as departments; all have university counterparts in the research on knowledge paradigms and departmental cultures. There is greater variation among departments than this sample represents: departments such as Bilingual Education or Special Education are organized around characteristics of students; departments such as Vocational Education are organized around characteristics of their expected careers and linked to the organization of work; departments such as Physical Education have members who often teach in other areas; and other departments, such as Industrial Arts, face extinction in the face of budget cuts or changing enrollments.[3]

There are, however, substantial differences within the narrower range of academic subjects; these are anything but homogeneous groupings. English and Math have very different paradigms, but both are single-discipline departments; Social Studies is a cluster of different, and unsettled disciplines (Economics or Psychology are sometimes included), generally from low paradigm fields. Science is high on both the number of disciplines and the tightness of paradigm, and nationally characterized by a shortage of specialized teachers. These four departments comprise the sample.

Within this study are the stories told by all of the department chairs, and many, but not all, of the teachers. Initial sampling design called for selecting teachers who might be expected to bring different perspectives to the issue: new teachers and those who had been there for years, male and female members, and teachers of different races or from different disciplines. Over the course of the field work that list both expanded and contracted. In several departments subgroups within the subgroup could be identified, and teachers from each were added to the list. When one department had a team-planning program in which 'most' teachers participated, one who chose not to belong to a team was identified and included. In other cases the categories contracted; in one department there were no female members, and in several there were no new teachers. In one department, whose members collectively declined, in the first year, to participate in any study which district officials had approved, the sampling list contracted to those few teachers who would, after repeated attempts, agree to talk at all. But that instance provided data of a different kind, about departmental politics and internal cohesiveness, and about the distinction between negotiating access to a school and access to its departments.

The central focus of this project is the department as a workplace for teachers. The study is drawn largely from their interviews, and, in some sense, it is these individual stories which comprise the department. Their individual histories, professional philosophies, and the leadership roles of individual chairs or teachers all play critical parts in constructing the particular culture of each particular department.

The first stage of this study was an initial exploration into the question of whether the department was worth studying, and whether departmental differences would be evident in teachers' explanations of their work (Siskin, 1991). A five-month pilot study of Math and English departments in a single California high school revealed these departments as comprising different worlds, exhibiting different cultures, and, surprisingly, as controlling 'key decisions about resources, professional tasks, and careers'. A follow-up survey of California department chairs suggested that this unexpected finding was a common phenomenon. Data from the pilot is also included in the present study as background. Primarily, however, this is a study of how departments work within the contexts of three comprehensive high schools: Oak Valley, Rancho, and Highlander.

The Schools

The observation, so forcefully put by Theodore Sizer (1984), that the fundamental 'framework' of schools across America 'is astonishingly uniform' has become a commonplace in educational research, and in many ways that characteristic 'sameness' is readily apparent in the three schools selected for this study (p. 6). Despite geographic distance, Highlander, Rancho, and Oak Valley all conform to the standard notions of the typical American public high school: all are good-sized comprehensive high schools where 2000–3000 students of the same age, wearing the same selection of clothing, move (with slight variations of speed and noise) from class to class as bells mark the fifty-minute hours till the arrival of the ubiquitous yellow buses. As one Oak Valley teacher put it:

> It's a very standard school in my impression. We don't do anything tricky, but I would say it seems like the archetypal comprehensive high school. We have all the programs.

Organizationally, too, they conform to archetypal standards: each school is set within a large district where an appointed superintendent and staff supervise two to eight high schools, along with several elementary schools and junior highs. All have principals (all of them male) in large offices, near to the front door but hidden from view by the protective barrier of the secretary. Each school has several assistant principals whose responsibilities are divided along student characteristics or needs (9th graders, discipline). In contrast, the faculty are organized along academic lines, although Rancho has tried to move away from this: large staffs of specialized teachers are divided into standard departments headed by designated department chairs.

Yet, at the same time, there are differences in these schools which are immediately, and almost palpably, evident. Each school has its own face and its own feel: Highlander, for example, with its imposing three-story 'Stalinesque' architecture sharply contrasts with Oak Valley's campus of scattered buildings. And, for the purposes of this study, it is the character of the school, as well as the structural arrangements of buildings, budgets, and by-laws, which create the relevant context for both teachers and departments. The professional pride of Oak Valley, the turbulence of Rancho, and the defiant optimism of Highlander make these schools markedly different places in which to work.

Oak Valley

> Well, I think that it's a place that's pretty pride-filled, if that's appropriate. I kind of view it as this wonderful little circle that is taking place, that real estate agents have an absolute heyday because they, our test scores, all those things that the public can seem to be so concerned about are good. So consequently, we have parents who move here, many of them the number-one reason was to have the kids go to these schools. So, then, if

you're going to have parents moving for the schools, then a lot of times that means you're going to have kids coming in the classroom who are being pushed to do well. And, at the same time, it seems like the teachers that [we] are able to bring in (I was the English Department chair for five years and I was very actively involved in the hiring process), and you would read that nationwide there was such a teacher shortage and the competency was so low and yet the people that we were interviewing sure seemed to be a heck of a lot better first-year candidate-type people than I felt I was. So the whole thing, it's, it's just such a wonderful little circle that it appears as though you have a community that is supportive of schools. You have teachers who are in general, enjoying their jobs and getting a reward from it. And you have kids who, basically are doing their job of being students and contributing, so . . . But I think it's all, it's all so interrelated. And from the outside going to conferences and all, it's, it's pretty thrilling to have people know that I teach at Oak Valley, and they'll, 'Ah, Oak Valley' and they've heard about us. So there's a sense of pride here that, I think, affects all the different levels. So that's kind of what Oak Valley High School is all about.

In the above interview Quentin Ivy, an experienced English teacher, provides his own personal reflection on 'what Oak Valley is all about', but it is a summation which was echoed over and over again as teachers and administrators alike almost universally voice satisfaction and pride in being part of Oak Valley High School. Not only is the positive evaluation of Oak Valley consistent, so, too, are the recurring themes of what makes it so: the community, the students, and a highly professional staff.

School History
Oak Valley is a sprawling suburban high school in southern California, with approximately 3000 students and 130 faculty scattered across a campus with more than twenty separate buildings. In the center is a large central courtyard, where during lunch hour push-cart vendors, student activities, and occasionally the prize-winning school band transform the otherwise quiet campus, and reveal, in a rare glimpse, the tremendous size of the total student body.

This was, until recently — and well within the memories of many of the current staff — 'a kind of back-woods town . . . kind of a country bumpkin place'. In 1963, remembers another teacher, out with the 'rattlesnakes and cows', this was 'a nice little quaint country school' with only 385 students. By 1989 it had almost ten times that number, as the mostly white commuters 'discovered' the area. The district added a second high school, and at the time of the study was constructing a third. Their history has been one of steady growth, and is generally told as one of steady progress as well, leading to a reputation for academic achievement and professional activity.

Just a few years ago this was not, for everyone, a good place to teach. One teacher recalls that 'we had a principal for several years who was in many people's minds just a tyrant and deceitful and many people didn't like working here at that time.' A department chair echoes the sentiment: 'we now know what it's like to live under a totalitarian regime, why people don't revolt.' That principal has moved on, but the stories of that 'regime' remain in circulation. The comments of another chair illustrate the persistent power of that history:

> There's a good bunch of the department that has a sort of built-in paranoia, because there have been some witch-hunts here in the past. So there's an 'us' and 'them' [between teachers and administrators] and that's unfortunate. But you can't ignore their experience.

He finds that experience one that can't be ignored — even though that 'experience' was several years before he even came to the school.

In general, however, teachers describe this school as relatively problem-free: relative to that recent past, to other schools in the state, and to an approaching and less certain future. The need for coordination in a growing district where decentralization was 'part of the culture' is producing some tensions for administrators and teachers. The effects of a third high school are a large unknown. Teachers notice the few minority students sitting together on the wall, and migrant workers moving into the neighboring town (where many of the teachers live) and wonder how the white escapees from the city will respond. Recent growth, which provides a strong financial base, also threatens to overwhelm the atmosphere. The balance here is fragile, and the sentiment expressed is not only that Oak Valley is a good place to be, but that this is a particularly good time to be in Oak Valley.

The Community

Like the school, the community of Oak Valley is sprawling, relatively affluent, and generally quiet. The area surrounding the high school still has a friendly, small town feel, although large new hotels, office buildings, and housing developments are beginning to dominate the landscape. Escaping from the distant city, developers and new residents find reasonable commuting distances (at least by recent standards), a high standard of living, and a remarkably sunny climate (at least to this New Englander). This is, to many newcomers, the epitome of southern California: bright sunshine, clear skies, relaxed pace — this is the school where the morning announcement ended with the call to 'have a kick-back day'.

On one of our early visits I asked an administrator what they do with all these students when it rains — a question which met with bemusement. He patiently explained that on the remote chance that this should ever happen, students could probably move under the overhangs or into classrooms, but that it certainly was not something they needed to prepare for or worry about.

A Science teacher, himself from New England, cited the weather as a major contributor to Oak Valley's atmosphere:

> I think it's multi-faceted. But I think the environment, the warm weather, not having to battle the elements relaxes people. It relaxes the kids. They're not quite as frustrated. They're not having to shovel the snow. They're not having to wear all those heavy clothes. It's very confining wearing heavy clothes. And I think the kids are more relaxed because of that.

The weather, the advent of new water technologies, and the reputation of Oak Valley have led to a period of rapid growth. One teacher recalls how when he came to the school he 'drove in on the road and said, "My God, what have I done to myself, in all these live oaks out here and these rattlesnakes and cows."' What he had done was to locate himself in what would become a thriving commercial and suburban town.

Policy Context

The growth, and the rising affluence, provide not only an enrollment push, but also a financial cushion. Here the 'wonderful little circle' acts not only to link local factors together, but to generate a protective sphere which buffers the district and filters external disturbances out. In California's 'Proposition 13' tax reform, citizens imposed a limit on the rate at which taxation levels could increase. But even with the rate of increase curtailed, the amount and the value of new construction in Oak Valley have protected this district from the financial hardships faced by many districts in California, with Rancho being a prime example:

> We have the best equipped labs of any district. The district supports us. (Voc. ed teacher)

> This district certainly seems well-organized from the top down. I mean there are a lot of complaints when people are negotiating, but when you look around at other districts, you look up in [another nearby district], they never seem to have enough

> money. Somehow this district, I don't know if it's the way it's
> managed down there, I mean everyone gets the same amount
> of money. (Librarian)

With steadily increasing tax rolls, and a district which teachers see as
supportive, the amount of money available to Oak Valley teachers
seems adequate.

Much of the small town atmosphere still flavors the district's
structure: administrators are typically promoted from within the district, and teachers report both familiarity with, and access to, the central
office. Making that easier is the style of the Superintendent, who for
the past twelve years has been an active advocate of decentralization,
which 'is now part of the culture' as an assistant superintendent observed. The limits of that culture, however, are being tested as the
continued growth leads to increasing numbers of schools and raises
new issues of coordination and standardization. The district has brought
teachers from the two high schools together to choose textbooks for
each course, and courses for both schools. At best this has brought
compromise; at worst it means physics teachers who cannot order new
textbooks because they cannot arrive at a compromise, or a new program which one principal almost salivates over but cannot convince his
counterpart to try. Whether a third school added to the political equation will lead to battles, administrative fiat, or an opening of diverse
offerings is unknown, and puzzling to both school and district officials: 'As far as trends, as we grow we run into the "loose/tight
philosophy" . . . how much should we control and how much should
we restrain?' At the time of this study, that question remained to be
answered.

The Students

This has been not only a period of growth, but growth of a particular
kind, as the conditions and the reputation of the district prove strong
attractors to those families particularly committed to schooling. This
'wonderful little circle' produces what one might call a 'Lake Wobegon'[4]
effect: where the staff are hard working, the town is good looking, and
the children are all above average. As another English teacher puts it,
echoing Quentin Ivy's observation,

> the students are really a cut above. They're typical in the sense
> that they moan when there's an assignment given but they'll
> also do the work. I've had success and enjoy working with
> them. It seems to be a good area here: good cooperative spirit
> with the parents and community spirit.

They are 'a cut above' on all kinds of measures: they produce prize-
winning athletic teams and cheerleaders, and by all accounts 'the band

is terrific'. But most important, for the purpose of this study, is the strong sense that these students are 'a cut above' academically. The circle draws parents who have high ambitions for their children and high expectations of their schools; this pushes Oak Valley, and particularly its academic departments, toward a collegiate orientation. From their perspective, one teacher notes,

> as a general term their kid is college bound whether he has the knowledge or not. So there's a push from the community to be conscientious about that. And to have this kid ready for the SATs, for the entrance exams, and so on.

The push from the community affects the course offerings within the school, since, as the principal explains, with a

> higher socio-economic class moving in, [there are] higher expectations for college. We're losing 600 kids, but physics is up forty-five. That's true for science, math, foreign language. Kids are choosing academic electives, what looks good for college, rather than just what they might want to take.

They are choosing higher level academic courses as well. One biology teacher admits, a bit reluctantly, that they still do use tracking in the science sequence. Life science is a general course, while biology has traditionally been for the college bound. But unlike many schools, the distribution of students across these courses is heavily slanted toward the college-bound end:

> we have sixty kids in life science, 659 in biology . . . It's 11 to 1. That's the ratio of our school. 11 to 1 think they're going to college, think they can handle a college level biology. That's what it is; it's a college track.

The circle also shelters this district from the changes in demographics which challenge many California districts. Not only are the students college-bound, and relatively well-off, they are almost exclusively Caucasian and English-speaking; there is little need for the bilingual teachers or classes which in some schools cross departmental boundaries. One teacher guessed that perhaps 3 percent of the students might be minority status, but no one seemed to know. An administrator noted that most of Oak Valley's 'immigrants' are from the Mid-west.

Professional Climate
Not just the school but the staff, too, is enfolded within this 'little circle' that defines Oak Valley as a good place to work, and extends its

reputation, and attraction, well beyond district boundaries: a new principal tells of his excitement at coming to this 'wonderful' district; a new teacher relates how 'when I came here I thought I'd died and gone to heaven; this was such a lovely place.' And another experienced teacher echoes the value of Oak Valley's reputation:

> It feels really prestigious to be an Oak Valley teacher. I mean, I'll come in contact with other people or friends of my husband, and they'll ask me where I teach and I'll say at Oak Valley High and they say 'oh gee, I've heard so much about Oak Valley' and it's always been in the newspapers.

Oak Valley not only is attractive to new faculty, it also has a reputation for selecting, and retaining, a highly qualified staff. Like the students, they tend to be ambitious, and academically oriented. Many teachers mentioned the 'modular scheduling' that a former principal brought to the school in the late 1960s, as an additional filter: demands for time and innovation were high, and a number of people left, so, as one recalls, 'Oak Valley was left with a real strong faculty. People were sold on what they were doing and came in and worked.' The sense is that this was a staff who were adventurous and could take the grueling pace when 'we saw 200 students in a day. It took a lot more work.'

Part of the definition of work here extends well beyond the school day, or the district boundaries. Teachers are actively involved in subject associations, sit on state level committees, pilot programs for state officials, and a number publish in professional and literary journals. Through such activities the teachers at Oak Valley continue to extend, and to earn, their reputation.

Departmentalization

While teachers may be involved in professional activities which take them across school and district boundaries, on campus they seldom venture beyond the departmental ones. The sunshine and clear skies of southern California affect the architecture of the school, which in turn has consequences for the departments within it: several teachers note this, for the campus is 'somewhat fragmented and large, and the way the school is designed we're departmentalized'. Although many of the buildings are recent additions to accommodate rapidly increasing enrollment, the original campus had twelve buildings and departments have always been physically separated. While there is a faculty lunchroom, it can only hold perhaps twenty of the 137 teachers, and so most eat in their department offices. Departments are thus quite distant from each other literally and metaphorically, and the hallway interactions of students and teachers or teachers and colleagues described at other schools almost non-existent — there simply are no halls.

Department chairs at Oak Valley are appointed by the principal, and serve as the chief administrators of what are fairly large divisions within the school. Academic departments range in size from the English department's twenty-four full-time members to Science and Social Studies' faculties of sixteen. Since each department has its own building, and an office or resource room of its own, and since decentralization has become part of the culture, these divisions tend to be semi-autonomous, developing strikingly different modes of interaction and of governance.

Having to coordinate curriculum across school boundaries but within subjects further decreases the sense in which the school itself constitutes a meaningful organizational unit, and perhaps strengthens teachers' commitment to their own departments. Many teachers cited the wonderful opportunities for professional development provided by the Oak Valley district, but those opportunities are most often within the subject area:

> This district has prompted my professionalism; there's no doubt about it. I mean they just gave me all kinds of opportunities and in anything that's done here, even for the remodeling of the English department, the architect even comes in and shows the English teacher the plans. (English teacher)

This sense of subject orientation and departmental isolation is something the new principal is trying to overcome, creating committees, working toward a Humanities program, and calling a series of 'period meetings' where all teachers with the same planning period are brought together to discuss school issues. At these meetings, one teacher reports, 'you can't sit at the same table as someone else in your department.' The principal sees this effort as being received with enthusiasm: 'I have a staff that is dying in communication and dying to be able to have conversations with each other about things that matter.' As an example he offers the story of the Physics and Math teachers 'who were both teaching vectors [although] neither of them knew it.' The meeting allowed them to begin a collaborative effort.

A number of teachers, however, are wary of any strategy which threatens departmental boundaries. Some remember, from the 'totalitarian' era, that the worst 'punishment' the prior principal gave out was that 'you would have to teach a course you don't want to teach, or you will be taken out of your department' and given courses in an unfamiliar subject. That history, as well as the more obvious conditions of size and architecture, produce in Oak Valley a highly departmentalized school. On the 1989 CRC survey, the Oak Valley faculty showed the highest level of departmental identification of any school in the sample.

Rancho High School

We had a year to plan this school. Then we had what we call the 'We Agree' with the staff, commitments, and then moved from there. And the structure was that every four years you recommit . . . kind of a fine-tuning thing . . . that was nice, because we were a SIP (School Improvement Program) school, and we could use SIP days, and then the Board took those away, and said no, we do not want to have students that are not going to school, we want them in school for longer hours. And that was devastating. So, but that was only one thing. It was sort of like a contingency universe. You touch this one little thing there didn't seem in and of itself all that significant, but it really had a rippling effect to all kinds of things. And yet I think the school functioned fairly well. I think last year was really hard. It's like all kinds of organizations — you can't see the dry rot for quite a while, and then you get to the point where you're really kind of, you know, dead in the water. And last year I think was a really tough year. Other schools had the same kind of year, but they weren't coming from the position where they had seen the possibilities. I think maybe that's even worse, when you can see the potential it can really be a different kind of a model for schools.

At Rancho one dominant story is of the school that might have been: its ambition was to design a whole new organizational structure in which the traditional subject-centered organization, and orientation, would be replaced with a child-centered advisory one. In this 'contingency universe', however, an overwhelming series of external forces kept 'touch[ing]' little things here and there, converging to create an atmosphere a veteran teacher describes as one of 'strife, stress, [and] chaos' (Siskin, in press). The assistant principal who described the course of events above was involved with the initial planning of the school, and was a site administrator in what she refers to as the 'Camelot period'. Since then she has spent several years in district-level posts, and has come back to Rancho at least for a semester — her stay is uncertain. Uncertainty, and a constant press of rapid, external, and unpredictable change, are predominant characteristics of this school.

School History

In 1976 a team of administrators and teachers, selected before the school was even built, were authorized by a supportive district to 'be something different', and to develop a new program. This was a growing community, with a fairly stable, middle-class population; the team spent the first planning-year analyzing local student needs and devising structural alternatives. Although they relied primarily on local taxes for funding, they obtained extra state funds available through a program for what was then called 'School Improvement' — grants for schools which would put forward innovative proposals that would include, in some form, community involvement.

After a year of planning the team had their innovative 'Rancho Plan'. As one of the original members, an Art teacher, remembers it:

> At that time there was a strong message from the district to decentralize. Rancho was supposed to be different. The School Improvement Council was supposed to be a viable, powerful body. As a teacher I would have input over what happened in the school. We had leadership training, training in conflict resolution, shared decision-making. We were on the cutting edge. We could generate our own curriculum to match student needs; we had resources, time, money.

Through the 'Rancho Plan' the staff were actively involved in designing a new model to fit their particular student body: new staffing patterns, curriculum, even the plans for the building itself. Through district support and state funding they were given the resources to put their designs in place. They saw themselves as creating 'a special vision in terms of educational design'.

The vision which this team developed called for deliberate restructuring of traditional organizational design, replacing departmental divisions and hierarchical levels with a program of participatory decision-making, and a staff divided into three advisory units. All staff, including administrators, eighty-five teachers, counseling, and clerical staff, were divided into these units, called 'learning houses'. Each unit would operate to some degree independently, but all shared the same central function: advising students.

But following quickly on the heels of the 'Camelot period' came the series of unforeseen, and unforeseeable events which created the period of 'strife, stress, and chaos'. Actions taken by the district, state, and even the courts have played a critical role in shaping events at Rancho.

Policy Context
Rancho, unlike Oak Valley with its 'wonderful little circle' to protect it, is described by teachers as 'an island' in the midst of stormy seas, buffeted continuously by threatening waves from policy context, community, and student demographics. Larry Cuban (1984) has suggested the 'metaphor of a hurricane' to understand educational change, comparing the waves and winds on the surface to the theories and rhetoric of reform, while below, classroom practice remains 'an unruffled calm' (p. 2). Rancho's teachers, however, locate their school and themselves

at the surface, and thus subject to the full force of the storm. Turbulent sea images occur frequently: one offers the image of the school as 'an island' being 'hit by waves'. Another ventures, even more precipitously, that 'this district is an absolute, utter mess. Can I be frank? Rancho is the raised flag of a sinking ship.'

While Oak Valley has a district which has been able to buffer the school from external pressures, at Rancho boundaries are open and fluid. After a declared bankruptcy much of the district's fiscal authority became subject to state surveillance. Contract disputes have been turned over to external arbitrators. Additionally, a federal court has assumed direct control and close supervision of many aspects of the district since a 1985 desegregation order. The decisions of these outsiders reach directly into teachers' professional lives: paychecks, expenditures for supplies, rules for curricular choices, the composition and transportation of the student body — all are directly influenced by outsiders. The last ten years have been turbulent times.

The district not only 'attracts turbulence', as a district administrator suggests, its circumstances make it extremely vulnerable to these forces. Proposition 13, the California taxpayer revolt, hit particularly hard: in its wake, the district laid off over 500 teachers, cut the high school day to five periods, and eliminated the counselors who had been crucial to the Rancho design. Without this support, the teachers found themselves on overload, as 'they changed the names but the work remained.'

When next the state, in turn facing fiscal shortfalls, declared that districts with declining enrollments would receive no increases in aid, the district situation worsened, for enrollments were dropping. The School Board closed seventeen schools and moved the 9th graders into what had been senior high schools, assigning into Rancho a new group of teachers who were neither selected for nor committed to the advisory program. At that time too, as labor relations became increasingly tense, teachers began what would become a persistent tradition of 'work-to-rule' practice — refusing to perform any but contractually-specified tasks. Such an action creates a hardship in any school, but particularly in one which depends on a model of participatory decision-making. Department meetings, unit meetings, curriculum development, work on developing a new peer observation program — all came to screeching halt, since all such activities are dependent on teachers taking on more than they are obligated, or paid, to do. As one Rancho veteran put it, 'we aren't going to kill ourselves when we don't feel there is any payoff there.'

Rancho was also particularly vulnerable to the district's move to centralize and standardize curriculum to ensure equal opportunity. From the Superintendent's perspective, the desegregation order made this essential: there was no choice. We need to be consistent. We have to standardize access and curriculum. It is not a matter of philosophy; it is a matter of necessity. Suddenly, people at the district level are working on aligning, standardizing, etc. Teachers resent this.

The teachers at Rancho clearly did resent this, for it undermined the essence of what they thought their school was all about and removed the sense of control over decisions critical to their work:

you had staff input, shared decision-making; you felt like you had control of your fate. When they centralized they took away the control of the school; they made edicts outside the school. It just goes on and on and you felt totally helpless . . . As the board became more and more conservative and started to become centralized, it started reviewing some of [the principal's] decisions. And once you did that he had to take the responsibility for our decisions and he started overriding decisions that the School Improvement Council made, or not using the SIC as a vehicle.

Finally, and during the time of this study, came the effects of state curricular reform, as state policy SB 813 began to hit the classrooms in a series of 'framework' guidelines covering texts, content, and teaching techniques, and developing tests to monitor their adoption. While this bill was adopted in 1983, it has taken several years for the actual guidelines to reach the schools, and the progress has moved with varying speed in different subjects. The arrival is stressful, for while they have had little chance yet to work with the specific guidelines, Rancho teachers have come to expect the worst. One chair vividly depicts the sense of conflict:

the people involved with this are kind of a distinct breed — real cloak and dagger stuff. [The district] wanted us to sign a paper saying we agree to this before they would give it to us. Even at the state level it's supposed to be a secret; you're supposed to go to summer training workshops [before you can see it].

Increasingly, then, policy-making is seen as centralized, standardized, and distanced from the classroom and the school decision-making structures — and antithetical to school needs. It is a policy context in which only two things are constant: that there will be some external crisis, and that it will be bad for the school. One teacher resignedly explains that 'I've been here seven years and each year it is something unusual. There's always some crisis in the district.'

For some time, the relations between teachers and district have been characterized by such stress, and by an overall atmosphere of distrust. Labor relations have been repeatedly tense, with the district charging the union with unrealistic greed and the union charging the district with hiding assets. This is a situation that a new administration is trying to change, and both sides are moving toward new forms of negotiations. Over the three years of this study, the policy context, in terms of district relations, has shown some evidence of that change (Bascia, in press).

Community
An important part of the Rancho Plan was its deliberate attempt to fit the particular needs of its community, a middle-class area at one edge of a large city. Less fashionable than the nearby suburbs to which executives and engineers have moved, the neighborhood is a mix of residential, commercial, and manufacturing areas, bounded by one of California's huge highways. Built when the city, and the school re-source base were expanding, and designed to fit into this growing community, Rancho now finds itself divorced from its neighbors. Under the desegregation order the immediate community (the neighborhood) and the school community (the students and parents) have been separated by court decree. Students now come from homes distant not only from the school but from each other; even students from the same family may be bused in different directions to achieve racial balance. Many of the local parents are fairly active by district standards, according to the principal, but there is no program to reach out to the more distant ones. Their absence is strongly felt, for Rancho's design called for community involvement and built an expectation of parental support. For many teachers, their child-centered approach requires getting to know not only the child but the family as well, and for them the loss of community is a high cost of desegregation.

Students
The desegregation plan dramatically changed the student body, dis-persing the neighborhood students whose needs the plan had been designed to serve, and bringing in new students, with new sets of problems. As one teacher says, 'we've gone from being a school that was very, very middle-class and upper middle-class to a wide range of students and all the problems they bring.' The busing that brings the students in made altogether impossible the extra contact, the before- and after-school conferences with teachers which had been a corner-stone of the program. It creates logistical nightmares for teachers and students alike:

> the court monitor should ride the bus for one solid month, every day, to see what it's really like for these kids, and to be

subjected to the same gang aspects on the same bus, and to be subject to the insults and the inconvenience.

With the new students, many of whom do not speak English, teachers have found themselves having to develop new skills to teach new assignments — ESL classes, transition classes — where they wanted to maintain the school goals of personalization and caring, but were not always sure how. One teacher recalls how she had a problem with one student:

> She was being abused, and I said, 'why don't you come home, you know, feel that you can stay at my house if it gets really bad' . . . that night there was the daughter, there was the mother, and there was the son. They moved in. Of course, I allowed it to happen, but they moved in. They stayed with me so long (about six weeks) that I was afraid that I was going to have to buy a six-foot Christmas tree.

The small gestures of caring that were appropriate to a Camelot era are simply incommensurate with the needs of Rancho's new student body.

Professional Climate

The staff who were chosen for this school, and who chose to come to Rancho, were by all accounts a special group of people — in a number of ways. They were strong academically. They were also, as one remembers, 'leaders, opinion setters'. A second describes them as 'the risk-takers. It was a very innovative school; it was going to try to set a brand new trend in education.' Yet another describes them as 'boat-rockers' and 'rebels' — among other, more graphic terms ('shit-disturbers') — and adds that their former schools were at least as happy to be rid of them as Rancho was to welcome them. They either came in as, or were quickly converted to, advocates for the special mission of caring for students.

Their energies, initially channeled toward devising programs for their students, have in recent years centered around protecting those programs, and each other, against the unwelcome intrusions of the external forces.

Departmentalization

Departmentalization is a complex issue at this school, closely tied to emotional issues of loyalty. On the one hand, it is equated with loss of the original mission of the school; on the other, it provides a 'comfort zone' to teachers under stress.

The original design of the Rancho Plan set out deliberately to break down traditional departmentalized boundaries: 'That was the whole idea, to have the units to get away from each department for themselves.' The administrators saw strong departments as a threat, both to what they wanted to accomplish for students and to developing a sense of school commitment for faculty. One explained that

> the three administrators who came here when the school opened were all strong department chairmen, in their own schools. And I think we all saw the dangers of a school that has a department, for whatever reason, that becomes sort of the tail that wags the dog.

For them, the units were a way of avoiding the fragmentation, and the competition, which they had seen in their own experience:

> The units were really a way of having teachers structured in a non-departmental fashion . . . And the idea was that you would force teachers, because of the set that you would put them in, you would force them to really look at the total student . . . To also look at the school as a whole, just as an administrator does, or a counselor. Most teachers don't have that experience in high school.

In the beginning, the teachers, and the units, did 'tend to somewhat fulfill these roles'. The organizational chart of the school listed the names of all staff members in three columns, one for each Unit. Within each they were further divided into 'learning areas' — such as Communications or Scientific Skills — with department affiliation reduced to merely a parenthetical label. It was the Unit which was to provide a sense of community, to serve as the site for conversations about students and about cross-disciplinary curricular innovations. The form of the chart still remains, but under the stresses of recent years, and without the financial, policy, and community support systems to hold them together, the functioning of the Units has weakened considerably.

In their place, the departments which were originally identified as part of the problem have re-emerged as teachers struggle with new problems never anticipated by the Rancho Plan. It is within the departments that teachers grapple with the subject-specific guidelines of the state framework. It is as departments that they receive the district's efforts to standardize curriculum, and fill out reports for the court-appointed monitor. Increasingly, they turn to their subject-colleagues for support, and for common understandings of the challenges they face. Departmentalization, at Rancho, is an emerging feature of the school, alternately cast as a retreat from the vision of what might have been, and as a necessary mechanism for survival.

Highlander High School

How could you send your son to Highlander? How could you
teach at Highlander?. . . I tell people, 'you ought to come to
Highlander. I'm proud of Highlander. You ought to come to
Highlander someday. You ought to walk the halls. You ought
to come and see my class sometime. You've got to be in the
halls. Sure, there's 2,000 kids walking the halls in the building,
and sure, most of them are minority students. But most of
them are going to school to get an education.'

Highlander is a large urban high school, located in Burton, Michigan.
Burton is dominated, physically and economically, by large auto plants
which once ran around the clock, but now sit strangely silent. Many
of the commercial and office buildings nearby, and the shops that
supplied the suppliers, are closed or struggling to survive. It is a
challenging environment for a school. The above comments by a Social
Studies teacher highlight in rapid succession the central themes of
Highlander as a place to teach: the presence of family, the tone of
defiant optimism and pride, the recognition of the problems of an
urban minority school, the chaotic schedule of a large and complex
student body, and the will to survive in the face of those challenges.

School History
The building which houses Highlander is a large three-story structure, built in what one researcher called 'Stalinesque' architectural style:
heavy, and imposing. It sits like a fortress in the midst of the community, presenting a stolid face and a reassuring presence. The school staff,
however, locate their school in a history which extends even beyond
the 1971 construction of this building, to the 1928 establishment of the
original Highlander High. There is a strong sense of school identity
here. While Oak Valley works to establish its identity and Rancho
seems in fear of losing its, Highlander is a school with a deep sense of
its own traditions, its own history, and its own special mission. The
principal is 'proud of the fact that I'm the fifth principal' in all that
time, 'and that tells you something about Highlander'. His conversations
are, as are many in this school, filled with references to Highlander's
'history', its 'tradition', the sense of 'continuity'.

The original Highlander opened as the second school to be built
in the Burton district. It is the school which would, throughout its
history, serve the 'underdog' part of the community, the most recent
arrivals in a series of immigrant waves drawn to the assembly lines. In
that history they find a special sense of purpose, and pride: 'we were
always the underdog, [with] a lot of determination, so they've always
had a lot of success, always had a pretty good racial harmony because

for sixty years people have become accustomed to working together, because of their differences.' While a number of staff remember 'the racial disturbances' of the late 1960s, they remember those years as an anomaly in the school's history, fueled by national rather than local conditions.

Highlander has always been the school which served minority community, although as the Principal notes, over the decades the particular minorities have changed: 'It was the Czechoslovakians, then the Mexicans, all the underdogs, a few Blacks, and so over the years that has been the history.' At the time of the study 85 percent of the students were of minority background, most of them now African-American. The teaching staff has long been racially mixed, and the current principal and vice-principal are both Black.

It is a school which takes special pride in the success of its graduates, and its graduates credit the school with preparing them well. Alumni return to the school to provide role models, and to tell students how they have made it. They also have set up a growing scholarship fund to help current students achieve the same success, despite economic problems. In 1986 the Alumni Association provided three $500 scholarships; in 1989 they gave twenty-two of that amount, and one of $750. Overcoming challenges is presented as a Highlander tradition, and skill.

Community
What drew these immigrants for many years was the auto industry, and the promise of a better standard of living — the essential American dream of upward mobility. But as Burton epitomized the American dream of industrial progress, it also epitomizes the recent economic crises. Built almost exclusively on the fortunes of the auto industry, the area now suffers from massive lay-offs and plant closings. Vacant houses, for-sale signs, and eviction notices dot the streets. With unemployment high and revenues falling far below needs, one Michigan mayor spent $20,000 to bring in an evangelist to pray for recovery. Few local or state officials offer more promising alternatives.

The school is tightly tied to the local community, and the economic problems affect the school in a number of ways. School officials describe increasing problems with drugs and security in the city: 'the last few years with the drug thing across our community, too many kids are living amongst the drugs and the violence, the crime, they see so much of that. That is always a challenge for us,' but most report that the 'schools are still safe'.

The school works to stay safe. Classrooms are kept locked for 'security' reasons, and teachers carry bunches of keys for access. The issue of security is an important one for teachers, for, as a twenty-year veteran explains, 'you have to have good security guards all the time.

A good security guard is worth quite a bit; I would put him right up there with administrators. A building climate where I can do my job is important.'

The school, however, has not locked the community out. The traditions of the school as meeting-place, as resource for community activity go back a long way, and the principal reports that, despite budget cuts, the school still stays open and in use till ten o'clock at night. Building community remains an important, if increasingly difficult, role for the school and staff.

Policy Context

What is more important than a climate where teachers can do their jobs, recently, is the issue of having a job. As the recession spills over into lower resources and declining enrollments, Highlander teachers, like the autoworkers, are experiencing massive lay-offs. This one issue dominates the interviews, and it dominates all aspects of teaching in this school. The district, according to all, is 'in dire stress in terms of money'. In 1987 192 Burton teachers were laid-off; by contract requirements, lay-offs proceed in order of seniority within certification areas. At Highlander among the most junior teachers now are those with eighteen years seniority. Faculty have learned to keep track of their tenure in terms of months and days: 'she has two months less seniority than I have' notes one who is at the bottom of the list. Another reports that he is 'the low man on the rung of the entire school system in Social Studies' now that his colleague with only seventeen years has been let go. He describes his own distress, and the system's confusion, when fall enrollments turned up even lower than projections and it became clear that Highlander would have to let more teachers go:

> In a twenty minute period, depending to which assistant principal I talked to, I was here; I was gone; I was here. I talked to three different administrators, got three different stories . . . Then we got a note passed from the Principal: 'We're going to lose somebody in Social Studies and/or English. Would any of you like to volunteer to go someplace?' I'm entrenched in this place. My mother graduated from Highlander High School. I graduated from Highlander High School. My son moved to Highlander High School. Played ball here. I've coached here. I'm pretty entrenched in this place. If I wasn't, as soon as my coaching days are gone, my son is gone, maybe I'd say yes; try something else. I didn't want to go.

And in fact someone else did volunteer. But this teacher remained at the bottom of the list, anxiously awaiting the next year's numbers.

Perhaps because of the immediacy of the lay-offs, or perhaps because of the traditions of local control, few other policies, from the state or district, turn up in teachers' discussions of their work. Instead they stress their independence. Both the state and district are fairly loose in terms of controls, with paper requirements that appear to have little direct effect on practice. The state requires competency tests for graduation, for example, but most students pass them in the first year so the high school teachers are hardly affected. The district, too, has policies and curricular guidelines, but 'we have guidelines but I would say they are fairly loosely structured'. There are district-wide textbooks, chosen by committees of teachers, but then individuals can add their own materials or change the pace: 'they tell me what chapter I should probably start on, but I can skip around, you know, as I choose.' District policies are sent to the school, where they are modified, and then given to teachers, who are free to modify them again:

> There's a master plan for the district, then there's one more suited for our own school. We sit down at the beginning of school, decide what's taught, you teach whatever you want to teach, but we emphasize certain things. We all try to stay within certain parameter. Rather than overlap, we try to go side by side . . . I'm given a great degree of freedom to teach. In fact it feels good. (Science teacher)

> As far as what we can and can't teach, I don't have any problems. There's a lot of academic freedom around here,. . . they pretty much leave us alone. (Social Studies teacher)

> I view the classroom as my domain. I am the professional. I can make the decisions for my class. (Social Studies teacher)

In general, teachers agree with this English teachers' assessment that 'there is a movement to standardize a little bit more', but in the end 'we go inside the room and close the door'.

Rather than as a directing programs, or as yet another layer of bureaucratic management, teachers at Highlander talk repeatedly about the district as a support system — one personified through individual district directors and coordinators. In these references the district people are quite distinct from the impersonal 'district' which hands down the budgets and pink-slips. Like Oak Valley, there is a small town atmosphere which pervades the relationships. The principal reports that he 'has the most contact' with the director of senior high schools, someone who was previously a principal in the district, 'so he has been there', is well-known, and can be turned to for support. Faculty, directly or through their chairs, turn to the district coordinators for each subject area. These are district officials whose responsibilities include supervising and supporting teaching, but more often they appear to manage the system for the teacher. They find and deliver needed resources: one Science teacher who often finds himself running over budget on supplies will 'find that I'm often short. All I have to do is call my science coordinator and say I need such and such and it's there.' Another, whose need for computers far exceeded available resources, called the coordinator — together they located an external funder, worked through the grant process, and brought in $20,000. It is through such contacts, rather than through formal policies, that classroom practices are most obviously affected by the district.

Where district policy does turn out to have direct effect on classroom issues is in terms of student attendance. In the 1970s, the district devised a magnet program to increase racial balance and avoid the possibility of a desegregation order. Highlander became a magnet for Math and Science; another high school for English and Social Studies. It was a plan which drew top teachers in these subjects to the magnet schools, and according to the principal, 'pretty much brought in a whole new Math and Science department here'.

The Students

The magnet program was also a policy that bought in new students. It substantially altered the composition, and the logistics, of the student body. High achieving math and science students come from all over the district — not for the whole day, but just for specific classes. Only the Math and Science teachers work with these students. Approximately 20 percent of Highlander students go off to other magnet courses in other schools; Vocational Education students travel in still other directions.

The notion of a student body here is highly complex: it is almost impossible to figure out who Highlander students are, where they are coming from, or where they are going. At Oak Valley a set number of primarily middle-class kids arrive together, study together, and expect to go on to same future — college. At Rancho, students come from variety of neighborhoods, and countries before that, but their day is fairly standard once they arrive at school. At Highlander, according to the counselor, students come from a mix of neighborhoods: 'we draw from the very poorest to the very upper middle class.' They also come and go from school to school for a variety of programs, in a complicated schedule which guarantees that there are always lots of students on the way in or out.

The principal's attempt to explain how that schedule works took one and a half single-spaced pages to transcribe: it includes three lunch periods, whose bells do not match class bells; the incoming magnet students 'are coming and going all day long, . . . most of them take two or three classes, so one group left here at 9:30, another . . . at

10:30; also at 9:10 our Skill Center kids leave our building and go to the Vocational Center'; there are also the Highlander students who attend magnet classes at other schools, who 'are coming back every hour almost'. He concludes by explaining, somewhat unnecessarily, 'I'm just showing you, it can look confusing sometimes.' Despite the confusion, the halls remain remarkably quiet.

The school administration keeps hallways quiet in part by direct supervision, but also relies heavily on symbolic strategies. While the district does not have a dress code, the school does, insisting that students need to look like they are ready to learn. Routine messages reinforce the theme: 'every day on the P.A. we talk about character . . . we keep saying "you become what you do." ' The ritual closing to the deputy principal's morning announcements reminds students daily that it may 'only take a minute to get into trouble, but a lifetime to get out'. The one morning that she neglected to include this phrase, the secretary reports that students came crowding into the office to find out what was wrong.

Teachers, too, stress such strategies, which provide both continuity and a message of caring to students whose needs for support systems are increasing. They worry about the external pressures students are bringing into the schools: 'that's one of the pressures they're feeling; that economically you can't survive.' Students are seen as overwhelmingly pressured by economic concerns, tempted by drugs and drug money, and increasingly difficult to teach:

> You hear kids talking pretty roughly. People are being killed and it doesn't seem to be a big deal . . . I don't know how rough it is. And if a kid goes home and is worried about not going outside because they might get shot, or they might get . . . maybe survival. If you had to choose between survival and education, I don't think there is any question which I would pick. I would pick survival. Maybe we are in a situation at this point, and I don't know if we are or we aren't, that kids truly have so many things going on that education really isn't on the top burner; it is kind of on the back. God, I hope not, that it is not the reason, but you know, every once in a while you will find some history behind one of your kids and gees, you know, it is a wonder that the kid even was coming to school, let alone coming and misbehaving and then doing all those things. (Social Studies teacher)

Most teachers, like the following Math teacher, seem committed to meeting the challenge in one way or another: 'you have to deal with a lot of things that I would say are not directly related to content . . . you have to listen to things that are going on in the community, things that are going on in their lives.' The challenges here are constantly demanding, and highly stressful.

Professional Climate

At Oak Valley the professional climate centers around scholastics; at Rancho it centers around survival. Here at Highlander teachers can be characterized by their commitment to service. There is a strong sense of the special 'calling' of teaching, and of serving the needs of students and community. This is a theme carried by the administrators and teachers alike: there are repeated and strong hints of church language, sometimes directly connected to religion, more often metaphorically to education as religion. The principal uses church language around education: he worked for a year in business, 'but found out during that year that teaching was my calling, and I had a difficult time driving by a school' so he came back to teaching and has remained at Highlander since 1965.

Other interviews echo the church language repeatedly. One teacher, who would prefer to be teaching in a small school, 'thought about transferring, but the principal is a good man, he is a man I can trust, a Christian man. I am a Christian too, and like that aspect of it.' Another explains that he became a teacher because of positive experiences as recreation leader with church youth groups. And a Science teacher uses preaching strategies in the classroom: ' "If you want to survive, not end up in [the state prison] you will prepare yourself." I preach that everyday for about two minutes. They buy into it.'

Teachers and administrators here do have job descriptions, but also the expectation that they will go beyond those tasks when demanded, to help students or each other. As the deputy principal says, there are job descriptions which state the responsibilities for each person, but they don't really reveal what people do, 'because if you limit yourself to those things, then there are things that won't get done'. A secretary talks about how at Highlander they handle the inevitable disasters with non-functioning xerox machines: 'we've only had service out here twice. We also have about six male teachers, particularly Science, Graphic Arts. Normally they can fix it in a matter of minutes.'

By the same token she usually leaves school when her scheduled workday is over, unless:

> well, if there is something going on, where you just need a little extra help. Like next Tuesday, for instance, and I'm not trying to brag, but I do think you need to know what goes on in a school like this, next Tuesday is what we call an appreciation luncheon. This luncheon is given to department chairmen, to advisors, to people who throughout the school year have done a little extra, they've given of themselves in one way or another,

to make us a better place to work in or to study in. That luncheon will be held here in the building. So we will be doing a lot of preparation for that.

But pink-slipping, in the anxieties of fearing for one's own job and in supporting those who are losing theirs, is clearly beginning to take a toll. One teacher observed that it's 'almost like they're different people' now, that after eighteen years at the school 'you don't consider job changes', but should be thinking about retirement. But other kinds of job changes occur when teachers experience and anticipate the stress of lay-offs. Some speak not only of no longer going beyond their jobs, but of an inability to function even at minimal levels: 'I don't really care what goes on. I'm just going to stay here, . . . do whatever I want and if it's good for the kids, fine; if it's not, who cares.' The professional climate, at the time of this study, was clearly stressful.

Departmentalization
Departmentalization at Highlander is complicated by the fact that Science and Math are constituted as district magnet departments. In these departments faculty were selected from across the district as the best in their field, students are brought in to take special courses, and classrooms are literally as well as figuratively 'at the top', up by themselves on the third floor. Teachers here turn to each other for social, professional, and intellectual interactions; they devise new programs, evaluate ongoing classes, share materials and support.

English and Social Studies, on the other hand, house teachers who were not selected for their magnet programs, and export many of the students who would take advanced classes. Their physical segregation is weaker: Social Studies shares a wing with teachers in Foreign Languages and Special Ed, and it is in this wing that Joan Frances, the English teacher cited in the introduction, has her room.

Highlander is referred to repeatedly as having a strong departmental organization — which means that the divisions between departments are strong. This is particularly true for the magnet departments, whose members seldom come downstairs, but also characterizes interactions more generally. It is a large school, the largest in the county, and teachers have little time to get to know each other. The comment made by one, that 'in this building there are many teachers I do not know', was not unusual. Classrooms are grouped by subjects into separate wings, so teachers report much contact within the department, but very little across departments. An English teacher points to the additional influence of the lounge area, 'which is right in the middle of the department, so that you eat lunch with those in your department, if you go to the restroom it will be those in your own department, so it's good, it's really good'.

The principal contrasts Highlander with other schools in the district, which use their department chairs mainly to take care of supplies. He says that at Highlander they use chairs as 'instructional leaders' and the job description, which is printed, matches this. But one chair reports that she 'handles supplies for the department and that's about it', and another administrator complains that there is no mechanism for removing chairs whose 'leadership' is less active. Chairs at Highlander, according to another, 'are not administrators, they are teachers who receive a stipend (perhaps as much as $1000 based on department size) for being chairs'.

Much of the administrative, and instructional leadership responsibility lies with the vice-principal, who is in charge of instruction and of the day-to-day operations of the school. She meets regularly with department chairs, and frequently attends department meetings. She is actively and closely involved in department and instructional matters of all kinds, regularly greeting teachers at the door in the morning to provide encouraging words and to scan for problems: 'it's just on their faces. Some people I can tell by the way they walk what kind of day they're going to have', and sometimes, just by listening or giving a few well-chosen words, she can change that day. Her attention to detail extends to 'small things, such as getting all of your male department heads to wear ties . . . there's only one department head who does not, and he knows we're working on that. And I think it's going to happen.' On the days of my interviews there it did happen.

District policies and organization, particularly in the form of subject coordinators, reinforce departmentalization, in the sense of strengthening subject identification and divisions. Each department reports to, and appeals to, its own official. These coordinators, like the school administrators, function to strengthen the divisions — yet they simultaneously weaken the division's strength. They serve as a site for expertise and support which lies outside the department, an alternative to the department chair or collective.

With all of this supportive context, there is little sense of department center, or cohesiveness, as a result of anything the department is doing, and less perceived need for leadership from the chair. Teachers describe socializing almost exclusively within the department, and give instances of sharing materials, techniques, support — but they describe these as accidental occurrences rather than deliberate ones. There are few formal or routinized informal mechanisms for sharing information as a department. One teacher tells how he asked for, and his department will try, a meeting where faculty share 'tips and techniques' that have worked for them — an experiment in collegial sharing. He describes their regular monthly meetings as a 'waste of time', partly since they see each other so often anyway, but also because nothing of substance happens there. His chair comments on the same experiment, saying that this kind of discussion is something she has tried to have in the past, but has been unable to accomplish. She reports being 'glad' the suggestion came, and came from a teacher — maybe now it will work.

Departments at Highlander are formal mechanisms, and architectural divisions, but they are tied together by a powerful sense of school as community, and by the active involvement and control of the administration. Highlander provides a case where departmentalization is strong, but the departments themselves are not.

Conclusion

These are the three high schools in which the study took place. All are comprehensive high schools, all fairly large, all reasonably typical of what American high schools are like.

At the same time the three schools create quite different contexts in which departments operate, and are clearly quite different places in which to teach. What resources are available and for what purposes they are most needed, who the students are and where they are going, how much discretion teachers have over what they teach, all can be understood as school characteristics. Teaching at Highlander is not like teaching at Oak Valley. Yet looking at the schools gives only part of the story, for teaching in the English department at Oak Valley is not like teaching in its Science department either. The following chapters examine the roles the academic departments themselves play in dividing schools and creating distinctly different contexts for the teachers within them.

Notes

1 A full list of interviews which were used for this study, and an explanation of the coding used to identify the sources, can be found in Appendix A.
2 Survey items are included in Appendix B. The index referred to here looks at the degree to which teachers identify with the department rather than the school. The range is 4.6 (in an alternative school with nine teachers) to 9.5 out of a possible 12 points.
3 These departments and their stories are included in the larger CRC study — see, for example, Little and Threatt's 1991 analysis of vocational teachers in 'Work on the Margins'.
4 'Lake Wobegon' is a fictional Minnesota town created by writer Garrison Keillor in the 1980s.

Chapter 4

Boundaries and Barriers

> For let no one be deceived, the important things that happen in
> schools result from the interaction of personalities. (Willard
> Waller, 1932, 1967)

> There are major interactions here in the department: little cel-
> ebration, but here in the department we coordinate, we col-
> laborate, we have kind of a modified team-teaching type
> situation. We share materials and curricula. Not much at all
> outside the department . . . For myself, I just don't leave this
> wing that often, unless I have to go to the office or run an
> errand. I have the materials I need here. I'm comfortable here.
> (Yancy Dean, Science teacher, 1989)

Willard Waller began his *Sociology of Teaching* with the assertion that
what is most important in understanding the 'concrete realities' of
schools is the 'web' of social relationships amongst those who inhabit
them. He set out to tell 'what every teacher knows, that the world
of the school is a social world. Those human beings who live together
in the school, though deeply severed in one sense, nevertheless spin a
tangled web of interrelationships; that web and the people in it make
up the social world of the school' (preface, p. 1). But while teachers in
this study confirm the importance of social interactions, both in constructing their own sense of professional identity and in influencing
what they do while in the 'deeply severed' confines of their classrooms, their sense of the 'tangled web of interrelationships' and the
boundaries of their social worlds differs sharply from that which Waller
detailed sixty years ago. For, as Yancy Dean puts it, and as so many
of the teachers in this study attest, the social world of the school has
expanded to such a degree that it has finally contracted, or splintered,
to where the department rather than the school effectively marks the
bounds of 'major interactions' for most teachers.

This chapter examines the boundaries departments create within schools, and the barriers they present to school-wide communications and interactions. Oak Valley and Highlander provide examples of highly departmentalized high schools. In those settings boundary strength can be understood in terms of:

- the continuing need for social relationships;
- the increasing size of schools (which makes the full faculty too large to satisfy the need and leads to the development of subgroups);
- the architectural design (which creates barriers to school-wide or interdepartmental relationships, and makes the department the most likely subgroup); and
- the institutionalized pull of academic orientation (which makes local attempts to restructure schools to break down those traditional barriers unlikely).

Rancho allows an opportunity to examine departmental strength from a different angle, for that school has made a concerted — but not entirely successful — effort to break down departmental divisions. Finally, network analyses of Oak Valley and Rancho provide graphic illustrations of how departmentalization 'looks' in the 'webs' of social relationships within these schools, and shows that variation in the strength of departmental boundaries can be not only a school-level phenomenon, but a department-level one.

Boundary Strengths

Social Relationships

In the sixty years since Waller's benchmark study, teachers have come to 'live together in the school' for longer and longer periods, as both the school day and school year have increased, and as more and more teachers have stayed for far longer careers. Nationally, the median for years of teaching experience rose from eight years in 1976 to fifteen in 1986 (NEA, 1987). Within these three schools tenure is even higher. The average number of years in teaching is 24.2 at Highlander (where lay-offs have almost eliminated teachers with less than eighteen-years experience), 22.2 at Rancho, and 17.7 at Oak Valley. These are teachers, then, who have been 'living together in the school' for long periods; many have come to know each other well, and can justifiably claim, as they do at Highlander, that they are 'like family'.[1]

These are conditions under which relationships can develop to a remarkable degree of intimacy, and teachers in all three schools, in interview responses and in observed interactions, demonstrate detailed knowledge of both the personal and professional workings of each others' lives. In fact, in several instances they report having married colleagues. Conversations in faculty rooms and hallways move quickly from children and funerals to which student has done what in class; frequently first names are enough to identify what are clearly familiar subjects. In such conversational shifts, the lines between personal and professional aspects blur.

Attending to such conversations, Judith Warren Little notes, 'calls into question the crude distinction between "social talk" and "teaching talk" ' for the two 'become intertwined' (Little, 1991, p. 9). Often the two aspects are interwoven in a single exchange, difficult for speaker or researcher to disentangle. A Home Economics teacher, asked to describe her department, begins with the formal language of the professional, 'we're very fortunate in that we have four in our department', but moves quickly to the personal, 'I'm a very close friend of [another teacher] anyway, so I usually see her after school hours, stay in touch. But it is a fairly close knit group', and finishes with a mix of the two, 'we do develop curriculum somewhat. At least we interact with each other, to bounce things off each other.' Through informal exchanges, this 'bouncing things off each other', teachers establish norms of what should be taught and how, and of what it means to be a teacher and a colleague.

In another example of how the 'important things that happen in schools result from the interaction of personalities' and how personal and professional aspects intertwine, a Math teacher at Rancho describes the value of a friendship in which he and two colleagues have come to know each other, and to 'work together as a team', since they have been teaching together for 'almost twenty-five years'. In fact, when one was transferred to the then new Rancho, the other two soon followed. This teacher attests to the importance of that social relationship, not only to his personal life, but to his classroom performance:

We used to spend our lunchtimes together, talk about calculus, and how to present a particular problem, how to make it clearer, different kinds of problems that he'd used in the past that he thought were really neat. We used to do that kind of thing. In fact, the idea of a limit, I never, I went through that kind of in cookbook steps when I was in college, but it wasn't until we got over to Esperanza [his former high school] and I had to teach that and math analysis, and calculus. And Dan and I got together and we spent hours after school going over it, until finally we had really an understanding of what it was about. And we could teach it.

71

Social relationships remain central to these teachers, personally and professionally. With longer tenure in schools and in teaching, these interrelationships take on special salience and meaning, and the bonds between teachers are strong.

Size

While the time to form social relationships has expanded, teachers find that the size of the social world the school represents has grown faster, and exceeds their capacity to form relationships. Despite occasional and temporary staff reductions, as at Highlander, the general trend throughout the century has been one of consistent expansion in numbers of students and faculty (Meyer *et al.*, 1986). The High School and Beyond data suggest that the typical high school in the 1980s has 1200 students. Rancho, the smallest of these three schools has 1800 students; Highlander has 2100. At Oak Valley, the largest of the three schools, and large even by today's standards, there are 3200 students, and 137 teachers. And size, as a Highlander teacher who has taught in a smaller school succinctly puts it, 'makes a hell of a difference'.

Such numbers, whether the 1200 of a typical school or the 3200 of Oak Valley, make it impossible for teachers to maintain relationships, or even to have interactions with all of their colleagues. They report repeatedly that there are too many teachers, too much space, and too little time for them to know other teachers by name, let alone to develop a sense of 'living together in the school' or sharing a common enterprise. With so many teachers, the close relationships they maintain with a few teachers contrast sharply with the more general sense of one's colleagues as virtual strangers.

This is particularly evident at Oak Valley, where the size of staff and the sprawling architecture of the campus make the problem dramatically apparent. Here an unknown teacher posted a 'letter to Santa' on the mailroom door, with 'my wish list for Christmas' including wish 'No.3: to know who I work with (who's the tall guy with glasses?).' One teacher described attending a state conference, where she was pleased to meet another teacher who seemed to share some of the same problems she was facing — but then was embarrassed when she asked what school he was from, and he responded 'Oak Valley'. Another incident revealed the opposite side of the same problem: on an early visit to the school, as I sat in the mail room, a teacher came over to conspiratorially whisper that the woman who had just walked into the room was a Stanford researcher — he assumed that though I was an unfamiliar face, I must be another faculty member. As one teacher observed, even when teachers do meet, and would like to get to know their colleagues, they often seem like strangers:

'sometimes . . . we walk up to the office, and you talk to people [from] across campus, [saying] things like "gosh, you still work here?" '

While Oak Valley is the largest of the schools in this study, the same lament echoes in the conversations of teachers across the sites. Although at Highlander all teachers are housed in the same building, the presence of 100 teachers overwhelms the teachers' capacity for getting to know each other. One noted that he 'went to a . . . meeting this week and talked to another teacher from this building, but I barely knew his name'. And when asked about the faculty, a Social Studies teacher responded that 'in this building there are many people I do not know, so it's a pretty large staff'.

The problems of dealing with a 'pretty large staff' are not unique to these sites. High schools in general tend to be large organizations with 'pretty large staffs' of largely unfamiliar colleagues.

Subgroups

The combination of teachers' desire for social relationships with a school size which exceeds their capacity for socializing encourages teachers in these large high schools tend to form smaller, closer 'webs': subsets of colleagues with whom they have particular interests or characteristics in common. The recent educational literature has tended to portray two extreme, and contrasting visions of the social worlds of schools, but neither satisfactorily captures the high schools these teachers inhabit. On the one hand are the models of the school which display what Huberman calls 'the vision of the school house as a bonded community' — the vision which is encouraged in the literatures of effective schools and of restructuring, and is characterized by shared goals and collaborative norms (Huberman, 1990). Nias (1989) describes the workings of such communities, in her observations of smaller elementary schools, which create a 'culture of collaboration' through collective activities such as the school assembly (p. 2). Examples of such school-wide communities exist in the Center study of high schools, in the smaller, 'special-mission' schools (McLaughlin, Talbert and Phelan, 1990). At large high schools, such as Oak Valley, bonding activities such as school assemblies are impossible: there is no space which can even hold the entire staff.

On the other hand are the images of those researchers who suggest, usually deploringly, that schools display what Andy Hargreaves (1993) calls 'isolation, individualism, and privatism, (p. 54)'. These are visions of alienating environments, with 'egg-crate' or 'cellular' classrooms staffed by isolated teachers engaged in 'parallel piecework' (Lortie, 1975; Johnson, 1990b; Metz, 1990). Consistent with this model, though more positive in tone, Huberman suggests thinking of teachers as 'artisans' who 'work alone, learn alone, and who derive their most important professional satisfactions alone' (Huberman, 1990, p. 11).

The teachers in these high schools take a more pragmatic view of community and schools. They acknowledge the logistical constraints of size, time, and space which make it impossible to establish a school-wide 'bonded community', but also the value of social support and collaboration which makes it impossible to settle for 'fragmented individualism'. Instead they negotiate a middle ground, one in which there are fragmented communities — the smaller social worlds of social 'subgroups' within schools which have been largely neglected in the literature (Huberman, 1990; Little, 1990a). While the trends in career length allowed for long-term relationships to develop, the time intervals for establishing such connections remain small: twenty minutes of preparation before school, five minutes snatched between classes, forty minutes for lunch. They can't know everyone, but want to know someone, so, as one puts it: 'I work well with a few colleagues.'

There are a variety of such subgroups in these schools, small clusters of 'a few colleagues' who find each other and maintain close and consequential interactions. Some, such as that described above by the Math teacher at Rancho, draw their relationships 'from my first years of teaching' and continue over time and even across schools. Another cluster at Rancho describe themselves as sharing a 'pedagogical philosophy' which binds them together. These are a self-selected group who come together almost every day at the same lunch table, who tend to volunteer for low-level classes, who spend much of their lunch hour talking about teaching as an art, or about the needs of their students, and who have an amazing repertoire of slightly off-color jokes. At Highlander one of the most clearly defined clusters is the smokers, who congregate in the one room where their habit is allowed every chance they get. The value teachers place on such collegial clusters is perhaps best exemplified by a teacher who quit smoking several years ago, and now can't stand the smell of the room; she still spends every possible break in the smokers' lounge with her 'support group'.

These support groups mediate the alienation of being lost in the crowd at large high schools. Subgroups provide sites for dense and close 'webs of interrelationships' to form.

Space

For most of the teachers in this study, the smaller web of interrelationships, the subset which dominates the social world of the school as they know it, is the department. While the combination of size of school with the desire for social community makes the formation of some form of subgroup likely, it is the addition of architectural layout that makes the department the most likely form for that grouping to take. For, as one teacher observes, the Oak Valley faculty is a 'young staff, very professional, very caring to students and for each other, somewhat fragmented and large, and the way the school is designed we're departmentalized'.

The 'way the school is designed' has particular significance, for departments are architecturally divided from each other in all three of the schools studied, a physical condition which has major implications for bounding social interactions. Again, as with size, Oak Valley provides the most obvious illustration, for classrooms and offices are in separate buildings, clustered by subject, and at considerable distance from one another. This separation is reenforced by the absence of any common area for staff to congregate (except a small lunch area with room for about twenty teachers); faculty tend to spend what free time they have within the confines of their departmentalized territory. The combined constraints of small segments of time and large distances to cover largely preclude or make a 'hassle' any interaction beyond departmental boundaries, even for those teachers, such as the union representatives, who have special incentive to establish them:

> During break I go to the [department] resource center. During lunch I go to the resource center, and that's usually all the contact I have . . . I've been trying to get out, I haven't always been successful, to get over to the faculty lunch area and talk with other teachers and see what's going on with them [in her role as union rep.]. But it's an effort on my part, it really is. (Math teacher and union rep.)

> We're too big [for contact with other teachers]. We're spread out in different buildings; there is no central area for teachers to meet and be together; the lunchroom is minute; and I know many people never set foot out of their faculty rooms in their departments, so I never get to know them. (Science teacher and union rep.)

> It gets to be such a hassle to try to go and have lunch, 'cause we don't have much time, and we do have a nice facility here and a nice group of people, so it's nice . . . it's mostly here. It's mainly because it's so hard to get over to the other area and eat. (Math teacher)

The sense of 'effort' required to 'get out', of the 'hassle' departmental boundaries create, appears in slightly different form at Highlander, where the school is smaller and occupies a single three-story building. Here the classrooms are clustered in 'wings' and referred to by the name of the subject which predominates: 'we call it the Social Studies wing, but we also have Foreign Language in that wing.' Each of the departments has a separate lounge, although Math and Science, the two magnet departments which have the entire third floor, have separate ends of a large, shared, lounge. Joan Frances refers to this physical arrangement when she talks about how 'they haven't moved my room. I'm not in the English wing. So I'm kind of out of the realm.' Although she is officially an English department member, her classroom is in the Social Studies wing; as a result, she has less contact with her department colleagues than she would like, and fewer opportunities for collegial support.

This physical concentration of department members is consequential not only for Frances, but is a recurring theme in Highlander teachers' comments, for with limited time outside of class they find it difficult to venture out beyond the spatial constraints of the departmentally bounded wings:

> It's geometry. It's physical layout. And so we have a nice convenient little [area] up on the third floor in one end where you've got a lot of Science people all working. Then right adjacent to us there's a lot of Math people. So, you know, I see a lot of those people regularly. To find other people, you really have to go some place and look for them. That's largely the way the thing is arranged physically. If you're busy, if you're working, you don't think about trying to meet all hundred teachers in the building . . . If you asked me to start naming all the teachers in this building, I'd have a horrible time. (Science teacher)

> Because one thing we, I, noticed when I came to this building, is that because of the way it's set up, Social Studies is in one wing. English is in one wing. Science, Math, there's not really much communication between the departments, compared to the situation I was in before, which was a junior high situation . . . Now we've got a lounge for every department, and there's really not much you can do. There are some teachers, I don't know, you know I see them in the hall, I may say 'hi' to them. There are some teachers I really don't know [what] their names are, because of the way it's set up in the structure. (Social Studies teacher)

> I see a lot of the Math department because we are up on the third floor, and you just don't go up and down a lot. (Math teacher)

You're departmentalized [here]. I don't know what's going on in other departments. [You] only have an hour lunch and an hour of planning; in that time you have to phone parents and prepare for the next day, grade papers, etc. You just don't get out in the building. (Social Studies teacher)

The physical layout of the buildings, the grouping of classrooms around subject lines, and the provision of departmental 'lounges' at Highlander and 'resource rooms' at Oak Valley, create significant barriers to school-wide, or to interdisciplinary, social relationships. With too many things to do in too little time, most often, it seems, 'you just don't get out' of departmental territory, even if you try. Departments become isolated from one another, lessening the possibility of school as community. While the existence of potent departmental boundaries is most obvious at Oak Valley, and nearly as apparent at Highlander, it is most intriguing at Rancho, for here the school's unit structure deliberately tried to break down these barriers.

Breaking Barriers at Rancho

Rancho provides a case which testifies to the strength of these departmental boundaries — and to anchors other than size and space which hold them firmly in place. The model which the original Rancho planners developed took into consideration the issues of size, space, and time in designing the advisory units which were to break down departmental barriers. Yet the departmental boundaries, temporarily and partially submerged beneath the unit structure, have resurfaced.

One of the purposes of the Rancho Plan was to deliberately break down departmental boundaries:

It was designed in order to allow people to meet people outside of their department. It was to get away from The English Department, The Math Department. So people were in units where they were mixed . . . that was the whole idea to have the units: to get away from each department for themselves.

The units were to provide the alternative, to fill the same subgroup needs which departments did, but to center around students rather than subjects. As an administrator recalls,

the units were really a way of having teachers structured in a non-departmental fashion. And the thing they had in common was being advisors, and the focus was the role of the advisor. And the idea was that you would force teachers, because of the set that you would put them in, you would force them to

77

really look at the total student. And to look at the educational experience from an organizational point of view. And so when you talk about organizational changes, or thrust, or looking at a new magnet focus, or trying to decide how to realign advisory, you do it through that arena. Now there are still some things that you can discuss in your department. The department focus is fairly narrow, isn't it? It has been. They tend to look at English as the only thing that is of concern. And you know, perhaps that's the way it should be. You need to have some of that kind of an ethnocentric way of looking at it. But we wanted for each teacher to play both of those roles. To also look at the school as a whole, just as an administrator does, or a counselor. Most teachers don't have that experience in high school.

The plan was designed around student needs, but it was also attentive to the needs of staff for collegial interaction. Units would provide what an English teacher calls 'a sense of community', that the school as a whole was too large to provide. Many of the teachers link the value of the units to their own need for a social group: 'the unit provided a structure for community, a means of support' observed a second teacher; 'it makes the school smaller and mitigates alienation' noted a third.

The unit plan addressed not only size, but space. In classroom assignments subjects were, at least to some degree, scattered, and department offices non-existent. Instead Rancho set up unit offices to serve as central gathering places, as sites for teachers to store their belongings, to make phone calls, or to work between classes — to be literally a 'structure for community'.

These unit offices, where teachers had their desks, began to fill with the trappings to make them more attractive, and more of a home base: coffee makers, a microwave, a comfortable couch, posters and pictures. And each Unit began to take on a distinct identity, a personality of its own: 'Unit 3 is argumentative; Unit 1 has strong personalities; Unit 2 is the good guys . . . [we] find it easy to make decisions, we get along' reports a perhaps somewhat biased member of Unit 2.

If size, the need for community, and space were the only thing holding departments together, these divisions probably would have collapsed. To some degree they did. But these were not the only forces at work, and the Rancho planners found department boundaries to be extremely resilient lines.

Institutionalized Boundaries

From the beginning the staff apparently recognized that factors both external, in the expectations of the wider community, and internal, in the orientation of subject-specialist teachers, would push and pull on the unit structure. In interviews these teachers referred repeatedly to their sense of belonging to external, subject-based communities — to the need 'to go to science conferences and things like that', to their friendships and professional contacts with teachers from within their fields but outside the school, to the demands of subject-based exams such as the College Boards and Advanced Placement tests, and to the feedback of returning students who report on their performance in the subject in college. One of the original English teachers remembered the push 'from outside — colleges, district mandates', observing almost wistfully that Rancho was 'intended to be interdisciplinary' but 'the secondary school was simply too entrenched in their [traditional] structure', particularly in terms of curriculum, so that 'everyone was willing, there was extra money to make it work, but the plan just didn't materialize'. They 'couldn't resist the weight' of the push; it was just 'too much to take on'.

And a vice-principal commented on pull from inside — from the strength of the individual teachers' orientation to subject:

> we had representatives from the units, that were elected by their constituents, they were to kind of represent the student and the school as a whole. And of course, none of that is that clean . . . no teacher is ever going to think about his role as an advisor and forget that he's a social studies teacher. But it's interesting, when people are given roles, they tend to somewhat fulfill those roles. I think that kind of happened.

For a while, despite the push and pull of subject-specific pressures, of institutionalized roles, routines, and expectations, an uneasy compromise was reached where it was not 'that clean', but it 'kind of happened'. The staff, as they remember it, worked hard to make the Unit structure work.

Comfort Zones

In the beginning, the teachers, and the units, did 'tend to somewhat fulfill these roles'. But following quickly on the heels of the Camelot era came the turbulent times. The support systems which had built the Units began to collapse: counselors, extra funding, district encouragement to 'do something different', and eventually the energy and commitment of the teachers. Being able to 'do something different' requires extraordinary resources.

In the ripples of policy turbulence, under conditions of stress from the external educational community, people returned to the familiar, the externally supported and legitimated system they had tried to escape. At Rancho teachers retreated into the traditional departmental divisions which they had originally defined as part of the problem.

For the departmental boundaries at Rancho have been, and are being, reasserted. The members of each subject area are increasingly returning to the familiar territory of the department. One of the department chairs notes that even administrators tend to gravitate toward their former subject areas: 'more attention is given to that department. I'm sure it's because it's their comfort zone; it's where they feel most comfortable' while with the other departments they 'feel like they're out of their league. I don't mean that as a put-down; I just mean that's the way it is.' And teachers in such a turbulent environment clearly find themselves in need of a such a 'comfort zone'.

Science was the first to go, breaking off even before the state guidelines hit. Despite the initial aim of breaking down departmental divisions, the Science classrooms were architecturally clustered around the water and gas lines of their lab-stations. Although they were assigned originally to desks in the unit offices, the Science teachers found themselves as connected to their lab-stations as the gas lines were. Built as spokes around a central common area, without walls, the architectural structure meant that Science teachers early and inevitably became closely connected. They could see and hear what was going on in each other's classes, and found it necessary to coordinate planning, so that one class would not be taking a test while the group next door was listening to a clearly audible lecture.

With their close contact, and early frustration with the 'they' that could not understand their needs and had provided them with inappropriate conditions and materials, the Science teachers quickly coalesced into a distinct and distinctive subgroup: a former Rancho teacher explained that 'they were nicknamed at one time, the swarm.' They found that as a group, as a 'swarm' of Science teachers, they were able to make demands on the system that none of them could have made alone.

Their independence, and activism, are readily apparent. Several teachers told, with relish, the story of how, early on, they came into the Unit offices and took their desks (all are men):

You can't do your preparation away from your materials. And so we just, one at a time, carried our desks over here. And the principal at the time was real upset about it. He didn't say anything to us, but he was real upset about it, the fact that we had left our unit offices and come out here and isolated ourselves.

They literally picked up and left the unit offices, and now report that they have little reason to venture out from their stronghold. The boundaries around this department are like high stone walls.

While Science may provide the most dramatic example of the department re-forming as a distinct and strongly bounded community, these teachers are far from alone in their departmental solidarity. In the Math department, teachers are tightly tied by the strength of their common assumptions, and also by the length of their shared experience — several of the leaders have been teaching together since the late 1960s, and they have 'brought [the others] in' across a number of schools. But rather than as a 'swarm' which directs activity outward to school and district politics, the Math department seems to observers to have retreated inward — to where they can count on a common understanding. The result 'is an unhappy feeling, is it not?' observes one teacher from his vantage point outside the department. He later refers to the department attitude as 'this sort of inward withdrawal . . . it's the same syndrome of always fighting the last war sort of thing.'

The sense of embattlement is very strong here, for in the recent movements to district standardization and state guidelines, the Math department both has the most to lose and is the most likely to lose. Within the department teachers share a set of assumptions about testing, placement and tracking which are seen as essential — but which are actively opposed by school, district, and state officials.

In the first year of this study, the Math teachers had concluded that this was a war they could not win, and they were no longer actively fighting to change the opinions of those outside the department. Instead, they prepared for a siege, determined to hold out against the changes as long as they could, and barricaded themselves behind departmental walls. As a group, they refused to participate in a number of school activities, ranging from the first-year interviews for this study to a meeting called when the principal found he had additional monies to distribute. As the chair describes his response to that invitation, 'I told him "I don't want to come to your meeting; we'll just take what we agreed to . . . you'd think he would welcome it; there's never enough money, and this was one less voice fighting for it." ' The reasserted barriers of the department keep others out, at least temporarily, but they also preclude these teachers from speaking in a variety of school discussions.

In English, the anger over recent changes is least obvious, and the retreat into departmental boundaries seems least deliberate — it just seems to have happened. A former Rancho teacher characterized this department as only having two or three activists around any issue, the rest 'whatever happens, happens'. But while they have not directly rebelled or withdrawn from the unit structure, what they have done is to quietly congregate within the unit to which their chair is assigned. When the administrators realized that this unit had a disproportionate number of English teachers (teachers had been given some choice of membership) they changed the official assignments, but the teachers have crept back, unofficially and quietly.

For the English teachers the importance of the departmental community is described not in technical or in political terms, but in social terms of friendship, of individual rather than categorical identification (this is discussed more fully in Chapter 7). It just happens that most of their friends are other English teachers. When asked about who her colleagues would be, one began 'Peggy, who's one of the other English teachers, and Denise, who's next door who's another English teacher.' The department happens to provide a group of people who share common interests, and with whom these teachers choose to spend their time. They back into the departmental boundaries, almost without noticing them.

The stories these teachers tell provide brief glimpses into how departments have re-emerged as distinct communities within Rancho, and also of the variety of functions that those communities can serve, even within a single school. Departments are, as the English teachers suggest, the site for personal connections which support and sustain individuals. They can be, as the Science teachers demonstrate, a base for political action, for pulling in resources and for pushing agendas. And, as the Math and Science teachers attest, they provide a mechanism for getting desired work accomplished — and an arena for having it valued — with colleagues who understand the subject-specific nature of their work. Departments provide a 'comfort zone' within the school, where friendships, interests, and assumptions are shared.

Departments also represent institutionalized boundaries, familiar to the teachers within them and linking them to distant colleagues in the wider community of the subject area. These external pressures also contribute to the strength and resilience of these boundaries. Echoing the progressive reformers of many years ago, for example, these teachers point to the potent press of college entry requirements and expectations. Others identify the state frameworks, standardized tests, professional associations and conferences — all of which are based on an assumed subject organization of curriculum, teachers, and schools. All in all, they suggest that the push 'from outside' was indeed, as the English teacher put it, 'too much to take on'.

Despite deliberate and careful attempts to dismantle them, despite alternative structures to deal with size and space, the departmental boundaries were reenforced by both the external push and the internal pull. As the Rancho case illustrates, academic departments remain a likely, and resilient, site for clearly defined and potent internal communities to form within the school, and a resistant barrier to school-wide community.

Drawing Boundaries: Communication Cliques

Departments are not the only subgroups of importance within these schools, but they are a likely locus for important subgroups, particularly in terms of teachers sharing talk about teaching. From the stories of teachers in these schools, it is also apparent that the strength of these boundaries around social interactions varies. Oak Valley, where a teacher mistook me for a faculty member, is more departmentalized in this sense than Highlander, where teachers say they know each other by sight, if not by name. Rancho's Science department, whose teachers have 'isolated themselves' in their department space, is more bounded than its English department, whose teachers at least go to the Unit office even if they bring each other along. The stories illustrate both the overall strength of these boundaries and the local variations. But stories are limited in how well they can 'illustrate' the relative strength of these boundaries.

An alternative way of viewing departmental boundaries is through network analyses, which translate survey responses into graphic images. Such a strategy provides a means of mapping out communication patterns among groups of people, and a device for tracking informal information channels. Researchers ask subjects for the names of those people with whom they talk, which are then 'reordered into cliques' by complex computerized algorithms (Rogers and Kincaid, 1981, p. 171). Patterns of communication proximity and density among respondents emerge out of the data, and are arrayed and displayed graphically, allowing analysts to identify cliques and their characteristics. One of the Center researchers has developed that strategy for use in analyzing communication patterns among school staff (Eaton, 1991).[2]

In the graphs shown in Figures 4.1–4.3 part of that process has been used to look specifically at departments as communication cliques. Instead of allowing patterns to 'emerge' out of the data, respondents were arrayed by department, before the analysis, on the horizontal and vertical axes of the graphs. The data then provide an opportunity to test the hypothesis that communication patterns of a school are organized by departmental boundaries.

In this graphic analysis, if the person named is within the same department, the corresponding square on the graph will fall close to the diagonal line. Squares farther from the diagonal indicate distance from the department. If the departments within a school restrict conversation to within their boundaries, the graph will show a series of clustered responses, grouped within square formations along the diagonal line.

That pattern can be seen clearly in the Oak Valley graph (Figure 4.1). All along the diagonal, departmental, line dense clusters of

Figure 4.1   Network Analysis of Oak Valley

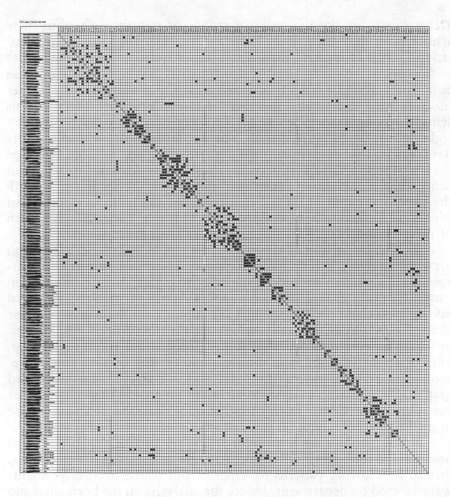

interactions occur. Away from the department there is little connection. Teachers seldom named, or were named by, people outside of their departments. Oak Valley is depicted as a highly departmentalized school.

For contrast, Figure 4.2 shows the pattern, or lack of pattern, when the departmental organization is imposed on the communication networks of one of the smaller CRC schools, where it does not fit. Most darkened squares do not fall close to the diagonal, suggesting that the key characteristic by which teachers choose their partners for talk about teaching is something other than departmental affiliation. This is the pattern of a non-departmentalized school.

Figure 4.2   Network Analysis of Non-departmentalized School

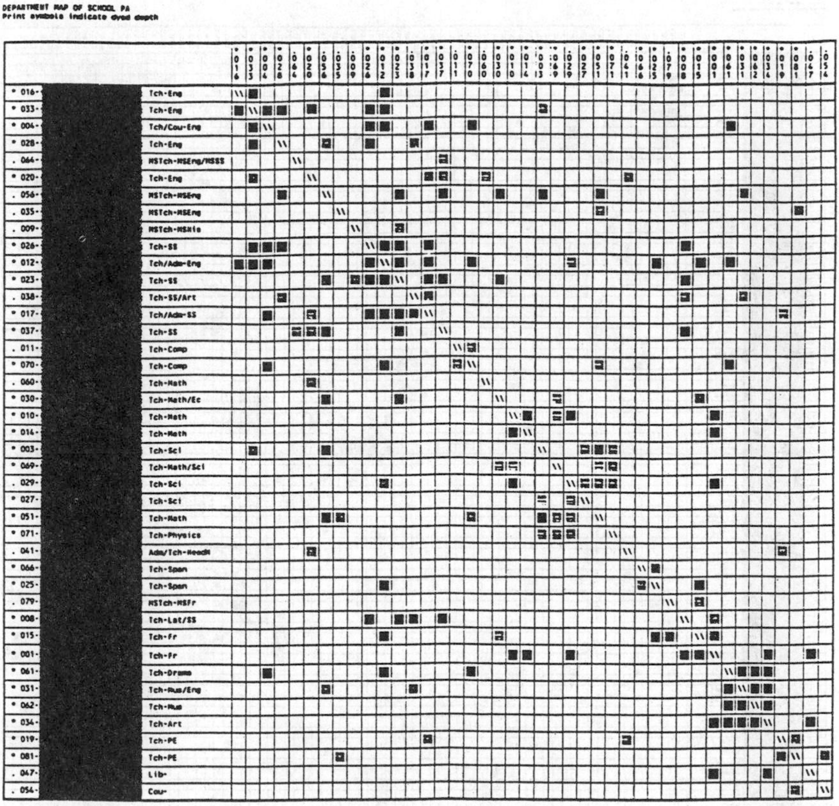

DEPARTMENT MAP OF SCHOOL PA
Print symbols indicate dyad depth

• 016 •	Tch-Eng
• 033 •	Tch-Eng
• 004 •	Tch/Cou-Eng
• 028 •	Tch-Eng
• 044 •	HSTch-HSEng/HSSS
• 020 •	Tch-Eng
• 056 •	HSTch-HSEng
• 035 •	HSTch-HSEng
• 009 •	HSTch-HSHis
• 026 •	Tch-SS
• 012 •	Tch/Adm-Eng
• 023 •	Tch-SS
• 038 •	Tch-SS/Art
• 017 •	Tch/Adm-SS
• 037 •	Tch-SS
• 011 •	Tch-Comp
• 070 •	Tch-Comp
• 060 •	Tch-Math
• 030 •	Tch-Math/Ec
• 010 •	Tch-Math
• 014 •	Tch-Math
• 003 •	Tch-Sci
• 069 •	Tch-Math/Sci
• 029 •	Tch-Sci
• 027 •	Tch-Sci
• 051 •	Tch-Math
• 071 •	Tch-Physics
• 041 •	Adm/Tch-HeadT
• 066 •	Tch-Span
• 025 •	Tch-Span
• 079 •	HSTch-HSFr
• 008 •	Tch-Lat/SS
• 015 •	Tch-Fr
• 001 •	Tch-Fr
• 061 •	Tch-Drama
• 031 •	Tch-Mus/Eng
• 062 •	Tch-Mus
• 034 •	Tch-Art
• 019 •	Tch-PE
• 081 •	Tch-PE
• 047 •	Lib-
• 054 •	Cou-

Rancho appears in Figure 4.3. The departmental boundaries here are apparently less strong than they are at Oak Valley, for a number of identified links lie outside the departments. But across the school, far more of the choices lie within the department than outside of it. In both of the schools within this study departments clearly represent substantial barriers to school-wide interactions. Data from Highlander are not available for this analysis.

The strength of department boundaries is to some degree a school characteristic: Oak Valley, with its larger size, detached buildings, and formal departmental structure produces boundaries which are stronger than Rancho's. Both of those schools contrast sharply with the smaller school, where departments are apparently too weak to contain or constrain conversations at all.

The network analyses also illustrate teachers' observations about important within-school variation. Departmental boundaries are not

Figure 4.3   Network Analysis of Rancho

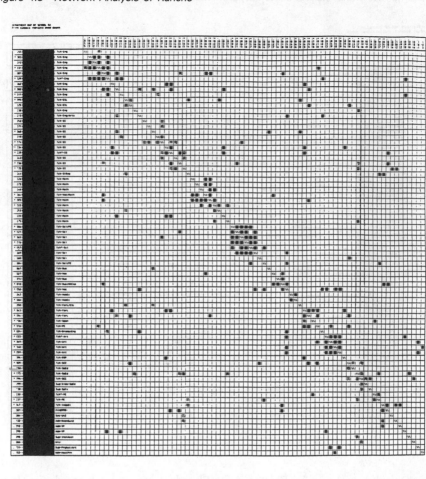

uniformly strong; they do not take the same form, or serve the same ends. This is particularly evident at Rancho, where the graph shows distinct differences in the patterns of different departments in the same school, under the same organizational conditions. Science, in the middle of the graph, is intensely interconnected: almost every member talks to every other member, and almost no one talks to anyone from outside. One teacher's reference to the 'stronghold' is apt; this department clearly has a strong hold on the communication networks of its members. In the English department, in the top left corner, every member is included within the cluster, but some also have external partners they named. In Math there is a dense subgroup within the subgroup — but some department members do not belong to the Math cluster at all.

Conclusion

Carved deeply into the educational history, organizational structure, and even the architectural layout of high schools, departmental divisions have become potent barriers to school-wide communication and community. In schools so large that teachers cannot even know all their colleagues by sight, let alone by name, the department becomes a manageable, and meaningful, 'web of interrelationships' where, as Waller pointed out, so many 'important things' occur. The stories these teachers tell provide testimony to the strength of these boundaries and to their resilience, and suggest the variety of functions, and kinds of interrelationships that those communities can serve, even within a single school.

What kinds of departmental interactions can produce such internal variations? How does it happen that Rancho's Science teachers, within their department, find such a strong and collective voice? Why does the Math department's collective signify, instead, 'one less voice' fighting for resources? This chapter, with its focus on the strength of department boundaries and the barriers they represent to school-wide communication and interaction, looked at the edges of departments. It provided only quick glimpses of their internal workings. The next chapter will look more closely at the people who inhabit these bounded territories, and at the kinds of social interactions which go on inside them.

Notes

1 The figures for years in teaching overestimate the number of years together, since not all years were at the same school. But the figures for years at the school (15.7 at Highlander, 11.4 at Rancho, and 10.78 at Oak Valley) underestimate them, since many teachers trace their relationships back to shared experience in other schools.
2 Through the survey, all staff in each school were asked with whom they talk about teaching, and were given five lines to fill in names. Those names were then linked to the identification codes, and the background information, of each person in the database. In this instance, only department membership was considered relevant background.

Chapter 5

Social Worlds

I would submit that the logic of using the school building as the unit of analysis and intervention, when we are talking about at least twenty-five to thirty teachers and support staff and 500 pupils, is a goofy logic. Why the school? . . . How much collaboration can we expect between 8th grade physics teachers, 11th grade English teachers and physical education instructors? . . . Why must we become, at virtually all costs, a socially cohesive community, when so few of the requisite conditions for becoming one are met?

From the artisan's logic, I would rather look to the department as the unit of collaborative planning and execution in a secondary school, or to the grade unit. This is where people have concrete things to tell one another and concrete instructional help to provide one another — where the contexts of instruction actually overlap. (Michael Huberman, 1990)

My experience has been that some people conduct their departments in a family atmosphere, let's say, and other departments lean more heavily toward a hierarchical [one]. Say the possibility of an established group, who do most of the directing [of] who'll teach what and so on. And it depends on the individual, upon the individuals involved, as to what type of structure you end up with in the department. How rigidly they hold on to policy, and to establishing policy emphatically or pedagogically, any way you want to put it. I feel there's a lot of that from one department to another, and that's very crucial in a high school setting. (Math teacher)

The high school as a whole, with its size, its fragmentations of time and space, its diversity of students and goals, and its structure of internal divisions provides few of what Huberman (1990) calls the 'requisite conditions' for becoming a 'socially cohesive community' (p. 32). While the literature on schools repeatedly finds attributes of cohesive communities, such as goal consensus, collaborative norms, and shared expectations to be essential components in 'effective' schools (Purkey and Smith, 1983), at least at the elementary level, those who look to apply those findings to high schools have found those same attributes markedly absent. Instead high schools are characterized by images of 'anarchy' (Firestone and Herriott, 1982), of 'shopping malls' with 'something for everyone' (Powell *et al.*, 1985), of 'fractionated' curriculum and staff (Sizer, 1984).

Departmentalization, as explored in the previous chapter, clearly plays a role in that fragmentation. In large high schools departments interrupt communication patterns and isolate small groups of colleagues into separate and separated divisions. They organize the anarchy of the high school into particular, and fairly regular, configurations. In stories centered around the quest for school-wide coherence and collaborative community the departmental barriers which divide and conquer play a strongly negative role: 'the villain is the specialist system' (Sizer, 1984, p. 209).

Looking for Communities

If, as Huberman suggests, we resist the 'goofy logic' of focusing on the school, and instead 'look to the department as the unit' a different story emerges, one in which the realm of knowledge of the academic department becomes the potential site for social and professional community. For the boundaries of departmental realms are not only lines which divide the faculty, they can also be seen as circles which enclose colleagues together within them.

To look for 'a socially cohesive community' it may well be best to look inside the department, 'where people have concrete things to tell one another and concrete instructional help to provide one another' (p. 32), and where the arrangements of time, space, and common tasks are more likely to provide the necessary preconditions. It is within the department that collaborative community is most possible, and through the collective efforts of that group of people, 'the individuals involved', that different kinds of communities are created.

In describing their departments, teachers often refer to them as 'we', as the particular group of individuals with whom they work most closely. They talk of how 'we' spend time together, how 'we' share materials, how 'we' get along. The resulting variation in atmospheres of departments, teachers tell us, is 'very crucial in a high school setting' because it can substantially alter the experience of teaching in a particular school.

How much cohesiveness can we expect in departments which, in this study, contain as many as twenty-four teachers, which offer courses as diverse as remedial science and AP physics, and which contain disciplines with as little in common as economics and psychology? How much collaboration or community building is there time for when teachers spread their scarce out-of-class time among student needs, extra-curricular activities, committee assignments, coaching, and a host of other demands? The answer, perhaps surprisingly, is quite a lot. What appear in these teachers' stories, with remarkable persistence, are accounts of interconnectedness among colleagues: formal teaming arrangements at Oak Valley allow Math teachers to collectively plan courses; informal mentoring partnerships at Rancho bring new teachers, or experienced teachers with new assignments, into the classrooms of their more experienced colleagues; Science teachers at Highlander bring classroom problems into the lounge for collaborative analysis and practical suggestions. Common across interviews at all three schools are such examples of what Judith Warren Little (1982) calls 'teachers teaching each other the practice of teaching' (p. 331).

What is surprising about these examples, and the persistence with which they appear, is that they run counter to what has become commonplace in school research: 'teaching is a lonely profession' (Sarason, *et al.*, 1966); it is characterized by 'the persistence of separation and low task interdependence' (Lortie, 1975, p. 15); teachers follow 'the rule of privacy' (Lieberman and Miller, 1990, p. 158); 'most teachers' lead 'professionally orphaned lives' (Rosenholz, 1989, p. 73). Where collegial, collaborative schools do occur, they are celebrated, but these instances are rare in general and even more rare in high schools (Little, 1990a).

Yet in all of the departments in this study there were frequent appearances of collaborative efforts among individual teachers, and in most there was the sense of the department itself as a cohesive community, with a strong collective identity, routinized norms of cooperation, and shared orientation. If collegial environments are so rarely found in high schools, even when researchers are seeking them out, why were they so frequently reported and observed within these departments? Is it, as the teachers above suggest, a matter of the 'individuals involved', are these odd schools, or does the difference lie in the methodological choice of the department as the unit of analysis?

Part of the answer may lie in a paradox observed by Dan Lortie (1975), still one of the most widely cited sources on the 'isolation' of teachers. In his study,

> teachers . . . work largely alone; there is little indication that they share a common technical culture. *Yet we have observed* that they turn to one another for assistance and consider peer

help their most important source of assistance [my italic].
(Lortie, 1975, p. 76)

Analyzed as a profession, or even as a school faculty, teachers clearly
have proportionally little time to spend with proportionally few teachers, with whom, as Huberman points out, they have little in common
anyway. Framed at the level of the department, however, those same
brief exchanges, when teachers 'turn to one another for assistance',
repeated with the same few department colleagues every day, present
an opportunity for a 'most important' network of collegial relationships in a small group with a common technical culture.

To the teachers in this study, the department is first and foremost
the group of people with whom they work most closely, those to
whom they are most likely to turn for assistance, collegial support, or
simply another adult voice. School-level conditions do much to create
and bound the territories of departments, but it is in the interactions of
the people involved within these small groups that routines, norms,
and values develop in distinctly different ways, creating 'social worlds'
with distinctive and shared perspectives (Shibutani, 1955). As social
worlds departments both provide a potential site for strong and
meaningful membership within a collegial community, and out of that
community generate a cultural mechanism which can reinforce, mediate, or transform school culture.

This chapter looks to the department as a site for cohesive community and collegial interactions, first turning to 'the individuals involved' who comprise and construct these relationships. The next
section explores the multiple forms and meanings of departmental
community which come out of teachers' own stories. Finally Shibutani's
discussion of 'social worlds', and the distinctions between exclusiveness and inclusion, on the one hand, and demand for loyalty and commitment on the other, provide a framework for distinguishing among
these departments, which represent very different kinds of social and
professional communities: bundled, bonded, fragmented, and split.

The Individuals Involved

Who are the individuals involved in these accounts? What might make
these teachers more likely to value and participate in cooperative or
collaborative interactions? Across all three schools, the people in these
academic departments tend to be experienced, career teachers. Unlike
prior generations, they came and stayed in schools, as the teaching
workforce became 'more mature and less tractable' (Rury, 1989). They
have been teachers for a long time: the average at Oak Valley is eighteen years, at Rancho twenty-two, and at Highlander twenty-four. They

share particular histories, remembering the comings and goings of different generations of students, of policies and reform efforts, and, with the exception of Highlander, building administrations. One Oak Valley teacher, who has been at the school thirteen years, notes that 'I have probably seen seven principals in that period of time.' It is among their faculty colleagues, in contrast to their students and administrators, that these teachers find the stability which permits close and long-lasting relationships.

At all three schools, among the generations of policies that teachers have seen come and go have been experiments which required or fostered collegial efforts. Oak Valley tried 'teaming' arrangements for a while, and now sends teachers out to negotiate curriculum with their subject area colleagues across town. Rancho's design included faculty in the original planning team, 'community building' as a goal, and 'participatory decision-making' as a governance device; Highlander brought in strong Science and Math teachers and asked them to develop a magnet program which would draw students from across the district. These are teachers who have experience working together in a variety of settings and teams — the stability lies in the colleagues and their shared histories rather than in the tasks.

These teachers are, by and large, a generation who report entering teaching when it was still understood as one of the few careers to which females could, or should, aspire. In this study of academic departments, however, there are few women, for while the numbers of male and female teachers in the high school may be fairly even, they tend to teach different subjects (Acker, 1983; NEA, 1987). The Science teachers are almost all men at Oak Valley (77 percent) and at Highlander (82 percent), while at Rancho they all are. Math and Social Studies departments, too, tend to be mostly male. Only two departments, English at Highlander (78 percent) and Rancho (66 percent), have a majority of female teachers (see Table 7.1, Chapter 7 for percentages). This distribution pattern has some consequence for collaborative partnerships with 'like-minded colleagues', for almost all of the closest relationships which these teachers described occur between same-sex pairs. But given the small numbers of women in this sample, it is beyond the scope of this study to do more than note that phenomenon; there are too few female teachers for any patterns of community formation or collegial interaction to be linked to gender. It is at the level of the subjects themselves that gender becomes involved in consequential ways, and that topic is taken up in Chapter 7.

These are also teachers who entered teaching when subject specialization was becoming important — but was not yet discipline-specific. A few hold certificates in multiple fields: one Science teacher, for example, started out in Physical Education; a Math teacher began in Physics; one teacher holds a 'general secondary' certificate. Joan

Frances has moved from Social Studies to English. For the most part, however, inter-departmental backgrounds are rare, and these teachers identify themselves as exceptions. Most teachers are specialists in the subject matter of their department — although they define their subject areas somewhat broadly. As one Social Studies teacher notes, her course assignments 'could be geography, rural culture, or maybe civics, but it's all related, you know, to government and history'. Teachers move with similar ease between physical and earth science, for example, or literature and journalism, making them fairly flexible in terms of within-department reassignment or collaboration. In their department colleagues they find support and suggestions for the practical problems of defining new courses to accommodate such changes. Changes, in the sense of attempts to move them 'out of their subject' into other departments, however, have been disruptive, and resented. They see themselves, and expect to be seen, as subject-specialists, and the subject area as the realm in which they expect to stay.

In the departments in this study, there are few young teachers. Membership in a group of like-minded colleagues is no less important to them, but it is less certain. More specialized, and more academic in their orientations, the newer teachers struggle to find time to find their 'niche'. A third-year teacher, for example, has tried sitting with the 'radical' table in the corner of the lunch area, and with the 'married housewife, more middle-of-the-road' group at the center table, but 'I haven't found my lunch-niche' yet. To find their own 'niche' these teachers rarely have time or opportunity to explore the territories outside of their own departments; they turn to their subject colleagues for company and for support. A first-year Science teacher at Oak Valley, highly trained in biology, initially felt out of place in his department, and out of his element in his assigned remedial physical science course. By the spring he had found a more experienced colleague teaching the same course: 'he has one year; I had none.' The two 'have worked together fabulously', initially complaining and sympathizing, but soon planning, analyzing, and evaluating: 'there were no resources, so he and I got together and we started to create it, a lot of hit and miss.' In working together, they have re-interpreted the assignment into a challenging experiment, and have asked for the same assignment next year.

Such collegial relationships occur frequently within the boundaries of departments, as teachers come together in twos or threes to work closely on planning, special projects, or new assignments. An experienced teacher in that same Science department reports that a few years ago, when he was asked to take a new assignment, he 'audited all the classes' of those who were already teaching the course. At Rancho, a teacher of advanced algebra had two teachers who wanted to move into that class 'sit in on my classes, just to pick up on the curriculum'. Another Math teacher, when assigned a new course, sat in on the classes of a more experienced colleague, and followed along, one day later, in her own classroom. In confronting new materials, or new students, teachers have to develop or adapt skills quickly — they turn for practical advice to their department colleagues.

Collaborative arrangements not only result from new assignments, they can be an ongoing process of professional development or a strategy for load reduction. One of Oak Valley's two chemistry teachers related the story of their long-term partnership, a relationship in which 'we went' to student competitions where 'we were always one of the first three places' and 'we had developed our own pace' and supplemental materials, and 'we had worked on it for ten years.' Math teaming at Rancho allows coaches to escape much of the demands of preparing materials or tests during their sport seasons, and to return the favor at other times.

Such collegial interaction relies on two adaptive skills, for teachers are working with extremely limited amounts of time to carry on conversations, or even to pass along ideas. First, as with any longstanding relationship, conversational partners develop a kind of shorthand: a concise phrase or two can convey much that is largely inaccessible to an outsider. Second, what these teachers displayed in repeated interviews was the skill of picking up the threads of a conversation which might have occurred days before. Where I had to turn to my notes, they could remember not only what we had been talking about, but how far we had gotten in the conversation. In one instance, a Social Studies teacher picked up the conversation she had had with another researcher months earlier, remembering where in London that person had mentioned visiting. One of the Center's teacher advisors talked about this communication skill as a common phenomenon among teachers, where 'usually it's a serialized story and it gets told not through any specific appointment to tell stories, but in crossing paths with each other in the rhythm of our day' (Little, 1990c, p. 20). Throughout this study, we could observe that teachers frequently shared such 'serialized stories' as they crossed paths, but their paths seldom led them outside departmental territory.

Individuals, then, despite the structural restraints, manage to establish frequent and close relationships with colleagues within department boundaries, and through those connections shape and reshape their own teaching — and bring it into line with local practice. They practice what organizational theorists term 'adaptation under conditions of ambiguity' where teaching, particularly in new courses but also more generally, can be understood as a highly uncertain technology: practitioners learn from experience, 'but that experience requires interpretation' and interpretation occurs through relating events to those selected few who are likely to have experiences and attitudes in common (March and Olsen, 1979, p. 55). Teachers seek 'practical knowledge' of similar situations from people in similar circumstances (Lieberman and Miller, 1990, p. 158). Departments provide the site where colleagues with common interpretations and practical knowledge most often can be found. With structural restrictions and subject-specific understandings of what the circumstances of teaching are like, teachers turn most often to department colleagues. But departments are more than just the site for those interactions, they can, through those interactions, generate groups where the interpretation, the practical knowledge, becomes a shared and distinctive departmental culture. Such membership can have important consequences.

Departments as Social Worlds

It is as community, as a social group creating the atmosphere in which they work, that departments matter most to the teachers within them. While the department is also an administrative unit which makes critical decisions about teaching assignments, as discussed in Chapter 6, and the subject which they teach, as in Chapter 7, for teachers the department is most often and most simply the people with whom they work most closely, the social group in which they are members.

When asked to talk about the department, or often even when asked to tell about the particular school in which they work, teachers frequently begin with two points. First, they limit the conversation to their own department. Some, as the Math teacher at the beginning of this chapter does, contrast their department with others; his is a split department, with those 'in the established group' doing most of the 'directing'. As a former chair, and a one-time member of the Science department, he has first-hand knowledge of how the 'atmospheres' can vary 'from one department to another'. Most teachers offer qualifying statements rather than contrasts: 'I don't know about the other departments, but we are a pretty cooperative group.' In either fashion they illustrate the boundedness, as well as the variation, in departmental environments. When teachers talk about community, about colleagues, about working with other adults, it is most often to the department, or to a group within the department, that they refer.

Second, as in the statement above, teachers most often talk about the department as 'we'. As in the excerpts at the beginning of this chapter, they refer to the particular group of people to which they belong: the Math teacher's 'individuals involved' who make up the 'structure' and the 'atmosphere', the English teacher's 'us' who 'create the environment' in which they teach.

It is to that sense of membership in the group that Joan Frances refers in the comment with which the preface began, when she described the difficulties of being 'kind of out of the realm' of the English department since her classroom is in another wing. For Frances the department is more than the 'label of administrative convenience' which Cusick (1983) suggested, and more than a physical site; it is first and foremost a group of people, insiders with whom she could share materials, ideas, and collegial support — if only time and space would allow. The department provides a resource for concrete and relevant suggestions, and, as she sees it, 'in this day and age you almost have to be open to some suggestions because kids are changing dramatically.' It is also a place where she can draw on a shared outlook, and a common conception of teaching:

> as a whole I think we're interested in [individuals]. To some degree, how far you should go I couldn't measure that, but when we have meetings together we're all in agreement about certain things, what should be taught and what shouldn't be.

Membership in the department is thus more than location in a collection of people; in most departments it means being part of a collective community 'to some degree . . . all in agreement about certain things' — a social group with a distinct and distinctive set of values and norms.

Science teachers at Oak Valley, who have been 'scattered' to distant classrooms due to overcrowding, relate the same need to belong to, and participate in activities with, their department group. The Chair comments that 'the guys off in the [other] building, they feel isolated' but that he is 'surprised that they stay as close as they do, with the distances that they're required to move'. One such teacher complained vociferously that he had been assigned a classroom in the Math area:

> as far away from the Science department as we can get. So, Physics is Science. Physics is not Mathematics, and people don't seem to want to understand that . . . And it's a nice room, I've got no beefs about that. My only beef is that I should be down here, with everybody else.

For him, as for Joan Frances, the issue is not having friendly neighbors; it is being a full member in the community of like-minded colleagues who share the same subject area.

These are communities whose 'agreements' can vary markedly from each other, and sometimes from the school as a whole, as can the 'some degree' to which that agreement is shared. Departments are not just smaller pieces of the same social environment but social worlds of their own; they are sites where a particular group of people come together, and together work out distinctive agreements on perspectives, rules, and norms.

Thomatsu Shibutani (1955) elaborates on the use of 'social worlds' to designate social groups which make up the primary 'reference groups' of those who inhabit them, and which not only create an atmosphere, but in important ways shape the views and influence the actions of their members:

> Modern mass societies, indeed, are made up of a bewildering variety of social worlds. Each is an organized outlook, built up by people in their interaction with one another; hence, each communication channel gives rise to a separate world . . . Such communities are frequently spatially segregated, which isolates them further from the outside world . . . Special meanings and symbols further accentuate differences and increase social distance from outsiders . . . Worlds differ in exclusiveness and in the extent to which they demand loyalty of their participants. (Shibutani, 1955, p. 566)

Unlike Waller, whose view of the school as a social world largely accepted the formal organization as the bounded unit in which inter- actions occur, Shibutani presents a view in which social worlds are more open and more complex, simultaneously larger and smaller than formal boundaries would suggest. Individuals belong simultaneously to a 'bewildering variety' of groupings: social class, ethnicity, family, the 'academic world', the 'loosely collected universes of special inter- est' such as stamp-collecting, and the tightly bounded subgroups such as a military unit (p. 566). Each of these worlds

> is an area in which there is some structure which permits rea- sonable anticipation of the behavior of others, hence, an area in which one may act with a sense of security and confidence. Each social world, then, is a culture area, the boundaries of which are set neither by territory nor by formal group mem- bership but by the limits of effective communication. (ibid., p. 566)

With his emphasis on communication channels as both the transmitters and constructors of reference groups, for Shibutani 'of greatest impor- tance for most people are the groups in which they participate directly — what have been called membership groups' where rules of behavior and interpretations of events come to be shared (p. 565). Similar ob- servations have been made about organizational behavior: in small groups in organizations a person 'will tend to like what those with whom he most frequently interacts like' and to make choices based upon those likings (March and Olsen, 1979, p. 65; also Scott, 1989; Van Maanen and Barley, 1984).

Of particular importance to this study are three points: 1) that these worlds are made and remade through the normal exchanges of routine communication; 2) that since they arise out of communication patterns, the most local membership group is often of central importance; and 3) that they vary in exclusivity and in demands of loyalty. Teachers' accounts of their daily lives certainly demonstrate a 'bewildering variety' of multiple reference groups to which they refer: in the school faculty, the subject specialty, the union, political factions, or even groups of friends. All of these are important, in varying ways and at varying times, to teachers' sense of professional community and identity (Ball, 1987; Bascia, in press; Goodson, 1987; Little, 1993). As Judith Warren Little (1991) demonstrates in her pronomial analysis of a single interview, the referent for 'we' can shift several times even in one episode of a teacher's narrative as he attempts to explain what his work setting is like.

The department is thus not the only social world to which teachers belong, but in many cases it is the primary one. In these large high schools, as explored in the previous chapter, the divisions between departmental territories are deep enough, and the territories isolated enough, to make the department the 'membership group' in which teachers participate most directly, where communication links are possible, and where membership is most likely to matter. These departments come to develop substantially different 'social worlds' or 'atmospheres' for teachers — environments which do appear to be, as the Math teacher observed, 'very crucial in a high school setting'.

Different Kinds of Community

Shibutani also provides a frame to understand the differences among these atmospheres, when he points out that these social 'worlds differ in exclusiveness and in the extent to which they demand loyalty of their participants'. In the stories of these teachers, the differences among departments which are 'very crucial' are along the dimensions of inclusivity — whether the 'we' of the department includes all members or only a few — and the extent to which they demand the loyalty and the efforts of members — the commitment to a collective endeavor. Within this study four types of departments can be distinguished, which represent four very different kinds of social communities along those two dimensions: I refer to them as bonded, bundled, fragmented, and split.

Bonded departments represent the 'socially cohesive community' of Michael Huberman's challenge, where members all work collaboratively with a high degree of commitment toward departmental goals. *Bundled* departments are those in which inclusion is high, but commitment to a common purpose is low: teachers support each other when

Table 5.1 Classification of Social Worlds

Bundled	**Bonded**
Low Commitment	High Commitment
High Inclusion	High Inclusion
Fragmented	**Split**
Low Commitment	High Commitment
Low Inclusion	Low Inclusion

needed and coordinate their efforts, but still preserve much of the image of individual artisan. *Fragmented* departments are low in terms of both commitment and inclusion: they most closely resemble the 'labels of administrative convenience' which Cusick (1983) found. Finally *split* departments, like the Social Studies department described by Bruckerhoff (1991), are those which have strong commitments to common goals — but loyalties and inclusion are split between conflicting factions.

Most of the departments within this study fall into the category which I have called bundled: teachers are clearly members of a cohesive and bounded department, sharing concerns and acting together to co-ordinate and support each other's efforts. Norms of inclusion are high — all members are welcome at meetings, lunch tables, and all are included when departmental decisions are made — but individual concerns rather than collective goals drive decisions. These fall somewhere between Huberman's vision of a 'cohesive community' and Cusick's 'labels'. They are, in the words of one teacher, 'pretty intact'. These are departments where sharing occurs, but in more limited form, and at less cost to individual teachers' autonomy than in the bonded departments. Asked about sharing, one teacher from the 'bundled' Social Studies department tellingly replied that the situation is 'yes and no. We share resources, how you handle a particular unit, work with your kids project-wise, information about kids' but 'I have a lot of freedom in what I teach.' Another notes that they 'share knowledge' and are 'protective of one another' but he is still able to say 'I view the classroom as my domain.' What happens in sharing in these departments is that materials, ideas, information, or plans are passed from one teacher to another. The process is an exchange, an offering of a commodity which can be refused, as comments from another member of the same department illustrate:

> I have materials that he wants, and I make copies and give them to him . . . I'll try it [an idea from someone else]. If it works, fine. If it doesn't work I give it back to them and look for something else. But there's a lot of give and take among the department holders.

Through giving and taking, through talking in the lounges and hall-ways, teachers in these typical departments come to implicit 'agree-ments' about what practice is, and should be — but they retain the sense of being individual 'holders' of their own 'domains'. Teaching is not private — these teachers could describe in detail the pedagogical strategies of their department colleagues — but neither is it quite pub-lic. It is neither held up to collective scrutiny nor to the demands of loyalty of collective goals. Understandings, interpretations, knowledge of others' teaching skills and styles are spread by a contagion model through conversations among colleagues who casually, as one observes, 'almost every day . . . see every Social Studies teacher' — but who seldom collectively discuss teaching issues. In most departments the norms tend more toward cooperation than collaboration, the bonds of professional community are 'pretty intact', the groups are 'relatively close', and yet teachers remain relatively autonomous. Here, as Huberman suggested, 'people have concrete things to tell one another and concrete instructional help to provide one another' — but the answer to his question of whether departments are socially cohesive communities is, as the Social Studies teacher reported, 'yes and no'.

The potential of departments as socially cohesive communities, and the powerful effects that this sense of community can have on teachers, however, can best be demonstrated in the more extreme cases. In one school, for example, the contrasting contexts of a fragmented English department and a bonded Science department create strikingly different atmospheres, mediating and transforming the school culture, and provide dramatically different environments for teachers within them.

Transforming school cultures — fragmented and bonded

What one teacher spoke of as the differing 'atmospheres' of different departments, whether in terms of the 'sociocultural contexts' in which teaching is embedded (McLaughlin *et al.*, 1990), the 'ethos' in which teachers spend significant time (Rutter, *et al.*, 1979), or the 'cultures' in whose construction they participate (Schein, 1985), have received a great deal of attention in the educational and organizational literatures. It is a literature, however, which has largely assumed that the environ-ment or culture which teachers inhabit is a school level phenomenon.

One can readily distinguish the differing environments, and the dominant cultures which characterize them, of the three schools within this study. As illustrated in the initial case descriptions, these schools represent very different contexts in which to work, not only in the objective conditions of the schools, but also in the social ones — the 'ways we do things around here' and the values attached to what should, and should not, be done. These differences in school-level culture tell much about what it means to be a teacher in a given site, about what kinds of attitudes, actions, and interactions are supported, tolerated, or sanctioned. But what it means to be a teacher in a particular department in that school can be quite a different story.

Each spring Rancho puts out an end-of-year publication, widely distributed to the community. This is a celebration of the graduating class, with a 'last will' from the departing students and advice from the staff to them; it is also a celebration of the faculty, with the announcements and profiles of each class award-winning 'teacher of the year'. The winner of the award from the senior class, an English teacher for twenty-three years, is described as responding to the award with embarrassment, and with the following comment:

> My teaching is no longer outstanding. There is little motivation to be a good teacher, and no financial reward, no professional award, no reward from society, and only on rare occasions, an intrinsic reward.

It appears in some ways to be an extraordinary comment for an award recipient to make, but it is similar to many statements we heard in this school. No one familiar with the CRC sites would have much trouble identifying the school from which it came. At Oak Valley such a statement would be unthinkable; neither the conditions nor the culture would support it. At Highlander, where the 'objective' conditions are similar, it would be unspeakable, at least in public. But at Rancho, such a statement not only would be tolerated, but would be common; the dominant story is one of frustration, of overwhelming constraints, and of the lack of external support and appreciation. It is the kind of statement heard from a variety of sources, and from a number of departments — but not from all. For while the conditions this teacher describes are certainly school-wide, the impact they have is not.

This award-winning teacher is a member of what I have here called a fragmented English department. The newspaper reports that 'he enjoys his job for "the isolation, the lack of administrative interference, and his ability to avoid contact with his colleagues." ' His colleagues, in their interviews, confirm the sense of fragmentation and isolation which characterizes the department as well as the school. Norms of inclusion are remarkably low, for there is little in which anyone could be included. And the Chair's description of her role has little to do with community-building: 'I am responsible for the Scantron order for the department. Also the reader (clerical aides) budget. And, when there is a contract, I attend meetings.' The focus is on clerical duties, rather than curricular or professional ones.

There is little talk of the department as a unit at all; instead, these teachers orient more toward the advisory units. Even the Chair notes that the people she is most close to are her unit colleagues. It is in the advisory units that teachers have invested their sense of professional community. In those units, however, they see collective strength waning: 'You lose the sense of the whole [now] . . . we work more in isolation from one another; I miss it.' So far, however, the department has not provided an alternative sense of community.

Friendships and collaborative exchanges occur within the department and are important to these teachers, but they occur sporadically and incidentally. The department does little to promote or organize them, or to foster rituals of inclusion or a sense of commitment to collective endeavor. Those who, like the award-winning teacher, choose to isolate themselves find little to draw them out of their classrooms. This fragmented department, like the ones in Cusick's study (1983), simply does not do much as a department, and as a department provides no protection from the environmental stress of the school.

The Science department in that same school generates quite a different atmosphere, in a bonded community where norms of inclusion and commitment to collective endeavor are both high. Tied together by the design of the classrooms, which all open on each other, and by the regular sharing of materials and lesson plans, no Science teacher has, or seeks, the ability to avoid contact with his department colleagues — everyone is by necessity included in the group. Chairing this group is seen as too large a responsibility for one person, and is instead shared among four teachers — giving rise to both greater involvement in decision-making and greater pressure for all to commit to the decisions.

Teachers in the Science department speak with quite a different tone, as the norms and values of their social world mediate and transform those of the school. While they, too, deplore the lack of rewards, support, and appreciation from external sources, their comments translate frustration into anger, and helplessness into action. One agreed that 'the whole system needs to be bombed and rebuilt' but his response, and that of four of his department colleagues, is to volunteer to be a union representative and have a hand in at least the rebuilding part of it. Even a new teacher was quickly brought into the group discussions of school and district problems — and demonstrated his loyalty by taking on the extra duties of union representative despite the countervailing demands of a new job and a new baby.

The sense of collective identity and responsibility makes teaching in this bonded department quite different from teaching in the fragmented English department, even though both are in the same school. This department provides the rewards, and the demands, of a collective enterprise. One teacher, for example, like the English teacher above has taught at the school for twenty-four years. Like the English teacher, he, too, is particularly popular with the students. And again like the English teacher, he receives 'no financial reward' for his professional development or activity, since he is already at the top of the salary schedule. Still, he continues to take courses, even though he now pays for them himself, so he can contribute to improving the science program: 'There was a lot of pressure going on in energy, so I took eight or nine units in energy courses so I could improve the curriculum in that area.' He speaks of regular 'reality checks', comparing the progress of his classes to those of others in the department, and to other Science teachers from other schools. With his department colleagues he presses for changes in policy, for additional resources, for program improvement: 'We want to see the students have a good education . . . we're very vocal on things that count.' His popularity becomes an asset to the bonded department, since he 'can be moved back and forth to help balance loads'. This leads to a 'little frustration' and to a lot of hard work on his part — but he sees himself as part of the whole of the department, and the assignment as a demonstration of his commitment to the collective good. Running throughout the interviews with these teachers are references to the 'we' of a 'Science department [that] is very strong' that demands extra effort of its members, but that in return provides strong support and community to all of its faculty.

What happens in these two contrasting social contexts is that information from and about the system in which teachers work is markedly and consequentially transformed as the small groups collectively process the information. As a result, their attitudes toward their work, and sense of the possibility of what that work can accomplish are also transformed. The English teacher-of-the-year finds no rewards in a system that places little value on his efforts, and no compensating rewards at the department level. There is no sense of community to support him, no sense of a commitment to a common purpose. His department reflects, as a colleague explains, the 'feeling that we'll get screwed no matter what we do, so teachers just concentrate on what goes on in their classrooms', but even there they feel overwhelmed.

The Science teachers, supported by their inclusive norms and shared commitment to their work, continue to take courses, even though the district offers no financial rewards, because the department, and the students, need the expertise. Together they use that new information to adapt content and methods to fit a new population of students — and they see the strategies working. Even when the system goes against them, their collective sense-making reflects the attitude that working for change will bring results, and allows them hope 'for the longer term picture; okay, if we don't achieve something in a year, then next year, or the following year'.

Building community takes considerable effort from teachers. More committed to the advisory unit structure, the English teachers have not found the time or the energy to build an alternative support system in their department. The Science teachers here have considerable advantage in that they were less committed to, or integrated into, the unit structure. For them, the department has long been their primary reference group. At the time of this study, the contrasts between the two departments were readily apparent in the stories their teachers told.

Collegiality

More graphically, the differences in the kinds of social atmospheres of these schools, and the mediating power of the different types of departmental communities within them, can be seen through the survey data. In both the 1989 and 1990 surveys, the following set of items, taken from the High School and Beyond ATS study, provided a measure of collegiality:

- You can count on most staff members to help out anywhere, anytime — even though it may not be part of their official assignment.
- Teachers in this school are continually learning and seeking new ideas.
- There is a great deal of cooperative effort among staff members.
- Staff members maintain high standards.
- This school seems like a big family; everyone is so close and cordial.

The five items were combined in an index to create a measure in which collegiality is defined as one in which a staff not only gets along with each other, but is actively working together through collaborative means toward particular educational ends (see Appendix B).

Figure 5.1 includes data from the full Center sample, from an analysis by Joan Talbert (1991) looking at the boundaries of teachers' professional communities. The differences among levels of collegiality at the school level are both apparent and apparently rather stable; there is little change between the two sets of responses.

For schools such as the one labeled 04 on the graph, an alternative high school with a clear mission and only nine faculty, the figure of collegiality can easily and appropriately be ascribed as a measure of the whole school. But in an analysis of data aggregated to the school level, which is where such analysis usually occurs, whether the same assumption can be made of faculties such as Oak Valley's 137 teachers is highly questionable, and is beginning to be questioned (Talbert, 1991). It is the question Michael Huberman (1990) raises, and answers emphatically, in the passage with which this chapter begins.

In these sites it may not be entirely 'goofy logic' to consider the

Figure 5.1   Faculty Collegiality by School

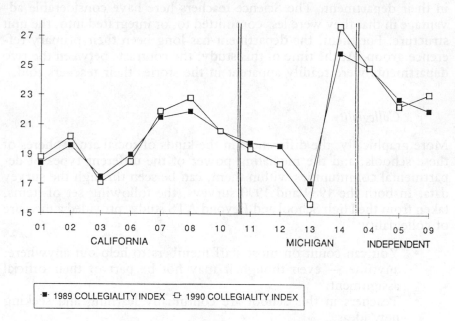

■ 1989 COLLEGIALITY INDEX   ☐ 1990 COLLEGIALITY INDEX

school as unit of analysis, even though the size of these schools is about four times as large as in Huberman's example. There are important differences in collegiality that arise around school level factors such as mission (or its absence), district and building administrative support (or its lack), and even level of fiscal resources. The lay-offs at Highlander (school 12 on the graph), the tense labor relations at Rancho (03), and the sense of community support and shared academic focus at Oak Valley (10) are all clearly contributors to their positions on the graph.

But what is masked in this excerpt from the Center analysis (and this is where most analysis stops) is the existence of differences in social worlds within the school, the internal variations which more closely approximate the social environment which teachers experience. If instead the analysis 'would look rather to the department as the unit of collaborative planning' as Huberman suggests (1990, p. 32), and as this research has shown, a very different picture emerges.

Figure 5.2, taken from a Center report which explores the multiple communities within schools more fully, reveals the added information which looking to the department can yield (Talbert, 1991). Here the data from one school, Oak Valley, (which had a 90 percent response rate) has been reanalyzed at the department level. And here, as the teachers have repeatedly reported, the graph shows that the levels of collegiality vary considerably.

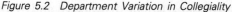

Figure 5.2   Department Variation in Collegiality

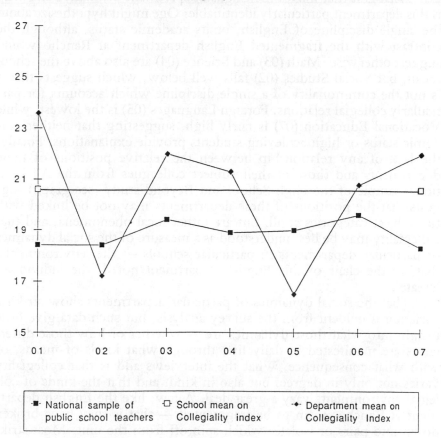

* Subject areas are represented by codes to protect the anonymity of teachers' responses to collegiality questionnaire items. Means are plotted only for departments with ≥ 5 teacher scores.

In this level analysis of the survey data, as well as in interviews and observations, the English department (01 on the graph) stands out as a distinctively collegial, and collaborative, community. Its reputation within the school provides another kind of corroboration. In feedback sessions where this data was presented to the faculty (with the department identifications concealed) almost everyone readily and correctly identified the English department as the 'most collegial' — they are fairly familiar with the reputation of this department, and could explain why they recognized it. They could not, however, necessarily identify other departments (sometimes not even their own).

What is it that makes the English department distinctive and why is this department particularly identifiable? One might hypothesize about the single discipline of English, or its academic status, although the contrast with the fragmented English department at Rancho would suggest otherwise. Math (03) and Science (04) are also above the school mean, but Social Studies (02) falls well below, which suggests that it is not the commonality of a single discipline which accounts for particularly collegial relations. Foreign Languages (05) is the lowest, while Vocational Education (07) is fairly high, suggesting that neither academic status or high achieving students provide explanations. Finally, the lack of any relationship between the relative positions of these departments and those of their subject colleagues from the ATS national sample of the High School and Beyond study (see graph) suggests that the positions of these departments may not be linked with the subject categories at all, but are rather local phenomena, and that collegiality may be best understood as a measure of the social dynamics of particular departments in particular schools — the 'environments' that, as the chair of this English department noted, the individuals 'create'.

That the social dynamics of particular departments show striking variation is evident from the survey analysis, but such data give little insight into what those dynamics are — whether or how those differences are manifested in daily life, through what kinds of means, or with what consequence. What the interviews add is that collegiality varies not only in degree, but also in kind, and that the kinds of collegial environments vary a great deal. A few, like the English department at Rancho, seem to be fragmented — that is they have broken down into pairs or isolates which spin off from the unit. Most strikingly, Oak Valley's bonded English department appears to be more like a strange attractor — collecting and holding its own members, reaching out to influence its environment, and even capturing passersby. This department provides an extraordinary example of the power and potential of a bonded community.

It was this department which drew Rick Youngman, who is currently department chair, to Oak Valley four years ago, and it was the people, and the cooperative atmosphere he observed who drew him to the department. He had been at another large high school before, and had come away with the feeling 'kind of [that] big is bad' but in his 'touring around' this department stood out as exceptional:

I came here and I was really impressed right away with the teachers that were here in the English department. They weren't the kind who were sitting back during the breaks, smoking cigarettes and complaining about kids and how bad they are and all that, and just bemoaning the fact 'oh, you know I hate this school; there is so much to do.' They were really energetic and involved in what they were doing, and more than anything else sharing ideas about what they were doing in class, what was working. Showing student's work, you know, 'here's a good example of this, don't you like it?' So it's not a feeling of trying to be better than anybody; there's not a competitive feel to it, it's very cooperative. And I would just credit that to the people there as well as [to] the leadership that we've had in the last two department chairpeople . . . So coming here I knew here was a school I wanted to be at.

Oak Valley is in general a school that people want 'to be at', but the English department has a special magnetism. Norms of inclusion are extraordinarily strong here, drawing not only job applicants but a wide variety of people who gravitate toward its center. Even the Center researchers tended to find the English resource room an attractive lunch spot, and were always warmly welcomed into collective conversations. One substitute teacher, who frequently works at the school, though in a variety of assignments, described how she almost always comes here for lunch, saying 'I like to be part of this group.' Even a teacher who left last year, moving to another state, had his continuing membership in the group celebrated. The department proclaimed a special day, and posted a large banner announcing it: teachers wore his style of clothing, ate his preferred snacks, and then sent pictures of the event off to him.

Creating, and maintaining, this 'magnetic' quality has costs, most obviously in the individualism which these English teacher prize. These inclusive norms create an atmosphere which increases the publicness of what each teacher does, and the interdependence. Teaching in this department, as in the collaborative communities which Jennifer Nias (1989) has observed, is 'personal but not private' (p. 28). Decisions, however, are less accommodating of personal interest than in many departments; course offerings are debated for what they contribute to department good, and teachers give up favorite courses in favor of a coherent program. One teacher, who had developed and was excited about a film course, had it demoted to marginal status, since the department determined that it could not maintain the course if he left. In meetings, at the lunch table, and in passing, the content and progress of particular students, classes, or projects are displayed and debated, with strong evidence of 'collegial pressure'. Remedial courses, in many departments assigned to new teachers, or to those considered weak, are here the shared responsibility of all, since according to the chair 'those are the kids that need the teacher with the most energy and the most enthusiasm.' Like Rancho's Science department, this one makes teaching a very public experience, and places public demands on individuals.

But where in the Science department it arises from structural conditions (the classrooms have no walls) which make privacy impossible and demand coordination, here it comes from the deliberate choices of the prior chairs, and the continuing choices (sometimes debated) of current members.

Again, as at Rancho, one can move only a few yards away, into the territory of another department, and find a starkly contrasting atmosphere. A Science teacher at Oak Valley describes his department as split: 'The department is split, Physical Science and Biology. It's split heavily.' As a new teacher, and one assigned to physical science, he finds himself cut off from the personal and professional support which the more senior biology teachers enjoy. Another teacher, one from the other side of the division agrees, although from his perspective the split is less of a problem: 'cliquish. Segmented. When something comes up that needs to be settled, we all work on it. A lot of cooperation, when the situation demands it. Day to day type [it's] small groups.' The 'all' who work together, however, includes the majority, but often leaves out their junior colleagues.

The department office has room for the desks of many teachers, but not all, and there is no space set aside for the whole group. Newer teachers teach their classes in rooms far from the department, and may have no place in the office at all. Here course assignments reveal not a sense of shared responsibility, but the privileges of the ruling class.

In the story of this split department at Oak Valley, the group in control, the more senior life-science teachers, clearly have a very different experience from the junior physical-science teachers. Not only do they associate with a different subset of the department, but through that association they have different levels of access to the resources, the course assignments, and the status which are distributed within the department. Their story is explored more fully in the next chapter, which examines the politics among and within departments.

Conclusion

Within this study are departments representing strikingly different environments for teaching, even within a single building. Their differences derive in part from the school contexts, and in part from the subject matter itself, but to a large degree the differences can be understood as the construction of the individuals themselves, and in the ways in which they interact collectively to 'create the environment'.

Most create communities of collegial individuals, bundled together under the name of the department. Here they find the colleagues with whom they are likely to cross paths, who have content in common, and to whom they can turn for support, sympathy, or strategies — if they choose.

The notion of a bonded, socially cohesive community, which Huberman suggested would be more likely found at the department level, is very much in evidence in departments such as Oak Valley's English department, or Rancho's Science 'swarm'. These are, however, as the English teacher observed, exceptional — not only in the sense of frequency but also in the benefits they provide for teachers and students alike (see McLaughlin, 1993). There is also the suggestion from these teachers that they are, like other collegial communities, 'fragile' (Little, 1987). The new chair at Oak Valley worries about pressures from the opening of the new high school, and about his own ability to maintain what has been built here. The Science teachers at Rancho worry about rumored changes in district magnet policy, and about the tenuousness of union – district relationships. In their worry, however, both the value they place on this kind of community and their attentiveness to its needs are evident.

Also exceptional, at the other extreme, are the two fragmented communities. These departments provide sites for friendship and support, but little sense of collective identity, collaborative effort to improve teaching, or common culture. Supportive friendships, and collaborative pairings occur, but the department does little to encourage or manage them. Like the departments Cusick observed, these fragmented communities don't do much as departments, at least in a positive sense. But the absence of community, of collaborative support, is a powerful contributor to the sense of frustration and helplessness expressed by even a Teacher of the Year.

These classifications provide a way of understanding the variation in kinds of atmospheres created by the individuals involved — and at a particular time. The Social Studies department which I have classed as fragmented understands current behavior as a response to a principal who is no longer there. With a new principal, one with a very different style, and with proposed projects such as a humanities program which will bring them together with the English department, this department may well look quite different in just a few years. At Rancho, where the Math department has been bundled, united first in developing a program and then in its anger at district and state policies which destroyed that program, teachers are speaking in terms of further retreat, of giving up the collective fight and closing their classroom doors.

A few departments are split: teachers belong not so much to the whole department, but to a clearly demarcated subgroup within the subgroup. Splits can occur along formal or informal divisions; in the case of the Science department above, the distinction is primarily based on experience and disciplinary specialization. In Charles Bruckerhoff's (1991) study of the teachers within a single Social Studies department, he illustrates segmented subgroups of a less structural kind, as the 'coaches' come into conflict with the 'academics'. The Math department at Oak Valley demonstrates this kind of pattern, with a clear if unofficial group who talk together, go out on week-ends together, and distribute teaching assignments together while another group is left out. Such split departments, more obviously than others, reveal the critical micro-political aspects of these social worlds, which will be examined in the following chapter.

Chapter 6

Power and Politics

The business of the sociologist is to explore the systematic social relationships on which this artificial contrivance [curriculum] depends. He will examine subjects both within the school and the nation at large as social systems sustained by communication networks, material endowments and ideologies. Within a school and within a wider society subjects are communities of people, competing and collaborating with one another, defining and defending their boundaries, demanding allegiance from their members and conferring a sense of identity upon them. (Musgrove, 1968)

The department is split, Physical Science and Biology. It's split heavily. The Physical Science courses are taught in [an undesirable location] . . . Our department is seniority based. And Biology based. Based on those two things. If you're a Biology teacher, and you have seniority, then you're going to be here [in the best classrooms]. Believe me. I've complained a lot . . . It's just the way the department makes the decisions . . . That's just from my perspective. My department head would shoot me if he knew I was talking like this. (Science teacher)

The realms of academic departments create boundary lines which constrain high school communications, and social worlds which can sustain subject-colleagues within their small groups, but they are also micro-political arenas where critical 'material endowments' of funding, time, and space are 'defended' and distributed. The material resources and conditions which can affect teachers' work have been recently examined as important influences on teachers' attitudes and practice, but in the US such analyses, even where they look closely at teachers' workplace conditions, are constrained by relying on the school as the sole unit of analysis (i.e., Goodlad, 1984; Johnson, 1990b; Reyes, 1990; Rosenholz, 1989).

Johnson's study (1990b), for example, examines the issue of the 'politics of space and supplies' and points to the important effects these conditions can have on both attitudes and practice, providing striking contrasts between urban and suburban or public and private sites. For Johnson, however, these conditions are school-level variables, and what remains unexamined are the within-school politics of space. When a high school bilingual teacher tells how 'lucky' she is to have her own room, she adds that 'if you spoke to another teacher you might get a very different response. They have to go from room to room' (p. 61). Given the limitations of the research design, however, Johnson could not speak to another teacher, and cannot proceed with questioning which teachers are likely to get their own rooms, or how rooms are assigned — questions which in many high schools would have lead to the role of the department, and to authority and politics rather than luck (Ball, 1987; Siskin, 1991; Wilson and Herriott, 1990).

In teachers' accounts of how they get, or do not get, what they need to teach at their schools, the department intervenes in two critical ways: it plays a primary role in the accumulation of resources (some departments get more than others) and then again in their allocation (some teachers get more from their departments). Thus even at Highlander, where school-level fiscal stress is readily apparent, Science teachers can say 'there's never any problem with money.' Even at Oak Valley, where the financial and professional supports create that 'wonderful little circle' for most teachers, a Math teacher finds a department 'power structure' shuts him out of planning meetings and keeps him out of advanced courses, making his life 'almost devastating if I'd let it be'. What complicates the issue of school workplace conditions, and explicates much of the difference in how teachers experience them, is the specific department to which they belong. In the workplace of the high school, some departments are routinely and systematically advantaged, while others struggle to survive. Some pass along their advantages to all members relatively equitably, while others create internal hierarchies and status ladders.

This is quite a different aspect of a department than the social circle of like-minded colleagues described in the previous chapter, and may or may not be contiguous with that group of people. It is referred to in a different vocabulary, less direct and less personal, but no less important. While the social and professional rewards of membership — support, sympathy, suggestions and humor — are valued resources for teachers, the department, as a formally sanctioned administrative unit, has the authority to command and dispense far more tangible rewards and sanctions. It is in this sense that teachers, such as the Science teacher cited above, talk about 'the department', and 'the way the department makes decisions' — as the official unit where a surprising number of rules are set, decisions made, and resources acquired and distributed. Which courses will be offered, and which required, who will teach them, at what time, in which room, and with what materials — these are micro-political decisions which are immediately and concretely consequential to teachers, and they are decisions in which departments play critical roles.

In some cases departmental realms become fiefdoms, as Ball (1987) has shown, vying to acquire for their members scarce 'material endowments' such as classrooms, schedule priority, or money; in others, like the 'split' Science department described above, the most salient competitions lie within the department, as it differentially allocates those resources. While conflicts may not escalate to the point where a teacher needs to fear that a 'department head would shoot' him for 'talking like this', the rewards of membership, and the punishments for treason, can be very real. In the routine decisions of department politics teachers can win and lose desired courses or students, the materials to make their jobs easier, or even the jobs themselves.

Norms of Silence and Political Language

This kind of pattern, which Musgrove recommended examining as the 'outcome of social interaction' might be more aptly classified as the result of political action. But while teachers speak frequently, easily, and directly about the social and intellectual aspects of their departments, they are far less likely to use the language of politics to describe the rewards of department membership, or the reasons for departmental decisions — even when they do not fear being shot for such talk. The consequences of such decisions appear frequently in their interviews, but, as in the quote from Johnson's 'lucky' teacher, the players and processes of that decision-making are less apparent.

Instead of the inclusive 'we' and the informal first names which they readily use to describe the social worlds of departments, teachers explaining the more material conditions and procedures affecting their work tend toward a depersonalized, and distanced vocabulary: 'the department' has a policy on tracking; 'the department makes decisions' about classrooms; 'the chair' assigns the courses. Sometimes referents and pronouns blur or disappear altogether, as the formalized administrative unit of the department takes over, and individuals are generalized in role and passive in voice, as in this Oak Valley teacher's explanation of how his schedule was assigned:

For example, my background has always been Biology. But when I was hired here I was asked to do a Physical Science

. . . And then, the following year there were a couple of open-
ings in Chemistry and you were sort of asked, you know,
'What's in your background. Can you teach Chemistry?' So,
from that my schedule became primarily Chemistry. And I just
never have gone back into the Biology. So, it's more or less the
slot that they happen to get you into. And in the meantime,
they've always hired when there was a Biology vacancy, they
always brought in somebody for Biology. So you never really
had the opportunity, and I didn't push hard.

In such stories the department which has the power to hire, to assign,
to dispense rewards, and to require actions shifts from the social 'we'
to the unspecified 'they', and even the teacher himself to a generalized
'you'.

When pressed about who it was who decided how classrooms
would be assigned, another Science teacher, one who was not as 'lucky'
as Johnson's teacher in getting his own room, similarly assigns responsibility to this disembodied character of 'the' department:

Interviewer: 'Now who is the "they" that wants to do this?'
Teacher: 'Just the way the department is.'
Interviewer: 'It's not the school administrators, it's just the
              department doing this?'
Teacher: 'It's just the way the department makes the
              decisions.'

When it comes to political aspects of departmental decisions, such conversations might be characterized as demonstrating norms of silence:
teachers are often reluctant to 'push hard' on who is doing what, or
how, accepting instead that it's 'just the way the department is'. It is
only through repeated visits, pushing interview questions, or in comparative analysis of their comments, that the politics of departments
emerges. This is not the story as they would tell it, but it is one which
emerges from the stories they tell. The decision to impose the analytic
frame of politics is my own deliberate and political strategy.

As Larry Cuban (1988) has argued, the language of politics has
been, and continues to be, an uncomfortable vocabulary for American
educators: 'many educators still wince over the use of the word political in reference to schools, much less a teacher' (see also A. Hargreaves,
1990a). Through the professionalizing reforms of the twentieth century,

the language and the open practice of partisan politics among
school officials was banished . . . political behavior continued,
of course, but was referred to by another name. Moreover,

professional norms emerged that made partisan activity in the community and the very use of political vocabulary virtually taboo. While those taboos have eroded over the last few decades, strong feelings about schools being special and removed from the familiar tussles within the larger political arena continue among many educators. (Cuban, 1988, p. 31)

Political vocabulary is not quite taboo in these departments, but it is rarely used by these teachers, and even more rarely used to describe their own actions. Without such a vocabulary, however, it is difficult to fully articulate the power relations and processes behind what are clearly consequential decisions, to legitimate complaints of unequal distribution, or to push too hard to change them (Ball, 1987).

The description by one Science chair of what was clearly understood as a political battle stands out as an exception, as he explained how he came to be chair: 'Well, there was a coup.' According to him, the two prior chairs had incurred resentment amongst the faculty because 'they were dictators', and so, eventually, a rebellion occurred in which the teachers went to the principal. Four years ago, 'twelve of the fourteen members signed a petition to remove the chair' and install the current chair instead. His job, once he had gained the position, was to relax the battle lines, and to end the vocalized strife: 'They didn't like being out of power. But they have relaxed because there was no retaliation.' Even here, however, that political vocabulary disappears from his narrative once his position had been won, and people could 'relax' into the more normal modes of silence. What makes this excerpt unusual is not only that it classifies teachers' behavior in the 'taboo' vocabulary of political terms, but that it so classifies the actions of his own coalition, and a victorious one at that.

More frequently, the vocabulary of political interests or strategies is used pejoratively, ascribed to the actions of others, and invoked by the losers. A Science teacher at Rancho disparages what he sees as an unfair decision by labeling it as politics: he 'put in [for the mentor program] and the district supervisor was very surprised that I didn't get the position because I have more longevity, I've got better training, and so on, but it went to somebody else. So it appears it was politics built in.'

Similarly, another Science teacher, this time at Highlander, refers to the closing of the school his own children attended as a consequence of 'the political things that happened . . . and that's what they were, strictly political'. For him, the term carries negative connotations, implying that the decision was made inappropriately. In other parts of the interview, when he explains how he has been able to garner what some might consider a disproportionate share of school resources for his own chemistry classes, the vocabulary is quite different. These decisions are explained in terms of what is good, and necessary, for his students: 'it facilitates individual learning' or it's a 'way of giving kids an opportunity' to do something extra, and those administrators who agreed with him 'could see beyond the ends of their noses'.

Another teacher, a former Math chair and 'insider', sees his current banishment to the outpost of low-level classes as a case of political, and inappropriate, decision-making: 'In my case at least, there are very strong political undertones.' Like the Science teachers above, he is reluctant to attribute this to any persons, but instead assigns responsibility to 'the power structure' of the department, observing that 'it has a very rigid approach to teaching math.' His own rule for assigning teachers to courses, when he was chair, is given a different kind of explanation, and the occasional inequitable distribution of courses 'excused', in his recounting, as a function of the rational criteria of expertise:

> a lot of times it was a matter of training, for instance, again, if they didn't have any math background the highest thing they usually could teach was algebra. And, in fact, they usually didn't want anything beyond that level . . . But, excuse me, generally speaking, I tried to balance it as much as I could.

The Math chair at Rancho, too, illustrates this same turn of phrase, in which 'political' is the negative term used to characterize others whose choices are at odds with his own. In his case, the political threats come from outside the department, where 'the movers and shakers in the educational business, at least in this district, want to deny [that tracking is important] . . . They're just on a political kind of trip . . . folks won't admit that they should be more attentive to where they put kids.'

Although the specifics vary, the common thread running through these narratives is that by and large 'politics' is reserved to describe those who can't see 'beyond their noses', who don't understand, and who have made bad — but consequential — decisions. For these teachers, across departments and across schools, their own actions, and those of their like-minded colleagues are typically not classified as political — instead they are rationally and morally justified, lexically placed in another grammar, and linked to the interests of the 'kids'. Similar patterns appear in teachers' discussions of union actions, which are deplored as political and celebrated as moral (Bascia, in press). Where departments can buffer their members from the 'political trip' of outsiders, they are valued; where departments themselves become the 'political' arena, the results can easily be 'almost devastating' for teachers, since there is no likely buffering between 'the department' and its members.

Despite the reluctance to use political vocabulary to describe school decisions, 'political behavior continued, of course, but was referred to by another name' (Cuban, 1988, p. 31). What, then, should we understand as 'political behavior' in and around departments? The intent here is not to look solely at the processes of politicized behavior — what Hoyle (1982) called the 'organisational underworld' (cited in Ball, 1987, p. 7), although these rare instances provide particularly vivid examples of how teachers understand their work to be affected by political decisions, but to look more broadly at the politics of outcomes — the routine and common arrangements of 'who gets what, when, and how' (attributed to Laswell in Pfeffer, 1981, p. 5).

Teaching is an occupation in which there are few 'perks' or rewards to get, few opportunities for individuals to get salary increases, bonuses or promotions, or even the more symbolic markers of status — reserved parking spaces, corner offices — available to those in corporate life. Under these conditions even small distinguishers, such as whose classroom is close to a phone or who got the advanced math class for how many years in a row, take on heightened import, for, as one teacher admits, 'there's always a little jealousy, which teachers get more money or have a key to the storage area.'

For teachers in these sites the most salient political issues translate into decisions about who teaches what, to whom, where, and how — whether named as politics, luck, just the way things are, or meeting the needs of kids. What courses are offered, who gets to teach them, who will take them, and where they are held — these are the micropolitical decisions which constitute primary conditions of work for teachers, which distribute tangible resources and status, and which are routinely and officially intertwined with the role of the department.

Departments play complex and multiple roles in the politics of teaching, and these roles act and interact on at least three different levels, which will be examined in the following three sections. First, there is significant and systematic differentiation in the resources afforded to different categories of departments, evident in the contrast between the 'academic' subjects, which are, an Industrial Arts teacher laments, 'what you go to school for', and the vocational subjects, where teachers refer to themselves as 'second-class' citizens. Second, there are more subtle, but still meaningful status differences among the academic subjects, with Science and Math typically 'on top' while English and Social Studies sit well below. Third, there are substantial differences even within departments, for while some share their resources among all members, others systematically privilege senior members over junior, insiders over outsiders, or biology teachers over physical science. These levels, moreover, are not merely stages in the distribution process, but rather are interactive, and dynamic. The modes of distributing resources and responsibilities within a department can change its position in the status hierarchy of subjects — at Oak Valley, for example, bringing unprecedented advantages to its English department and unfamiliar disadvantages to Science.

The Privileged Position of Academic Subjects

In important ways, the conditions under which teachers work derive from the status of the particular subject in which they teach, for while some departments clearly have 'clout and status' (Lightfoot, 1985, p. 261), others do not. Most visibly, physical placement can reflect political differences among subjects: which department has its own wing or building, good classrooms, or convenient location depends on its position in the subject hierarchy. At Highlander, for example, which is 'a Math-Science specialty school', Science and Math hold high status positions quite literally. They have the third floor of the building, up 'on top' where the noise of the hectic schedule is reduced and the security problems are lessened. While on the lower floors teachers complain about the noise and lock their doors against wandering students, up on the third floor one Science teacher commented that 'in fact this is one of the quietest schools I've been in.'

The question of which subjects get to be 'on top' and how they get there has been pursued by some analysts, particularly in Europe, where authors such as Bernstein (1973), Foucault (1972) and Young (1971) provide rich and broad discussions of the political issues surrounding the boundaries, ideologies, and control of knowledge. Ivor Goodson (1988b; 1987) has more closely examined the complex political processes, and the substantial rewards, of 'becoming a school subject' in secondary education. In such studies the contested nature of subject status becomes most apparent in looking at marginal subjects, or at times of historical shifts, reminding us that status is neither permanent nor natural, but rather the temporary result of larger political and cultural processes in which schooling is embedded.

For some subject areas recent years have brought painful reminders of the possibility of such cultural shifts. Vocational teachers at Oak Valley, hired when 'we were actually a growing and expanding department', remember back when they could 'build programs', when they would 'feel real positive about what we were doing', and 'had more students than we could accommodate'. Now defined as marginal to the central academic goals of the school, they are losing programs, students, and their jobs (Little and Threatt, 1991).

For the four subject areas focused on in this study, the only shifts in the last century have been upward: the steady entrenchment of Mathematics, the increasing acceptance of English and Social Studies, and the remarkable ascension of Science. Jacques Barzun (1945), writing in the middle of this century, could look back to remind us that

50 or 60 years ago science was a new academic subject. People
mistrusted its power to educate . . . mathematics was supposed
to train the mind; but the new physical sciences were first seen
as manual arts, messy and expensive, and with no more 'discipline' to them than a pair of elastic sided boots. (Barzun, 1945,
p. 88)

Over the course of this century the sciences have been elevated to a
position at least as high as that of mathematics, a position that they can
now take for granted. From the perspective of this generation of teachers, in these 'academic' subjects, in this country, however, such issues
are largely irrelevant. Those contests are ancient history, fought by
other people, in other settings. That they can be irrelevant, however,
is a function of the privileged positions of these particular subjects; it
is a luxury afforded only to some.

Science, Math, Social Studies, and English — these are currently
'the four basic subjects' in the words of one Highlander administrator,
and in the minds of most educators. No longer new, or mistrusted,
their disciplinary status is now secure, well-institutionalized, and relative to other subject areas, highly privileged. At Highlander, while not
every subject can be literally on top, these basic subjects are understood
to command their own wings, even if they do not have exclusive use
of the space: 'we call it the Social Studies wing, but we also have
Foreign Language in that wing, and we also have some Special Ed.'
The teachers, as well as this administrator, not only refer to the wings
in these terms but understand the wings to be the territory of these
departments, the 'realms' of these knowledge categories. It is because
she is located in this same 'Social Studies wing', despite the fact that it
houses a variety of subject-teachers, that Joan Frances identified herself
as 'out of the realm' of the English department in the interview with
which this manuscript began. Outsiders may reside in these realms,
but they do not quite belong.

These 'basic subjects' dominate contemporary high schools, not
only symbolically, but in quite concrete ways, in terms of their staff
size, their needs for space, their priority in schedules, and their budgets.
Thus, as the Science chair at Rancho explained, only when Science and
Math one year did not ask for School Improvement Grants, did the
less 'basic' departments stand a chance:

we had gotten the lion's share of the funding . . . and so the
P.E. department always complained that they didn't get their
fair share. With the two departments pulling out, it at least
gave the other departments a shot at getting their dipper in the
kettle . . . It gave the Art department and some of those other

areas a far better chance because the two biggest automatic point gatherers were not in the game.

From the perspective of the Industrial Arts department, another teacher at Rancho sees the same pattern: the four academic departments 'can yell for more money and they seem to get more money, or more of the pie than their fair share, plus some'.

Such dominance is not unique to these schools, or even to this country: from British studies Ivor Goodson (1988b) writes of the 'preferential treatment of academic subjects' (p. 179); in Canada, Andy Hargreaves (1990b) finds that 'the higher-status subjects, most notably the "academic" subjects, receive more generous time allocations, are granted more favorable scheduling slots, and are more likely to be made compulsory than the lower-status, practical subjects' (p. 306). If resource distribution is considered a game, the question of who is 'on top', or which subjects are currently the 'automatic point gatherers' is just that — largely automatic.

In a study focused on the academic departments, such a question might as easily be dismissed as irrelevant, as extraneous to the matter at hand, since contests for status with these other departments are largely extraneous to the conversations of academic teachers. In looking at the role of the department, however, such silences can convey as much information as what is said. That the Science and Math teachers at Highlander, for example, can perceive the 'fact' that 'this is one of the quietest schools', that they can not hear or have to deal with the problems of noise and security that others have to contend with, is a revealing indicator of their privileged position — but one which becomes evident only in the contrast between their silence on the issue and the pervasive references to noise and security from other teachers.

From their privileged position as 'basic' academic subjects, these departments have less need to actively enter the battles for resources, since it is generally understood that their needs will receive high priority, and little need to even acknowledge that such competitions exist. They are accorded the 'lion's share' when they enter the arena, and therefore develop quite a distinct perspective on how the resource allocation process works.

At Oak Valley, for example, the chair of the English department views school decisions as largely consensual: 'We don't have departments battling against each other over resources.' The chair of one of the vocational subjects, however, views the matter from quite a different perspective, and sees battles as a regular part of the process: often 'it does tend to get a little bit competitive' and when it comes to the specific issue of which courses can be offered and can recruit which students 'it's a dog eat dog sort [of competition] on electives.' Since electives translate into the existence of programs and security of jobs, and since the competition is one they are losing at all three of these schools, the difference is crucial to the way the non-'basic' vocational teachers experience their work (see also Little and Threatt, 1991).

The difference is crucial, too, to the work teachers are asked to do, which can vary considerably by department. Less visible than where departments are placed, but more critical to these teachers, is the issue of which students are placed within their courses, and again, the status of an academic subject can bring considerable benefits to its members. For most teachers working with students is a primary reason for entering, and for staying in teaching (Lortie, 1975; Yee, 1990), but here, too, departmentalization complicates school level analyses, since not only are departments housed in different sections of the building, they have different sets of students with whom their teachers work.

Teachers in academic subjects typically have to deal with the full range of students, since their subjects are most likely to be required, but the curriculum structure serves as a filtering device, gradually sifting out those who do less well, or who have less interest in the topic, and retaining those who are widely considered a valued resource. For Oak Valley's Math department that sifting begins quite early, since several sections of 'low' math have been shifted to the Business department.

That the work of teaching high level classes is quite distinct from that of teaching lower ones is a point made repeatedly by academic teachers, such as this Advanced Placement Math (college-level) teacher at Rancho:

> I kind of enjoy it [the AP course]. I like working with that type of kid. I don't feel as comfortable with the kids in the Intro class. I guess I don't relate to them as well. They're a different kind of person . . . a different kind of kid entirely. It's interesting; you get to know more about the general math kind of kid, at least I did. They're more open, and they talk about their problems, and the dating problems, and the problems at home . . . and the calculus kids are all business. I really don't know about their personal lives . . .

An English teacher, from Oak Valley, similarly distinguishes between the advanced classes where students 'are bright and demanding and are challenging' and the different demands and challenges of working with the 'quote remedial, non-college bound' kind of kid. Her department, under a policy adopted when she was chair, rotates the remedial classes, in part to provide high-energy teachers to those kids while preventing faculty exhaustion. At the other end of the spectrum, a Science teacher described the 'kind of kids' in his own exclusively advanced classes: 'on the other hand, when you have the Chemistry kids, you have the cream up here, and you can talk to them; you can probably impart some of your experience to them.' The ability to attract, and to offer to teachers, the 'bright and demanding', the 'cream' of students, is a privilege that comes with subject status, and it is a privilege many academic teachers would not willingly give up.

Teachers in the vocational subjects agree with the distinction, although the words used to describe the 'different kind of kid' and the value attached to working with them may vary. They agree, too, that low-level classes place greater, and different demands on teachers, not just in the logistical efforts to teach, but in the emotional efforts to reach these students. They find, however, that these are increasingly becoming the only kind of kid they teach — as one teacher puts it, 'in our department we either get non-college bound students, or at the most a two-year community college and that's kind of the level.' In these departments teachers see their work valued less for teaching than for housing those students the academic subjects don't want. At Oak Valley, for example, a Business teacher notes that 'Business Math is combat duty; these are the people the Math department just rejected'; an administrator, and former vocational teacher himself, echoes 'you will hear these are the rejects from the academics.' To be consigned to teaching the 'rejects', even if you value those students, is to be constantly reminded of your 'second-class' subject status.

These differences in status, in institutional support, and in students give teachers in the 'four basic subjects' a particular perspective on conditions in their schools that often contrasts with that of the teachers, who, in Judith Warren Little's words, 'work on the margins' of comprehensive high schools (Little and Threatt, 1991). A more thorough examination of those differences is provided in that study of vocational teachers in five of the CRC schools, including Oak Valley and Rancho. They are differences, however, of which academic teachers show little awareness, at least in these interviews.

The lack of awareness of the perspectives and positions of the less privileged departments derives not only from the general reluctance of teachers to engage the issue of politics, and the particular privilege of the academic subjects, but also from the departmentalized structure of the school itself, which, as shown in Chapter 4, prevents information from flowing across departments, making direct comparisons, and conflicts, less likely. As James March (1988) has observed, departmentalization acts as a 'buffer' which serves to 'narrow the audience for any particular decision process, and thereby restrict the realizations of potential conflicts across divisions' (p. 7). In high schools, as in other kinds of organizations, teachers simply have little access to what is going on in other departments: 'I just have no way of knowing. You're departmentalized. I don't know what's going on in other departments.'

The lack of information may restrict potential conflict, since those in one department often do not know what resources others have, but so too does the generalized acceptance of the right of some departments to have more than others. Even when teachers do know, or can guess, that higher status subjects have more resources, they are likely to accept it as inevitable, as just the way things are, since the support for academic subjects is overwhelming. As one drafting teacher in the larger CRC study so eloquently put it:

> Academics will support themselves. Academics is the kind of things that parents want. Academics is supported by the college-university regents. Basically, that's what you go to school for, reading, writing, arithmetic. Whoever said reading, writing, arithmetic and wood?

The academic subjects automatically receive the 'lion's share'; they expect and are expected to receive preferential treatment. They are 'supported by the college university-regents', by the parents, by their administration and the states, and now largely define what it is 'you go to school for'. Science, Math, Social Studies and English have become the 'four basic subjects', and the dominant, privileged subjects at each of these schools.

Relative Privilege Among Academic Subjects

While all of the four 'basic' academic subjects hold positions of privilege relative to the rest of the school, there are status differences evident even among these four, with Science and Math typically 'on top', as they are literally at Highlander, and English and Social Studies slightly lower. As one union activist from Rancho, talking about the relative political clout of different departments, indicated, 'some departments are probably very, very, weak; the English department, Social Studies department are reasonably weak' while 'the Science department is very strong' and the 'Math department is very active too'. The 'very, very weak' departments, which would presumably include the vocational subjects, are not even given names.

The same relative positions hold true at Highlander, although Math and Science have the added advantage of being district magnet programs. When asked directly whether some departments would get more money than others, a Highlander teacher with eighteen years experience had to stop and think. He then talked about how his Social Studies department has raised funds to meet its needs, but later returned to the question:

> I don't know. I really don't know. I never thought about that
> . . . Now we are a [magnet] school in Math and Science . . . I'm

sure they would get preferential treatment, so to speak, because that's what they are, but I would say generally speaking I have plenty of supplies.

What teachers at Highlander do think about is whether they will have jobs next year. Faculty lay-offs, decided by subject as well as seniority, have devastated many departments, and now threaten English and Social Studies, but as one teacher observed, in Science, and 'within the Math department, we don't have [lay-offs] to complain about . . . the Social Studies teachers have the right to complain . . . And the English teachers have the right to complain . . .' Again, in this interview, the other subject areas are not even named.

Science and Math

Science, no longer a 'new' subject, holds a particularly privileged position at all of these schools, and gets 'preferential treatment' even when it is not a magnet program. What holds it in its position 'on top' is a combination of features both inside and outside the schools: cultural, demographic, social, and material.

Now seen as traditional, and highly disciplined, Science is supported by cultural values that define scientific achievement as central to educational excellence and economic strength; science and math are the two subjects targeted specifically in the federal agenda for Education 2000. Industry, too, has recently played a vocal role in demanding school reform, and as a Highlander Science teacher reports, 'what they want from the schools is the kids to have a better background in math and science', which frequently means more courses for more students (and therefore more jobs), with more equipment.

Demographic factors reinforce the status of science, for the push for excellence demands specialized teachers, and the supply of these men, and they are almost always men, is low. Science teachers are well aware of their privilege as a scarce commodity, which as a Rancho teacher observed, 'to an extent the Science teachers are an endangered species' allows them to take risks other teachers could not. An Oak Valley physics teacher echoed this perception, asking

Do you realize how rare an Advanced Placement physics teacher is to find? You can't find physics teachers. They just don't hang around. Nobody's dumb enough to go into education; they go into industry to make money.

Being a scarce commodity is an asset, however, only when accompanied by the cultural value on your presence; vocational teachers are also an endangered species, 'a disappearing breed in these schools' (Little and Threatt, 1991, p. 28), but there is little public clamor to save them.

Those 'rare' science teachers that do go into education bring with them the socialized expectations of scientific observation, classification, and active control (or at least management) of their environment: 'Science teachers are more active', commented a physics teacher in this study, echoing a well-established view that those trained in the sciences are 'inclined to be impatient to see if something can be done' (Snow, 1959, p. 7). Reinforcing their sense of agency and control is the fact that, as shown in the previous chapter, these are the teachers most likely to be tied to their classrooms, and to each other — they make their demands on the system as a unified, valued, and mutually supportive, collective.

Finally, the material demands of science currently require that it be accorded a greater share of financial support. What was defined as 'manual arts, messy and expensive, and with no more "discipline" to them than a pair of elastic sided boots' in Barzun's (1945, p. 88) recollection has now been reconstructed as highly disciplined, still messy, and therefore necessarily expensive. Highlander's principal explains that in his budget Science 'always comes in at the top because of consumer items, that type of thing, and I allocate to them the dollar amount'.

As the Science chair at Oak Valley explains it, consumer items require that his department has the largest budget, which came to $7000 in 1988, almost double that of any other academic subject. Although 'other departments see that as a lot of money', for him, it is necessary since they will have '700 students dissecting frogs, that's $1000. Also live and preserved animals. The textbook is the least used of all our materials.' Science teachers' interviews are filled with references to their equipment — to chemicals, computers, and colorimeters — the material endowments necessary for their teaching. This argument makes Science necessarily more expensive than what have been classified as textbook-dependent courses, and it is an argument which is accepted, since it is widely understood that 'science teachers require more resources for good teaching' (Johnson, 1990b, p. 68).

This logic might also privilege other material-dependent departments as well, since, as this Science chair continued, 'Auto and wood shops have expensive budgets also. English and Math have lower budgets.' But since, in fact, Science has been drawing increasing numbers of elective students away from those subjects the issue is moot, and is justified with what is a recurrent phrase throughout conversations with this chair: 'Let's just do what's best for the kids.' What is good for kids in Science, however, is often purchased at the expense of what is good for kids in other subjects. Science not only begins with a strong position and a larger budget, it is repeatedly and consistently able to place demands on the system for additional or

unanticipated needs. Through formal mechanisms and informal negotiations, Science at all three schools is over-represented in budget allocations and in leadership roles, even given the fact that they are one
of the largest departments, and over-active in decision-making committees, even with the labs that take so much of their time. Science
at Oak Valley applies for, and repeatedly receives, the largest budget
from the school, and frequent grants from the Site Improvement
Council. At Rancho, they not only receive the 'lion's share' of school
grants, but working as 'the swarm' of activists, as 'the union department', they actively push to have other needs met. And at Highlander,
although they 'always comes in at the top' of school allocations, they
frequently and successfully call on their district Science coordinator to
replenish or increase supplies.

By such formalized mechanisms, these Science departments have
access to extra resources, but also by less formal or public routes. At
Highlander, for example, even in a time of 'big budget crunch' and
staff being laid off, Science teachers' stories repeatedly illustrate their
ability to get the additional resources they need. The chair talked of
appealing to the principal when he ran low on funds, and how the
chair of Physical Education was asked to give $200 from his budget
(which, according to both the Science chair and the principal, he did
willingly). Another teacher remembered going to the principal with
ideas for an innovative course proposal, 'talking about the needs, what
was necessary to accomplish this . . . and the principal kept saying "oh
yes, we can do that". . . so I've never seen the system become a problem'. Still another teacher described his proposal for a computer course,
which initially met with some resistance, but in general, 'there's never
any problem with money' for his needs:

> I was very set in what I wanted to do. At first when I proposed
> the idea they said 'we'll give you a couple of Apple computers
> for the classroom' but I said that won't work. I've got to have
> one computer for every pair of students. I said if I can't get that
> I'm just not going to do it at all. So we got the money.

Along with Science, the Math departments also tend to get a lion's
share, and to be 'on top' in each school, but like their subject, they
tend to be more entrenched than actively gaining. Math has an ex-
ceedingly long history as a dominant 'school subject', and like Science,
it is high on the list of reformers' agendas. Unlike Science, however,
here recent reform efforts have tended to turn not only to more time
for more students with more equipment, but also to less time on what
teachers have been teaching as math, less of the tracking that Math
teachers see as essential to their teaching (Ball, 1987; Siskin, 1991). If
science was once seen as lacking discipline, mathematics is currently

under attack for being too disciplined, too 'conservative' (Lightfoot, 1985; Little and McLaughlin, 1991). The cultural support for the subject is mixed with the cultural threat to what Math has been, and to what many of these teachers came into teaching to be.

Demographics work slightly differently for Math too, for while calculus is accepted as arcane and specialized knowledge, the curricular structure positions early math courses as what everyone should know, and many — as the move to Business Math demonstrates — could teach. And the material demands of Math, despite the National Council of Teachers of Mathematics' push for calculators and computers, remain low in these schools. While the Science teacher at Highlander was able to gain a computer for every pair of students in his classes, he sees in his colleagues' department 'a computer wasteland'. But there are no stories of Math teachers being denied these resources; instead, it seems they haven't asked. The Math department begins with a lower budget, has less need to call on the system to replenish consumable supplies, and is less likely to ask for additional items. Their posture, more typically, is a protective one: as a union leader from Rancho observes, 'as long as their curriculum process goes well most of them don't rock the boat.' Their budgets are seen, however, as adequate to their needs, and complaints about resources or status are infrequent.

English and Social Studies

Compared to Science and Math, English and Social Studies are, as the Science teacher pointed out, 'relatively weak', and complaints about status, courses, materials, and even job security, are noticeably higher among these teachers. At Highlander, several of the English and Social Studies teachers complained about the 'noise level', or how 'you can't find the security guard' when you need one on their floor, while as another sees it, 'the third floor [the Math and Science area] was perfect; third floor is perfect, no problems. A woman takes care of that.'

While students and community see Science and Math as the keys to economic advantage for society and for individuals, English teachers struggle to convince people that what they do is not what everyone thinks, or what anyone could do. They talk of fighting the perception that 'anyone can teach English', and the difficulties caused when, for example, Oak Valley district administrators operating under that assumption moved a teacher trained in Speech into their department. Stories of punitive moves of teachers from English to Social Studies, or vice versa, persist years after the event, and are retold even by those hired after the fact, illustrating their sense of vulnerability to the possible consequences of this perception.

Joan Frances, at Highlander, is another example of this assumed mobility — she spent the year prior to her interview split between English and Social Studies, the year of the interview in English, and was uncertain what the future would bring. At Rancho, too, an English teacher contemplated the fluid boundaries of her department, as the retirement of some of her colleagues approaches:

> it will be interesting to see if we can hire new people, or whether we have to get somebody else's cast-offs, and usually that's what happens, we get somebody else's cast-offs, and then it weakens the department.

This is a perception that frustrates teachers not only in these schools but also in the British schools studied by Ball and Lacey (1980), where teachers made similar comments: 'it's one [subject] that does demand specialists I think. I know that every teacher is a teacher of English, that old tag, but it doesn't work out that way' (p. 159). But while English teachers may 'think' that their subject demands specialists, it often works out that they don't get them, and in an endless spiral, that further 'weakens the department'. Here the political status of the subject affects the potential for social cohesion and community described in the previous chapter.

Social Studies teachers face the difficulty of a community unclear on what it is they do, or why it is relevant. Repeatedly they stress that for their subject 'the biggest problem that we have is to get the kids interested in it'. Recent reform agendas, rather than stressing more time with what these teachers have been teaching instead turn to new content, and for many unfamiliar disciplines, such as California's 1986 requirement of a course in economics. Rather than pressing for more equipment for these teachers, funders keep the departments 'technology poor' since, as a Chair complains, 'no one thinks Social Science needs computers.'

Coupled with the cultural uncertainty of the relevance of their subject and the additional uncertainty of collecting a variety of disciplines into a single department, is a job market in which there has been both little opportunity for these teachers to do anything else, and a sense that anyone could do what they do. Paralleling English, Social Studies teachers too, even when they change their name, report having to battle what one calls 'the old "anybody can teach a social science class"' perception.

Unlike vocational teachers, they can be fairly certain that their courses will continue to be offered, but unlike Science, they are less certain that they will get to teach them. Social Studies teachers at two schools complain that they 'have a lot of coaches' brought in, and fear that they will be asked to move out, as has happened when administrators saw a need for more English classes, or when someone with higher seniority moved in and 'bumped' a teacher out. And at Oak Valley there are vivid and painful stories of a past administrator using out-of-subject assignments as a weapon:

> you don't want to make waves, you don't want to say anything because it will become repressive, you will be punished in some way or another. You will have to teach a course you don't want to teach, or you will be taken out of your department. This happened to a couple of people in our department. A couple of our people were told at the very end of August, just before we came back, they were going to teach English courses. With no prior notice. Not having taught them.

At Highlander they have seen teachers with seniority transferred into their department from areas such as driver's ed — which meant that in 1988 five of the eleven Social Studies teachers, all who had less than eighteen years of experience, were 'pink-slipped' (notified that their contracts would not be renewed). As the Science teacher above observed, this does indeed give Social Studies teachers 'the right to complain'.

The differences in status among these departments work not only through the more obvious resource decisions such as staffing, or initial budgets and grant receipts, but also in more subtle ways. Where, for example, English and Social Studies departments have tried to move away from tracking and have altered their own course structures to implement the change, their attempt was largely thwarted by the decision of Math to retain tracking. The scheduling priority of Math, which means that students in calculus will tend to move through the day in a block, perpetuates *de facto* tracking despite the nominal change in other subjects. When, at Highlander, the state-required competence tests in English and Math have to be given, an English teacher complained, 'the Math teachers for the past several years have not had to administer it, just English teachers.' There, too, where the Science and Math departments turn repeatedly to their respective coordinators to advocate for their needs or find them supplies, English and Social Studies share a single coordinator. Through such repeated, though often subtle, workings, the hierarchy of subjects translates into status differences among academic departments, and among teachers.

What is at issue here is not simply the positioning of particular subjects in the hierarchy of knowledge, for that has been more thoroughly examined elsewhere, but how that position plays out in the workplace of a school, and the consequences for the teachers who occupy positions within each department. The status of the subject can bring additional resources to Science and Math teachers, can enable them to make claims on the system that their colleagues in lower status subjects would not even consider, can free them from the mundane demands of having to give up valued class time to administer a state test. It can leave English and Social Studies teachers struggling for the respect they think their subjects deserve, and uncertain of what, or whether, they will be teaching next year. But the status of the subject, and the resources given the department, do not necessarily translate into the status or resources available to a teacher within it — they simply provide the political base from which 'the department' can work, and different departments work in decidedly different ways.

Micro-politics Inside Departments

What 'the department' is and does is more than simply the resources it has to command; it is the ways in which it commands them. The status of the department tells a great deal about the amount of resources which is likely to be granted the department by the wider community, but less about the amount of resources which will actually reach an individual teacher. If the status of the subject satisfactorily explained the status and access to resources of the teachers within it, then we would expect to see better equipped teachers in high status subjects across schools. While to some degree that appears to be the case in these schools, that explanation cannot account for the highly privileged English teachers in one school, the 'almost devastating' situation of a Math teacher in another, or the Science department where so many faculty are actively seeking transfers out.

As Ball and Lacey (1980) and Ball (1987) pointed out in their studies of British teachers,

> rather than being a cipher of subject knowledge for the teacher, the subject department is in itself an arena of competition in which individual social strategies are organised on the basis of biography, latent culture, and situational constraints (Ball and Lacey, 1980, p. 151)

Just because a department receives a large share of the resources does not guarantee that every member of the department will be similarly advantaged, for at this level issues of biography (junior versus senior members), of specialization (physical versus life science), of latent culture (norms of cooperation, isolation, or competition) create and complicate a new round of micro-political decisions.

While the first critical role 'the department' plays is accumulation, the department is also the primary mechanism of, and the authority over, the allocation of most resources to teachers. The rooms in which teachers will work, the courses and students they will teach, the equipment with which they will do it, all are typically and officially distributed by the department, and different departments, even in the same school, develop strikingly different decision-rules.

Departments in these schools are not unique in the control they wield over the 'nitty-gritty' decisions which affect teaching. In a pilot survey for this study, of the Math and English department chairs in twenty-five California high schools a substantial majority report that they have authority over what materials teachers use (92 percent), what courses are offered (76 percent) and which teachers are assigned to those courses (73 percent) (Siskin, 1991; see also Wilson and Herriott, 1990).

It is in this distribution role that departmental politics becomes most immediate to teachers, for colleagues within the same subject area are most likely to need, or desire, the same resources, and there are few rationales sufficient to justify glaring disparities among department members, as there were to justify differences between departments. Moreover, teachers are immediately aware of who has what classrooms, schedule, or equipment, for while information may not easily cross departmental boundaries, within the department it circulates quite freely, and sometimes quite loudly.

Where the most noise is generated is around issues of the schedule, for within the department, usually within the province of the chair, reside decisions about schedule which touch most directly the concrete realities of teachers' work — who will teach which courses, when, where, and to which students. As one chair observes,

> I have the power of the schedule. And that's, you know, it's the nitty gritty. The department chair doesn't have much say in any way except for the schedule. And that's kind of . . . I mean some of the department chairs are real dictatorial with it; some are not . . . some don't do anything.

Actually, department chairs report having a say in a wide variety of decisions, from the hiring of new teachers, through setting school policies on students, to determining annual budgets. No set of decisions, however, takes more of their time or produces more reaction than the 'nitty-gritty' of the schedule.

The role of the chair in making such decisions — as distinguished from the role of 'the department' — is difficult to disentangle, and beyond the scope of this study. In these sites it is unclear to what degree the chair shapes the patterns of the department, or to what degree the department norms shape the selection and practice of the chair, but it is clear that the two are intertwined. For while at all of these schools the chair holds considerable authority over issues such as schedule, all of these departments — but particularly those with higher

Table 6.1   Classification of Political Units

Bonded departments	**Bundled departments**
high commitment	low commitment
high inclusion	high inclusion
leadership consensus based	leadership competence based
shared decision-making	chair decision-making
Collaborative leader	**Administrative leader**
Split departments	**Fragmented departments**
high commitment	low commitment
low inclusion	low inclusion
leadership in power struggle	leadership by default, burden
chair decision-making	unclear decision-making
Dictatorial leader	**Non-leader**

status — play an influential role in the choice of, and the tenure of, their chairs.[1]

The departments, as discussed in the previous chapter, exhibit quite distinctive social norms along lines of commitment and inclusion, and here these social styles of interaction translate directly into political modes of governance. The result is that bonded departments, those which have both high commitment to professional issues and high inclusion norms, have collaborative chairs and operate by shared decision-making; these resemble the university departments described by Johan Olsen (1979) as 'consensus dominated organizations' with an 'ideology emphasizing the duty of participation' (p. 284). In contrast, split departments, which have high commitment but low inclusion, resemble Olsen's 'power struggle' departments. These have chairs who make important decisions about resources, allow participation and dispense rewards to 'insiders', but are seen as 'dictatorial' by the 'outsiders' who want in.

Table 6.1 indicates the characteristics associated with each type of department, with leadership and decision styles roughly paralleling, and derived from, Olsen's study of leaders' and non-leaders' participation in university governance (p. 279). Departments with high commitment are those which, in Olsen's terms, see the decisions being made as important; those with high norms of inclusion are those where chairs (leaders) have low resistance to faculty participation in decision-making — and in this study these chairs welcome, and depend on, such participation. Which comes first, however, remains unclear, for only one department changed chairs during the course of this study[2].

This social and governance structure thus provides the mechanism through which the department's status and its resources flow, or are filtered, to reach the teachers. At the same time, the level of status and access to resources adds a critical third dimension which largely determines what it is that the department has to work with. It is in the interaction between the status and access to resources, on the one hand, and the social-political structure, on the other, that an individual teacher's experience is set in motion. As a Physics teacher with a wave tank might demonstrate, when the two are in phase, highs coinciding with highs, lows with lows, the two amplify and reinforce each other, producing remarkable peaks and troughs. At one extreme, where commitment, inclusion, and status are all high, as, for example, in the peak enjoyed by a bonded Science department, teachers find few problems they cannot overcome. At the other extreme, where all are low, as in a fragmented English department, teachers are likely to be overwhelmed, inhabiting a strikingly, almost palpably different environment even though they work in the same school.

Peaks and Troughs — Contrasting Contexts

Two kinds of departments illustrate the extreme contrasts, the peaks and the troughs, that the micro-politics of departments can create in teachers' working conditions. Those departments which begin with high status, and have a collaborative social structure, such as a bonded Science department, clearly are at the peak, providing tremendous advantages which flow through to all their members. In decision-making, chairs and teachers strive for consensus, and after decisions are made all accept the responsibility for making them work. Faculty in these settings work together, in one even sharing the tasks of chairing the department, since 'we don't receive any additional salary or release time for that here, and so the other members of the department share the duties'. They also share the results of that work, acquiring even the rare resource of a telephone:

> here in the department we coordinate, we collaborate, we have kind of a modified team teaching type situation. We share materials and curricula . . . I have the materials I need here; I'm comfortable here . . . it isn't my phone; it's the department's phone. There's eight of us here that share it.

In another such department, a Science teacher, cited above, talked of his individual effort to get computers, but collective benefits: 'I said if I can't get that I'm just not going to do it at all. So *we* got the money. [my italic]'

These are teachers who also know how and when to make their demands known in the larger system, as these comments from two Science teachers illustrate: 'Most of us who have been around a while understand how superintendents are, and which little track they're going down' and 'we're very vocal on things that count.' Those who haven't been around long learn quickly from their colleagues. Every interview from this department, including one with a third-year teacher, contained references to district decisions and budget allocations, including very specific dollar amounts: 'The district has hired a board member's wife to conduct a $25,000 study on why district enrollment has decreased', 'the district wanted a $4 million dollar ending balance', 'the district might be able to justify a $1–2000 difference, but this is a $5–6000 difference.'

Knowing how the system works allows these teachers to work the system to their own ends, even in a school which has generally been buffeted by external actions. When one district 'stacked' the committee to choose textbooks, and selected a biology teacher from a 'peak' department who would not have the expertise to influence the choices for other courses,

> he was good enough to understand the ground rules; he said 'I don't know diddly about chemistry or physics' so he came back and said 'okay, these are the choices, what do you want me to fight for?'

When the desegregation order brought mandates for standardized curricula, which they saw as 'cheating' students, these teachers found ways to 'supplement it with other kinds of things; we kept the program going'. The ground rules in this department require fighting for your colleagues and students, include relying on each other for information and support — and they frequently mean winning.

Scheduling decisions are made collectively, and with the expressed goal of benefiting the department, or the students, rather than individuals: 'We as a group had worked out the schedule.' Even when teachers do not get their preferred teaching assignments, they willingly accept the department need for their services elsewhere, as does this teacher whose popularity is a departmental resource, used to build up enrollments where needed:

> with the background that I've had there are pluses and minuses because I can be moved back and forth to help balance loads . . . I went back in and built chemistry. And now we're going into scheduling again . . . and they want me to move back out of chemistry and into physical science. I would prefer [not to] at this point, I'm just getting things down, all the lab materials and those kinds of things, all set to go.

But individuals clearly benefit, and this teacher, although weary, is not unhappy with his role.

While there are clearly 'pluses and minuses', bonded high-status departments provide a sense of power to their members. These are the teachers for whom 'the system is never a problem', for whom 'there's never any problem with money', or the teachers, who, if problems do occur 'just talk to the principal, just take a half hour and say these are the problems'. These are the teachers who can give an ultimatum that if they don't get the computers they need, they will not continue the program — and these are the teachers who get the computers.

At the other extreme, in the troughs of collegiality and efficacy are those fragmented Social Studies or English departments where teachers can count on neither the status of their subject or the strength of their group, and 'each person tries to avoid the costs of participation' (Olsen, 1979, p. 292). Interviews in one such department consistently reflect the familiar image of isolated teachers: 'I am the program', 'you're dealing with individuals', 'everybody has got their own thing.'

These few departments, and there are only two in this study, do little to command resources, and seemingly have no one in command. Chairs in these departments are not seen as strong leaders, or as dictatorial figures — instead these are, as one more active chair put it, 'some [chairs that] don't do anything.' Where chairing Science is seen as so large a responsibility that it has to be shared by four people, in these departments people describe the job quite differently. For the teachers, it is unclear what chairs do: 'I suppose the department chair does the scheduling of classes.' The chairs themselves hesitatingly describe just what their responsibilities are — it is in one of these departments that the chair reported, 'I am responsible for the Scantron order for the department. Also the reader (clerical aides) budget. And, when there is a contract, I attend meetings.' In the other, the chair remarks, 'the department chair isn't that much, just keeping track of things.' When the role of the Chair 'isn't that much', it is not only the social cohesion of the department that suffers, as discussed in the previous chapter, but also its access to resources and information.

In these departments it also tends to be unclear how one gets to be a chair, since it seems, as Olsen suggests, almost random. In one, 'I got it by default. But the department had absolutely no input in it at all. It was at the whim of the principal'; in the other, 'no one wants to be chair.'

While the Science teachers keep track of who is doing, deciding, and spending what across the district, these teachers keep track of little outside their own classrooms. One teacher, with ten years at the school, had a hard time even keeping count of the members of the department: 'I think about n . . . I think there are n of us now, more or less.' Even a chair of such a department sees herself as 'ignorant' of how the system works:

on a scale of 1–10, I'm quite far down there as far as considering myself really knowledgeable even of the process. I'm really very ignorant of the process.

Not knowing how the system works, teachers in these departments do not know how to go about getting resources, or how to manage them. There are a lot of decisions being made, but 'I'm not privy to any of the details' comments one chair, and not being privy to information prevents participation in those decisions. One chair has written grants for computers, only to watch other departments get them — and is not sure why. She reports no attempt to find out how others had gotten theirs through the system; instead she simply 'resubmitted' the same proposal the next year, and was again turned down. The other chair has declined even to put in the necessary proposal, which,

> is just kind of a hassle, and I kind of avoided it. I really couldn't get behind the computer and the thousands and thousands of dollars it was going to take to do what we wanted . . . so I just kind of put it on the back burner. It has stayed on a back burner for a year or so. I mean, we've done nothing . . . I mean, if I'd been committed I wouldn't have cared, I would have gone right ahead and pursued it, but I wasn't committed . . . And I think it becomes contagious if a department chair says 'hey, I'm not into this.' But it's been hard for me to get behind it, it really has, because you're not talking about a mistake worth a couple of hundred dollars, you're talking thousands.

Rather than make mistakes, rather than take the risk of being turned down, rather than fighting, these department chairs tend to retreat from the battles for resources, and the attitude is contagious. Here teachers' statements sound quite unlike those of their colleagues in the 'peak' departments above: 'people just don't want to invest the time' in decision-making, or 'numerous people on the faculty who are not content . . . just do a perfunctory role'.

In these departments teachers have little sense of control over their own professional careers, and little confidence in how the schedule will treat them:

> I've taught a brand new class every year for eleven years. I've taught it once, and then it goes away and I never see it again. I don't think I'm singled out; I think it happens to everyone.

With the department as an effective barrier to communication, and with these teachers showing little inclination to venture beyond the barriers, she has little way of knowing that it certainly does not happen to everyone in her school.

In such departments teachers have little sense that anyone will listen to them, and instead of turning to a chair or a principal, they tend to retreat into the isolated cells of their individual classrooms.

These teachers talk about retreating, about defeat, about distrust of their environment, and, perhaps most critically, about the impossibility of truly teaching their students (see McLaughlin, 1993). Several mentioned being uncomfortable with the taping of interviews, since even though rare, being listened to can be dangerous:

> I'm only distrustful [of the tape recorder] because I'm afraid you're going to take people's names I've used and misquote me, regardless of what you say.

They did not, however, ask that the tape be turned off.

These are the teachers who don't ask for much, and don't attempt much. They 'have a shaky feeling about some of the things that develop', they don't want to make waves', they seldom put in for grants, and when they do they have been repeatedly turned down.

In these two kinds of departments — the high/high peaks and the low/low troughs — the social structure of the department reinforces the status position of the subject, making some departments 'very strong' and a few more than 'relatively weak', empowering some teachers to demand and to perform while leaving others feeling powerless.

Most interesting, however, are the interactions between highs and lows which change teachers' standing — the split high status departments which make life 'almost devastating' for some of their members, or the bonded low status ones which empower all of theirs. The stories of two teachers, Brad Carter and Rick Youngman, hired into the same school in the same year, but into two such contrasting departments, provide a particularly vivid illustration of the consequences for teachers, and of the dynamic nature of departmental status.

Dynamics — A Split High Status Department

Brad Carter is a Science teacher in a split high status department. There teachers who are, in the words of one, the 'outsiders', have a particularly frustrating time. For them, resources are clearly present and tantalizingly close, but unattainable, and there is a group of faculty working together, but they can't get in.

In such departments teachers work together, but in small, conflicting groups rather than as a whole: 'we're cliquish, segmented'; or 'the department is split . . . it's split heavily.' Decisions are made, not by consensus, or apparently by chance, but by the deliberate imposing of those who have control on those who do not. Thus a Math teacher finds himself relegated to teaching low level classes, where he feels he can never succeed — but year after year, as the schedule confirms, 'the power structure' will not let him teach anything else.

Schedules dramatically reveal the divisions within these departments, for while all departments ask that teachers submit their requests, in these departments, year after year, some requests are not honored. Carter, with a reputation for excellence in AP biology at his former school, found himself consistently assigned to the 'Basic' classes his first three years, 'and I cannot believe how hard the Basic class is, if you want to teach them something.' This is the lowest level class, where students are 'lacking certain skills. Auditory, tactile, they can't write, can't graph, can't speak, I have all of that in that one class. Behavioral problems, I won't get into that.' Exacerbating the situation is the fact that he has a masters degree in biology, and this class is physical science. He has to learn new content as well as new skills, but those who have more background in physical science, and more experience, have all requested the life-science courses, where teaching is easier and resources more plentiful. In his department courses are awarded on the basis of seniority, not training. The chair was disturbed that a new teacher would even request anything different. According to him,

> Brad Carter, who's a brand new teacher, wants to teach AP biology. Well, that's great, Brad. Wait in line like everyone else. I mean, there are other teachers in the department that would like to teach AP biology but there's only two sections. If you're a first-year teacher I'm afraid you'll have to kind of wait your turn, even though you may feel that you're the top person to teach that.

Unlike the example in the fragmented department above, where resentments are lessened since teachers 'think it happens to everyone', here teachers know what the rules are, and to whom they apply. Carter knows the rule in this department is to wait in line, he just objects to the rule:

> Well, rule number one, and this is not just from my own experience, but a general rule, the worst classes are taught by the newest teachers. And you have the least access to those resources. Make sense to you? That's not an evaluation, [it's] an objective statement. In terms of direction, none. In terms of where you get it, you can do one of two things. You can get blown out, or if one takes an interest, you seek out the resources . . . The third person who teaches basic classes is Nate. He's also young. How much experience do we have? Dave one year, Nate and I none. So, who else teaches the Basics — there's a few who have but they've moved on to other things. Basic is a holding tank . . . it's the shit course nobody wants to do.

The worst classes get the least experienced, and they want to move on the most. There's no curriculum for it, no textbook, I don't have a textbook by the way . . . So there are no resources . . .

What frustrates these teachers most, however, is that there are resources, and they can see them used by their colleagues; they just don't have access to them.

One of the most critical resources in this school is space — teachers cannot all have their own classrooms, and are not all located within the realm of their department. Portable classrooms at the edge of campus now house an overflow of students and teachers. The rule for allocating Science classrooms is the same: seniority. A new teacher, but one of the few who can teach AP physics, finds that he gets the course he wants because no one else wants it, but cannot get the appropriate space to teach it. When I asked him if teaching in the room that houses the computers was an advantage, the question struck a nerve:

Why would anybody want to move and be stuck in the worst room that we possibly have. Can you imagine teaching in a science room [like] this room right here? Can you imagine what it's like for me to hook up my air tracks and all my lab equipment? I don't have a lab. I teach AP physics out of a room that's this size right here. You're looking at it. Every time I want to do a lab assignment with my physics courses it's incredibly impossible . . . You would think AP physics would have the hottest most technological best situation. . . . last year I taught it out of a foreign language room, and the choir was after me, so they brought the piano out, and they'd play the piano, and then they'd leave and I had to teach, and put the room back together again and shove the piano in the corner and teach. That's the situation I've had for two years. But that's because I've only been here for two years, so I'm low person on the totem pole.

Now my point is, you've taken Physics, AP Physics, which is the highest level science course we offer, in my opinion, and we have now located it as far away from the Science department as we can get.

By his reckoning, AP physics, by virtue of its subject status should have first claim on resources, 'the hottest most technological best situation'. That instead, as 'low person on the totem pole' of seniority, he is denied that claim, which leaves him with a sense of outrage.

That Science teachers have to deal with such conditions at all is the subject of outrage on the part of the chair, whose statements on the subject echo those of the AP physics teacher in what physicists call self-similarity — the repeating of the same pattern on different levels of scale:

> Science, with thirty pieces of equipment, fifteen microscopes, test tubes, glassware, and chemicals is being moved from room to room. Those rooms should be set first and then you can have an English teacher move from room to room with his briefcase. Let a Math teacher move from room to room. Have a Social Studies teacher move from room to room. They have to take care of those classes that have large groups and also large [hassle] first . . I already sent [the principal] a memo saying that, you know, if we're totally committed to science that ought to be the rooms that are set up first. Because, and then you wouldn't have this problem . . . And then if someone has to use that room in the off period, a non-science teacher can use that room, . . . a Math teacher or a language teacher can use that. People traveling to four different rooms — why can't a Math teacher go to four different rooms?

So far, however, the Science department has not been able to gain the support for such an arrangement. Given present conditions, then, the internal politics of the department determines which teachers it will be who get their own rooms. Here again, the decision rule in this split department operates to give those in control the classrooms, which some retain even during their free periods. Newer teachers use the five minutes between classes to race across campus pushing wheeled carts loaded with lab equipment: 'I have a little Rubbermaid cart that I travel around in.' This situation not only creates discomfort for teachers, it severely restricts the lab experiences they are able to provide students. According to the chair, who assigns the rooms, it is also directly responsible for the number of young faculty who want to leave the school:

> [the principal] wanted to know why all our young Science teachers wanted to go . . . it has mostly to do with . . . the carts. They're pushing carts around. They haven't had their own room, or they want to teach a specialty that they haven't been able to teach because there aren't enough classes to go around in that specialty . . . Some of the young people want to go because they wanted their own science room.

In his view, the problem is that the school does not give all Science teachers their own rooms, not that the department does not distribute them equitably.

In the eyes of the school administration, however, the problem lies in the inequitable distribution of the resources the department does have — and makes them reluctant to give more. The noise surrounding issues of scheduling and resources have echoed well beyond the confines of this department, and one administrator sees this as very much a problem:

> [the chair] had a hard time recognizing that there were a number of people who had a problem. I've been talking to him about it all year . . . he couldn't see it . . . He thinks seniority is the issue for how people get placed . . . they were doing a budget of $7,000 with $800 to physical science, the rest to life science. It's been that way for a number of years . . . Some people who had been teaching single preps [while a new teacher] they were giving two or three preps and five different rooms.

Weakened by the political struggles within, the Science department has lost ground in terms of its access to resources. In the past few years they found their budget share decreased, their requests for priority in classroom assignments denied, two new technology teachers scheduled (over the chair's objections) to be transferred in from Industrial Arts, and finally a principal who stepped in to replace the chair.

What occurred in this department over the years of this study demonstrates both the dynamic nature of departmental status, and the consequences for teachers while the department goes through such political struggles. These outsiders in privileged departments are teachers who are close to, but not in, the ranks of privilege in the school. They see themselves as 'second-class' as deprived of the full rights of citizenship in their own realms. Unlike the teachers in fragmented low status departments, however, they are less likely to retreat. These are the teachers who fight, and in this example may have won, or who leave.

A Bonded Low Status Department

On the same campus, quite a different context for teaching is created by the lower-status, but bonded, English department. While Brad Carter was drawn here by the general reputation of the school, Rick Youngman was attracted by the specific reputation and atmosphere of this department. As the chair observed, the English department is well-known as 'the best in the county in terms of a place to grow professionally'. That reputation has certainly proved well-founded for Youngman, who in the three years of this study went from new teacher to co-chair of the school-wide technology committee (and technology is a favorite project of the principal) to department chair. As Youngman recalls, he was really impressed right away with the teachers that were here in the English department. They weren't the kind who were sitting back during the breaks, smoking cigarettes and complaining about kids and how bad they are and all that . . . They were really energetic and involved in what they were doing, and more than anything else sharing ideas about what they were doing in class, what was working . . . So it's not a feeling of trying to be better than anybody; there's not a competitive feel to it, it's very cooperative.

The idea of people working together, and sharing ideas, and also sharing the demands, impressed him. He also knew that the 'rule' of the Science department, that new teachers get the worst courses, was not the case here: 'department policy is that everybody takes the basic courses . . . that was one of the selling factors [for] why I chose this [school].' While a number of chairs talk of sharing high and low level courses, this is one of the few departments where the schedules for the past few years confirm the claim. And this 'department policy' was mentioned, and affirmed, by almost every English teacher. Even a twenty-six year veteran at the school proudly explained that 'we rotate, so every semester it goes down the alphabet.' The chair herself had a basic class, commenting that 'it's an unbelievably wonderful mix of kids.' What happens though, once teaching 'the Basics' stops being defined as a low status assignment, is that a number of teachers who have gotten to know and like the students fall semester will ask to keep them for the spring.

This collective commitment to what Youngman calls 'democratic' rules does not come without costs. Like the teachers in the bonded Science department, these teachers talk of the 'pluses and minuses' of their decisions. Teachers have invested heavily in the time and energy that such a community requires, and they also pay the price of losing some of what have traditionally been their benefits. Department policy is that not only will the 'basic' classes be shared, but that all courses are the property of the department rather than the individual teacher. Felicia Yates, as the second chair in this series, began this policy by asking particular teachers to 'request' courses which had become the territory of others, and then 'I was able to say "these are people who would like a shot at that class." ' Then the policy became 'not to require but to encourage' teachers to take on a new assignment every other year, so that the department would be able to count on having people ready to staff every course they offered. In the process, some of the 'specialties' of the past were lost, and one prize-winning film teacher had his course demoted to an elective without college admission credit, because no one else would be able to offer the course if he left.

As a new teacher, such policies meant that Youngman was not

only given the chance to teach a mix of courses in his first year of teaching, he was also given the resources to make the teaching easier. A former chair describes this as another 'department policy', but one he thinks is shared across the school:

> a new teacher joins the staff and instantly they're paired up with a couple of buddies who are teaching the same [courses], and file drawers and computer disks and everything are just made readily available . . . [it's] the only way this school knows how to function now.

This school, or at least the Science department, does seem to know quite another way to function, as the stories of the new teachers in that department attest, but for the teachers in the English department it is seen as standard operating procedure — all teachers have buddies, because all teachers share ideas and materials regularly. Repeatedly, in observations in the department office we could witness such efforts as teachers sat around the central table working on strategies, or sharing stories of success — and occasionally failure. As Youngman described his experience, the buddy system appeared as collegial sharing rather than supervisory mentoring, since rank or seniority are not issues here. Instead new teachers 'don't see it as here's one expert teacher sharing their little perspective, that person is also hearing from three others' and Youngman 'got some neat ideas' from another person also teaching the course for the first time.

Classroom assignments, which created such difficulties for the new Science teachers, are less of a problem here, because the problem does not belong to the new teachers. Youngman does have to change rooms, but the rationale is that the rooms belong to the courses not the teachers — so that while he taught his second year in three different classrooms, he understood that 'part of that, I should explain, is because we have a writing lab and we want to share that as much as possible' and it's 'a trade off, it's not just negative'.

A variety of events which might cause stress or conflict in other departments are here 'not just negative' or at least are not grounds for giving up, for unlike those in fragmented departments, these are teachers who persist. The second chair of this department, for example, has been a strong advocate of writing, and has seen four of these teachers go off for special training in a prestigious writing program. When she began her 'writing across the curriculum' project by offering their assistance to other departments, 'the response has been zero. So what I did was I wrote up a grant' for after school workshops. This time 'again I haven't been able to generate any interest; a failure.' But again, with the support of her department, she persisted: 'I'm going to push ahead with the summer workshop.' That time she found about twenty

145

teachers willing to try. In the course of these efforts, she also found writing accepted as a school priority, and writing across the curriculum adopted as an official goal. Even an administrator who sees his job as to 'make the teachers more accountable' pointed with pride to the fact that

> one of the big changes we've made here is in the English department where we have cut down on class size, especially in the writing classes . . . I can verify that one time it wasn't uncommon to have a composition class or an advanced comp. class with thirty-one, thirty-two, thirty-three kids and now we're trying to keep those around twenty-six, a maximum of twenty-seven.

At this school, he also reports, most classes have thirty students, and in some, like music, 'I'm talking about fifty to fifty-five kids per section.' The advantages to the English teachers are considerable. He also notes 'I think we need to encourage writing across the curriculum', lending further credibility to her notion that people 'are responding to [the project] a little bit better'.

What is now the 'standard every day practice' of teachers bringing in and sharing ideas, of rotating courses and classrooms, of collective commitment to the good of the department, does seem to be the 'only way' this department 'knows how to function now', but it is not the way the department functioned in the past. As one person noted, 'we came off years of being a divided department' until the former chair, Quentin Ivy, 'brought it together'. Ivy himself acknowledges that 'most people will say that it's because of me, because when I became chair that's what happened', but he sees a more complex set of factors at work. Among them he lists his own 'gregarious, sharing sort of nature that set an example' but also the hiring of five new teachers who were not aligned with either faction, the desire of the other teachers to help these 'rookie teachers', and that these newcomers were 'receptive to being helped'. Over the next few years 'the culture changed' and 'what happens is that the more we share the better we get, so therefore it produces more sharing.' Other teachers do credit the 'communication skills' of Ivy with beginning the change, but the effects, from whatever the source, have been enough that the department has only continued to strengthen its collaborative orientation after he moved on to a district role, through two years with another chair, and then the first year under the newest chair — Youngman. At no time during our visits to campus, and in none of the interviews, was there any evidence of even remnants of the earlier 'division', and I never even heard what the dividing lines were.

The other change which has occurred during the tenure of these three chairs is that as English has built its sense of community it has risen in status in this school, and in its ability to command resources. The two former chairs have been promoted to district positions, and there is some evidence that Youngman is being groomed for a similar future. Gaining resources has a high priority here. When I asked chairs across the schools what their roles involved, most began by talking about the schedule, or about clerical demands, but here the chair began 'I've written grants . . . that put forward department goals, so that's the number one way.' Writing, once the pet project of the department, has become writing across the curriculum, and an official school-wide goal. While several departments have yet to receive their first computer grants, the English department has gotten two fully equipped labs.

This change in status shows up more specifically in the stories of the three chairs, who by contract receive a stipend for the job but no release time. When Ivy was appointed he went 'to the principal and said "now if you want me to chair this huge department, and you want anything new to happen, you're going to have to give me some release time." And the principal said "no." ' Six years later, when Yates was in her second year as chair 'the principal recognizes that the English department is a huge load, and sort of said "here, I'll give you a little bit of a break" ' in a release period to work on her writing project. One year later, when Youngman was appointed, the position came with a release period to pursue his interest — and the department's — in developing computer technology.

Bonded departments, even where they begin with less certain claims to high status, such as this English department, can empower themselves as a department and as individuals, and can move themselves up the hierarchical ladder. These are teachers who can go to the principal with new ideas, and find 'there was an assurance that it would be there, whether it came through [one budget] or he would have to find it through some other means.' When they find themselves moving from classroom to classroom, or giving up the security of their favorite courses, since they have been part of the decision-making they find 'it's not all negative.' These are teachers who recognize the 'challenge' of low level classes, but since it's a challenge they all take on together, these are teachers who can enjoy the challenge, and even succeed at it. Like those in the bonded Science department, these are teachers who continue to fight for the resources they and their students need even when they at first lose, and like those Science teachers, these are with increasing frequency finding that they can win.

Conclusion

Teaching is an occupation which requires of its members the continual investing and reinvesting of their own resources, whether in taking additional courses, searching out new strategies or materials for a new generation of students, or simply finding the energy to strive for a classroom where, in the words of one teacher, 'there is learning going on here.' It is also an occupation where these resources need frequent replenishing, whether from the district coordinator who locates extra materials, the chair who arranges the schedule to prevent burn-out, or the colleagues who can provide support and strategies.

Kilpatrick (1905) held high hopes that the 'ascendancy of the departmental plan' would create a system under which 'each teacher equips his department. The teacher of history is on the lookout for maps and charts, the teacher of arithmetic is collecting weights, measures, etc.' (p. 472). While departmentalization has not played quite the role Kilpatrick envisioned in bringing additional resources into the school, it has come to play an important and complex role in the patterns of resource accumulation and allocation within contemporary high schools.

Whether framed in the more idealistic language of 'what's best for the kids', or the more neutral bureaucratic language of 'just the way the department does things', what these teachers' stories reveal is that the department plays multiple roles in the politics of teaching. As boundary lines they divide faculty, keeping information from circulating so that teachers 'think it happens to everyone', even when it does not. As academic departments these are privileged in a system in which 'academics is what you go to school for' while other kinds of knowledge are considered 'second-class'. As literal 'realms' of knowledge, departments function as 'baronies' vying for 'wealth and territory' (Ball, 1987) in an arena where some academic subjects 'always come in at the top', others 'have the right to complain'. Holdless teachers, like Joan Frances, who are somehow 'out of the realm' find themselves at the mercy of shifting enrollment patterns and unfamiliar courses. Within these realms, departments become the authority for determining the mechanisms and norms of citizenship by which resources will be transmitted to, acquired for, or split between their members.

In such stories small groups, like the bonded Science department, or individuals, like Quentin Ivy, play an important part in affecting the conditions of teaching for themselves and their colleagues. Another critical part, however, is being played out by the knowledge categories themselves, in factors such as the status of Science, or the disparate disciplines of Social Studies. It is to those features of these realms of knowledge that the next chapter will turn.

Notes

1 At Rancho, while the formal position of department chair was cut by the district, faculty select a 'lead teacher' who functions as, and is known as,

the chair. At Highlander the chairs are appointed by the principal, but with input from faculty. At Oak Valley too, this is the normal practice, although in one department there is no evidence of any consultation, while in another the teachers' petition was granted in the 'coup' referred to earlier.

2   At the end of this study, however, two other chairs were replaced by the principal, after consultation with their faculties, in part as a deliberate attempt to alter the social and political climates of those departments.

Chapter 7

How the Subjects Matter

Mathematicians hunt elephants by going to Africa, throwing out everything that is not an elephant, and catching one of whatever is left . . .
Professors of mathematics will prove the existence of at least one unique elephant and then leave the detection and capture of an actual elephant as an exercise for their graduate students . . .
Computer scientists hunt elephants by exercising algorithm A: 1. Go to Africa. 2. Start at the Cape of Good Hope. 3. Work northward in an orderly manner, traversing the continent alternately east and west. 4. During each traverse a. Catch an animal seen. b. Compare each animal caught to a known elephant. c. Stop when a match is detected . . .
Economists don't hunt elephants, but they believe that if elephants are paid enough, they will hunt themselves.
Statisticians hunt the first animal they see N times and call it an elephant . . .
Senior managers set broad elephant hunting policy based on the assumption that elephants are just like field mice, but with deeper voices. (Peter Theobald, National Center for Software Technology, Bombay, India, 1991)

I've got a lot of respect for my colleagues in Math and Science, but it's all going in straight rows and straight arrows and straight answers to everything. (Social Studies teacher)

The expectation that different professions carry with them different ways of thinking, of looking at and understanding the world, is a familiar concept in the sociological and anthropological literatures, and also in common sense. It is the stuff of stereotypes, and of telling jokes. 'How was the operation doctor?' 'The operation was a success, but the patient died', allows us to acknowledge, in a humorous way, our expectation that doctors see the world, and even life and death, in a particular, and to the laity strangely detached, way. Professions have their own vocabularies, whether the Latinate terms of medicine or the arcane definitions of law, they set different priorities, and they engender different arrangements, even when dealing with the same task. We expect the doctor's office to look quite different from the lawyer's, although both are the sites for consultation with clients. That they are different gives us reason to make the jokes; that they differ in predictable ways lets the jokes make sense — even across national boundaries. So Peter Theobald (1991), a computer programmer in India, can suggest, in a slightly satirical article, 'a bold new proposal for matching high-technology people and professions' by sending candidates to Africa to hunt elephants, and comparing their behavior to the above classification-scheme (p. 46).

One question to address might be how teachers would catch elephants, or conduct their professional lives, in distinctive, but common, ways. The few available stereotypes of teachers turn on their modes of control — there is the 'teacher-look' one can give a misbehaving subordinate — but these are not particularly telling. When those interested in the professions, or in professionalization, turn to teaching, they are typically stopped short; they acknowledge, somewhat reluctantly, that teaching does not seem to have a common body of knowledge, a technical language, a distinctive way of thinking (Darling-Hammond, 1990; D. Hargreaves, 1983; Lortie, 1975).

The problematic nature of the assumption that as *teachers* secondary school faculty would speak *a* technical language surfaced in this study with the first pilot project of two departments in a single school, where it became clear that Math and English teachers were speaking quite different languages (Siskin, 1991). Secondary school teachers both describe and demonstrate the distinctive vocabularies, logics, and concerns of their subject specialties in subject-specific ways. A team of physics teachers, for example, works on a 'unified theory' of teaching science to non-academic students. Math teachers refer to 'tiling properties', or speak of making departmental decisions 'sort of by consensus by elimination, finding the common denominator that everybody could live with'. Despite teachers' attempts to translate for the benefits of uninitiated researchers, patterns across interviews suggest that these are more than simply idiosyncratic appearances of technical jargon; rather the discipline's language and epistemology are interwoven in the ways teachers — as subject-matter specialists — conceptualize the world, their roles within it, and the nature of knowledge, teaching, and learning.

Academic departments are realms of particular types of knowledge — these are English or Science, Social Studies or Math departments. More than simply adjectives, or 'labels' describing their position on an organizational chart, these subjects give departments their very reason for being. It is the understood differences among these kinds of knowledge which construct the boundary lines, which draw people together around common interests, and which justify differing sets of administrative rules and resource allocations. While teachers may, as in the excerpt above, 'respect' their colleagues, they are frequently cognizant of the differences among them, of which subjects go 'in straight rows', and which disciplines, in Becher's (1989) words, 'meander like rivers'.

For these high school faculty, their professional identity and sense of what Van Maanen and Barley (1984) call 'occupational community', lie not in teaching, but in the teaching of their subject[1]. Teachers frequently explain who they are, what they do, or how they do it by anchoring their identities, actions, and understandings in the subject matter itself. Science teachers are more active in union affairs — because, as one says, 'it may be the subject area. In science you're pushing large quantities of material; we have to be very highly organized', or because, another offers, 'there's something about mathematicians and scientists when they get this social conscience that seems to say "I know how to do this." ' An English teacher explains her department's readiness to try cooperative learning because 'our subject matter allows us to do that.' Sometimes the subject itself becomes the actor in teachers' explanations: 'Science said no, English said no, I can't remember what Math said.' Repeatedly the subject plays an active role in influencing teachers' actions and attitudes.

Even when teachers do not directly reference the subject matter, disciplinary background reveals itself in their choice of words, the structure of their arguments, or the goals they hold. To ensure that teachers share the teaching of less popular courses, a Math chair 'keeps a data bank of what people have taught' while his colleague from English explains that 'the courses that people don't want to teach . . . are rotated alphabetically.' Two teachers at Oak Valley make what is apparently the same unusual choice — they request the low-level course 'that people don't want' — yet their reasonings are quite different. The English teacher has gotten to know the particular individuals in the class fall semester, and wants to maintain the personal connection she has established, to 'stick with' the 'same kids for the whole year'. The Science teacher has 'requested it, because the problem fascinates me', but for him the request is to have the same kind of student (the 'Basics'), not the same individuals. At the end of his first year he had come closer to solving the problem, 'last time I talked to you I had no idea, I really didn't, but I think I do know, I have a much better idea of what I'm trying to do and how to get there.' What he has been working on is a 'theory' of how learning works for 'the basics', one which involves an 'incredibly complex matrix' of skills, content, and association and which requires a particular pedagogical style (with one of the fundamental physical science tools as his metaphor): 'The only route to accessing those kids is my content . . . If my content is good they understand; if they understand I have leverage; if I have leverage I can correct the discipline problems. You see that?' It's the challenge of the experiment, the joy of solving a difficult problem and developing a general theory that underlies his decision: 'It goes like [I'm] Mr Chemistry in the back of the house, playing with chemicals, saying "let's try this, let's try this" and I'm just having a blast.'

Subject matter differences show up in teachers' use of language, in their images and metaphors; they underlie different decisions and even differing logics behind the same decisions. The subject, in such complex and subtle ways, is an important influence in how high school teachers construct their norms of community, their standards of practice — their professional identity and behavior.

Subject Cultures

To return for a moment to elephant jokes, imagine the response if the question had been 'how do professors catch elephants?' It is a joke that won't quite work, not because of an absence of specialized knowledge, orientation, or technical language amongst professors, but because of the multiplicity of them. What are technical terms in one field may not be in another — 'significant' in sociology, or 'Romantic' in English. Like teachers, professors can be known collectively by vague behavioral attributes — talking in abstractions or forgetting mundane details — but the jokes only become telling when we specify the disciplines of the professors. The classification scheme offered above by Theobald depends on our understanding not only differences among professions, but more subtle disciplinary distinctions between mathematics and economics, or statistics.

Disciplinary Cultures

This notion that academics within different disciplines have quite different ways of thinking, speaking, and operating, that they inhabit different cultures, has a longstanding tradition in writings about university faculty. From C.P. Snow's (1959) 'two cultures' of the scientific and the literary, to Donald Campbell's (1969) proposal for a 'fish-scale model of omniscience' to replace the 'ethnocentrism of the disciplines', scholars have understood academic behaviors and languages to be subject-specific. Later works, such as Clifford Geertz's (1983) contemplation of the 'scattered discourse of modern scholarship' (p. 155) and Foucault's (1972) genealogy of the disciplines of disciplines, further exposed the construction and consequences of these discursive boundaries. In more current projects, such as Burton Clark's (1987) 'small worlds', and Tony Becher's (1989) 'academic tribes and territories', analysts have made more and finer distinctions among disciplinary cultures within and across universities.

Disciplines have been separated, clustered, and classified along dimensions such as the insularity of their vocabularies, the 'maturity' (Kuhn, 1970) or 'height' (Bresser, 1984) of their paradigms, their orientation to quantitative or qualitative modes of operation (Becher, 1989), or their political status (Pfeffer, 1977). These disciplinary differences have been used to explain differences in organization (Bresser, 1984), decision-making (Pfeffer, 1977), and standardization of textbooks (Levitt and Nass, 1989) — with a growing sense that these differences pervade not only the verbal discourse, but the professional lives of their members.

Becher's (1989) study of university faculties in the UK and the US provides rich descriptions of the pervasive differences among these 'academic tribes', in which

> a physicist might 'see everything from a physics point of view, 24 hours a day,' or a biologist could discern 'a biological analogy in almost every situation' . . . a number of historian claimed that their subject gave them 'a better feel for what is going on' and a human geographer remarked that 'geography gives you a way of looking at the world.' (Becher, 1989, p. 123)

Like their university colleagues, the teachers in this study see things from within disciplinary points of view, can discern discipline-specific analogies in almost every situation, and derive from their disciplines distinctive ways of looking at the world.

Unlike their university colleagues, however, they are organized around subjects rather than disciplines, and that difference matters.

Subject Areas

The subject cultures of high schools resemble, in many ways, the disciplinary cultures of the universities, but there are important differences, in terms of the people, the conception of practice, and the structure of departments.

High school teachers talk about each other as 'Science people, Math people, Industrial Arts people', as a way of conveying information about the differences among them. What counts is not simply *that* they teach, but *what* they teach. They see themselves as subject-specialists, and those subject specialties as consequential across a wide range of issues.

Many teachers talk of identifying their chosen fields at an early age, and remember childhood heroes: 'I've always loved Science . . . Mr. Wizard, I fell in love with Mr. Wizard when I was a kid' remembers one, 'I was always good in Math' recalls another, or 'I was 14-years old, a freshman in high school. I had a Math teacher . . . and I thought "I want to do that." ' As Susan Stodolsky's (1988) rich study of how 'the subject matters' in elementary school classrooms illustrates, the phrase 'get ready for math' has definite meaning not only for teachers' behavior, but even for 5th grade children, who understand that these subjects are quite different and have different codes of conduct (p. 23).

Many of these teachers have gone on to complete majors, and advanced degrees, in their subjects: at Oak Valley only 18 percent reported having taken fewer than ten college or graduate courses in their subjects, while 37 percent had taken more than twenty. Well socialized in their fields, even when they leave their teaching assignments they tend to take their subjects with them: one teacher asserts that administrators maintain particular ties to their own subjects, which are 'where they feel most comfortable'. An English teacher now assigned to computer classes maintains that she 'will still emphasize those [English] skills, that I am still an English teacher as well as a Computer teacher'. For such confirmed specialists, subjects are an important aspect of who they are.

Who they are also has an effect on which subjects they choose, for, as Sandra Acker (1983) has shown, there are strong gender patterns to subjects: 'Men and women typically teach different subjects to different groups of children . . . women [tend] to teach domestic subjects and humanities, men technical subjects and physical science' (p. 123). Nationally, according to statistics collected by the NEA (1987), English is a subject which women tend to teach, and in that area they were the majority (76 percent) of high school faculty. In the three other 'basic subjects', however, women were distinctly in the minority: only 45 percent of Math, 37 percent of Science, and 33 percent of Social Studies teachers were female. The same gender patterns show up even more strongly in the departmental demographics of these schools, with only English, the one humanities subject included in the sample, having substantial numbers of female faculty:

Table 7.1   Percentage of Female Teachers by Subject

	Rancho	Oak Valley	Highlander
Math	.23	.39	.28
English	.66	.41	.78
Science	.00	.23	.18
Social Studies	.36	.27	.20

Women are far more likely to have chosen English, and also to have seen that as an acceptable choice. One female Math teacher, who was 'always' good at math, remembers that she was 'stubborn' about her 'different' choice of field:

> I think I was kind of stubborn about that. People always said 'math major, girls who go to college aren't math majors. Girls are always English or social studies majors.'. . . I knew I was different in making the decision. I guess I liked math more than most girls . . . my senior year in high school we were in math analysis class and there were two girls and the rest were guys. But once you got to college, it wasn't quite that bad.

Her story illustrates not only her experience of math as a 'different' choice for a female, but also what was a recurrent pattern of very early identification with, rather than university level socialization into, a particular subject.

There are, however, people who came into teaching for other reasons, and who neither identified with nor were socialized into, a particular subject, for state certification agencies and public schools have not required that teachers hold majors in their fields. A football coach, for example, explains that he 'got into teaching because of the coaching end of it; I was pre-dental for three and a half years' before he changed direction, and 'ended up with a physical education major and chemistry and math minors' and a job teaching math. A physics teacher, who 'initially wanted to be a teacher' but found that his economics major didn't qualify him for Social Studies,

> went to the teacher credentialing people. And she said, 'well, you have calculus, why don't you try physical science?' And of course I thought physical science was like PE. So I said 'Ok, what is it?' And she said 'Physical science is physics, and there's a real big demand, you can get a job real easy.' So I said ok.

For him, getting into the subject was almost accidental, and secondary to getting into teaching. Some teachers hold certificates in multiple fields: a Science chair, for example, started out teaching in Physical Education; a Math teacher began in Physics; one English teacher even holds a 'general secondary' certificate, although, she acknowledges, 'you don't see many of those any more.'[2] And in the Social Studies department at Highlander, where lay-offs present a constant threat, several teachers debate changing fields to retain their jobs. For one veteran teacher, it's gotten 'to the point where I'm taking some biology classes so next year I can get in the Science department just to keep my job'. To leave the subject area is not, however, a decision made easily. For the most part, inter-departmental backgrounds are rare, and these teachers identify themselves as exceptions — and as now entrenched in their assigned fields.

Whether they found their subjects as children, in pre-service education, or in assignment within the departmentalized high schools, the identification of teachers with their subject matter is still strong. Even the accidental physics teacher now declares 'I teach the best subject in the entire school', and evaluates it on its own terms: 'as far as Science is concerned it's the simplest and most elegant science that there is, and it's enjoyable and interesting to me.'

The second major difference between disciplinary and subject cultures lies in the nature of teachers' practice, for in schools the concern is not with the practice of the discipline (they are not biologists or economists), or being, as university faculty often are, 'seekers of knowledge rather than communicators of it' (Becher, 1989, p. 3). For high school teachers the reverse is true — they are primarily communicators of knowledge, charged with the complex task of making it make sense to adolescents. To do this requires a specialized understanding, and special skills: as one chair put it, teachers 'have to be not only math-wise, but teacher-wise.' Lee Shulman (1987), exploring the 'wisdom of practice', similarly finds that teachers need not only 'content knowledge', understanding of the discipline itself, but also 'pedagogical content knowledge', the 'ways of representing and formulating the subject that makes it comprehensible to others' (p. 9; see also Grossman, 1990; Wineburg and Wilson, 1991). The same point was also made by Ball and Lacey (1980), in terms of their distinction between the 'subject paradigm' and 'subject pedagogy' of English teachers.

In the stories of these teachers, the familiar division between subject-centered and student-centered teachers blurs even further, and finally does not hold up as a useful distinction; teachers understand and value their subjects for what they offer students, and understand their students through the metaphors and assumptions of their subjects. An experienced English teacher, with a solid reputation for academic excellence and standards, claims that hers is the 'best' subject to teach because it 'is a subject that allows us an opportunity to really get to know the kids'.

Value is often defined in terms of what the content can provide to students: the kinds of comments made by English teachers in other studies, that English is '*the* most important subject', or that it is 'the key to everything . . . the most important' because of what it offers students, were repeatedly echoed by teachers in these schools (Ball and Lacey, 1980, p. 162, Grossman, 1990, p. 68).

In this study, however, since it includes four subjects, teachers tend to find four different 'keys', and define their own subjects as 'most important'. An English teacher claims 'that English is the foundation of everything' since even 'filling out an application for a job you need to know English', while to a Science teacher, 'technical education is the key; it's not the answer, it's the key' to 'what they're going to need in the future'. Each sees her or his subject as what students 'need'.

If teachers view their subjects through the lens of student needs, they also see students through the lens of their subject, drawing on the metaphors and methods their disciplines provide. One teacher with his masters in biology, for example, looks at the influx of minority students 'which I think is great, because, you know, the old gene pool thing', but 'I think it has to be recognized. And I don't think it is recognized', perhaps since few teachers have that metaphor readily at hand. An English teacher expresses her concern over today's students: 'before things get out of hand and get all blown out of proportion, we should deal with it. More, I guess we need — I don't know, how often do we update books? We should have some newer updated books with the teens dealing with problems.' She, too, draws on the conceptual, and material, tools of her discipline. In descriptions of Oak Valley (discussed more fully in the following section), an English teacher sees students in terms of their biographies, a Science teacher of their physical environment, and a Social Studies teacher of their socio-economic status. In high school teaching, these interviews suggest, students and subjects are inextricably intertwined; when the subject is the issue teachers still tend to be student-oriented, and where students are concerned, to be subject-specific.

The third major difference between disciplinary and subject cultures lies in the subjects themselves, what it is that teachers are specialists in. Departments in high schools are not necessarily organized around disciplines, but sometimes around clusters of them — disciplines which can have more or less in common. While English and Math contain single disciplines, Science as a school subject collects biology, chemistry, and physics teachers into a single unit — along with the occasional geology major. Although their topics of interest and levels of analysis differ, these teachers at least have similar methodological assumptions. Social Studies brings together a variety of distinct, and sometimes conflicting disciplines with disparate topics, levels, and methodologies. Social Studies, a Highlander teacher explained, 'talks about economics and philosophy and psychology and sociology and American history and world history'. Here Becher's comparison of each discipline to an 'academic tribe' takes on new meaning, for at Rancho, as one observer attests:

> there used to be a joke even by the department [chair] that it was a loose collection of warring tribes. There were three or four factions, and it didn't matter what it was, union activity, curriculum, you couldn't get agreement.

It is a collection in which one would not expect agreement to come easily. Even at the level of the individual teacher the disciplines mix in complex and sometimes uneasy combinations: one teacher's assignments 'could be geography, rural culture, or maybe civics, but it's all related, you know, to government and history'. How the subjects clustered in some non-academic departments are all related is even more questionable (Little and Threatt, 1991; Siskin, 1991).

And the subjects themselves are subject to change: electives such as 'Vacationland USA', once offered at Highlander, have moved out of Social Studies, while economics has moved in. Writing-process courses have come into English, computers into Math, ecology and oceanography into Science. High school teachers are thus likely to define their subject-specialties more broadly, and themselves more flexibly, than their university colleagues.

In secondary schools, teachers may be less systematically socialized within their disciplines, more likely to shape their professional interests around what they understand to be student needs, and more likely to be mixed in units with multiple disciplines. Despite these cautionary distinctions, many of the findings of the research on higher education were paralleled in this study, for, as Theobald's elephant exercise suggests, there are distinctive disciplinary patterns of behavior which cross institutional and national borders. As Stephen Ball (1987) has shown in his research on British schools, high schools, like universities, exhibit systematic departmental differences linked to the 'complexes of epistemological, pedagogical, and educational values and assumptions [which] constitute, in each case, a subject subculture' (pp. 40–1).

Subject Differences

When asked about the school in which they worked, three teachers from different subject areas provided tellingly different explanations of what makes Oak Valley a good place to teach, explanations which reveal the subtle influences of these subject subcultures. The first, as discussed in Chapter 3, gave the following account:

> Well, I think that it's a place that's pretty pride-filled, if that's appropriate. I kind of view it as this wonderful little circle that is taking place, that real estate agents have an absolute heyday because they, our test scores, all those things that the public can seem to be so concerned about are good. So consequently, we have parents who move here, many of them the number-one reason was to have the kids go to these schools. So, then, if you're going to have parents moving for the schools, then a lot of times that means you're going to have kids coming in

the classroom who are being pushed to do well. And, at the same time, it seems like the teachers that [we] are able to bring in (I was the English Dept. chair for five years and I was very actively involved in the hiring process), and you would read that nationwide there was such a teacher shortage and the competency was so low and yet the people that we were interviewing sure seemed to be a heck of a lot better first-year candidate-type people than I felt I was. So the whole thing, it's, it's just such a wonderful little circle that it appears as though you have a community that is supportive of schools. You have teachers who are in general, enjoying their jobs and getting a reward from it. And you have kids who, basically are doing their job of being students and contributing, so . . . But I think it's all, it's all so interrelated. And from the outside going to conferences and all, it's, it's pretty thrilling to have people know that I teach at Oak Valley, and they'll, 'Ah, Oak Valley' and they've heard about us. So there's a sense of pride here that, I think, affects all the different levels. So that's kind of what Oak Valley High School is all about.

An English teacher, he provides a story, peoples it with a cast of characters, provides their motivations and a bit of contextual background, and works through the plot to the climax of 'what Oak Valley is all about'.

Another faculty member, one who teaches biology and ecology, provides quite a different explanation:

I think it's multi-faceted. But I think the environment, the warm weather, not having to battle the elements relaxes people. It relaxes the kids. They're not quite as frustrated. They're not having to shovel the snow. They're not having to wear all those heavy clothes. It's very confining wearing heavy clothes. And I think the kids are more relaxed because of that . . . I think more kids go to college in the east because of the environment.

In his terms Oak Valley's 'environment', quite literally, produces its 'atmosphere', and its students become the species occupying a particular environmental niche.

A colleague from Social Studies provides yet another analysis of Oak Valley's atmosphere, interpreted through quite a different understanding of environmental effects:

Probably the most dominant characteristic of this school right now is its size. The pure number of students that we have here. They dictate a lot of things that happen. I think also the socio-economic placement of most of the students that are here. It's fairly high. And I think that characterizes the type of kids that we have. Because, you know, our hoods aren't really even hoods. They'd be scared to death in an inner city school.

These three teachers approach the same phenomenon — the good high school — but bring to their interpretations their own disciplinary perspectives, analogies, and language.

Differences in language, and the boundaries of meaningful communication groups, show up most strikingly when teachers use what are unfamiliar terms outside the discourse communities of their own disciplines — the 'Fibonacci series' of math, 'didactic journals' in English, or the 'colorimeter' of science, which they patiently translated for the uninitiated researchers. Less noticeable but more common are familiar terms in unfamiliar usage — the 'give and take among the department holders' in Social Studies, which requires a mental link to feudal systems, or reference to the American Association for the Advancement of Science (1989) report title 'Project 2061', a number which is meaningful only if you know that this is the date of the next pass of Comet Halley (or, as known to most non-scientists, Halley's Comet).

Woven throughout these interviews are the recognizable, specialized languages of subject-specialists, with common terms, referents, and images. A Science teacher's popularity becomes an asset to the department, since he 'can be moved back and forth to help balance loads'; another explains the appeal of teaching freshmen: 'I love that from September to December, the raging hormones, the growth spurts.' A Social Studies teacher uses the same simile three times in a single interview: 'we now know what it's like to live under a totalitarian regime, why people don't revolt', and others use similarly historical-political metaphors. English teachers recall 'the Camelot period', or joke about the state mandate for interdisciplinary connections by invoking aspects of novels: Roald Dahl's 'rats and sausages' as science, *of Mice and Men* as math.

For Math and Science teachers, a quantitative orientation distinguishes not only their content, but their ways of looking at their context. At Rancho, as discussed in the previous chapter, Science teachers had budget amounts readily available for their arguments; the English teachers never mentioned figures. At Oak Valley a Science teacher had a wealth of numbers immediately at hand: 'we have sixty kids in life science, 659 in biology . . . It's 11–1. That's the ratio of our school. 11–1 think they're going to college, think they can handle a college level biology.' In the building next door, the chair of the English department hesitated when asked how many teachers there are in the department: 'about twenty. Ask [the former chair] but I think maybe twenty-four.' For him, numbers are clearly not a major preoccupation.

The common languages and common interests which are associated with those who share the same subject area are part of what Joan Frances describes as missing from her everyday life at Highlander, since her classroom is 'out of the realm' of the English department. With her colleagues in English she shares a set of assumptions about the nature of teaching and learning, one that is not the same as those of her Social Studies neighbors: 'to some degree, how far you go I couldn't measure that, but when we have meetings together we're all in agreement about certain things, what should be taught and what shouldn't be.'

To look at the agreements which characterize subject cultures requires a shift from viewing departments as subunits of a school system to seeing them as subsets of a knowledge system, and teachers as members of subject-based communities that extend beyond school walls. In high schools, as in Van Maanen and Barley's (1984) conception of universities, departments are sites where school and subject come together — and sometimes conflict — in a 'confluence of organizational and occupational interests' (p. 332).

As Stephen Ball's interviews with English teachers at four British schools reveal, the occupational interest, the degree to which English teachers are all in agreement about what should and shouldn't be taught, can and does vary, and his caution that 'the extent of agreement and allegiance within subjects cannot be taken for granted' is clearly an important one (Ball and Lacey, 1980, p. 151). Disagreements and mixed allegiances were clearly evident in the previous chapter's analysis of micro-politics within departments. Nonetheless, without taking it for granted, 'to some degree' teachers in a given subject area are 'all in agreement about certain things', and it is quite possible to recognize the field of a teacher from an interview transcript without reference to the identifying labels. There are dominant themes and discursive patterns in subjects which show up not only across these three schools, but also in other studies which have listened to teachers talk about their work. What makes these dominant themes worth exploring, and worth recognizing, is that they translate into systematically different conceptions of the tasks of teaching and learning.

Social Studies

The subject of Social Studies, or Social Science as it is known at Oak Valley, is the most difficult to characterize, for while its assorted 'tribes' may not always be 'warring', it does seem to bring together people of disparate backgrounds who have difficulty reaching agreement — at least ten different disciplines were named by Social Studies teachers as included in their subject. In addition, complicating the subject even further, Social Studies has been the department where coaches have tended to teach, although as Bruckerhoff's (1991) case study of one embattled Social Studies department shows so vividly, they have not always been welcomed by their 'academic' colleagues. Certainly the level of agreement within this subject cannot be taken for granted. Of the four subject areas studied, Social Studies appears to be least likely to form bonded groups, least likely to wield political power, and least likely to speak with a common voice — although as a case study of one exemplary Social Studies department reveals, it can happen (Hill and Bussey, 1993).

In this subject area, not only are there multiple disciplines, but they come out of the social sciences, characterized as having low agreement on goals and procedures (Kuhn, 1970), and less likely to have established routines or clearly defined tasks (Lodahl and Gordon, 1972). Becher (1989), for example, finds sociology 'always contested — there are no consensual judgments' (p. 7). In high schools this is a subject where teachers are likely to function as fairly autonomous 'holders', where contests are frequent, and where everything must be locally negotiated, since there are few standardized assumptions about how things must be.

The resulting tensions are evident not only in the image of the 'loose collection of warring tribes' at Rancho, but also at Oak Valley, where the chair comments 'we're all vastly different personalities, and some personalities are not my kind of personalities, but it's ok.' Here too, the Social Studies department has seldom been 'all in agreement' about anything, and spent two years unsuccessfully trying to negotiate their response to new state guidelines. And at Highlander, where there is less sense of conflict, comments from Social Studies teachers repeatedly, as these examples from three different teachers attest, stress their differences, and their autonomy: 'I guess most of the people in our department, myself included, are pretty independent; we go inside the room and close the door'; 'I have a lot of freedom in what I teach'; 'I view the classroom as my own domain.'

Where Science or Math teachers check informally or form 'teams' to ensure that they are proceeding at same pace and covering the same material, in Social studies, one avows, 'we want latitude, we want to do it individually.' Oak Valley tried a school-wide teaming effort back in the late 1970s, but in Social Studies the experiment lasted only briefly: 'we didn't have it before and we haven't had it since.' Even in multiple sections of the same course teachers proceed at their own pace. One American history teacher describes how a colleague will 'fight the Civil War in about twenty-five minutes one day' and by the end of the year be 'up through the Iranian crisis and then the Ronald Reagan [sic]' while he himself 'would have just ended the depression'. Teachers may not even feel compelled to keep up with their own timetables, another reveals: 'some years I don't get through the whole curriculum; other years I do.'

There are no clear rules in any of the Social Studies departments about who teaches which courses, or even about who can teach what. For some the expectation is that teachers stay in their own specializations: 'I just deal mainly with the history part of this; my degree is in history so I didn't get economics, I never get political science.' For others, teachers are assumed able to teach almost any course: 'we've all taught different disciplines . . . most of us have taught everything in this department except psychology at one time or another.' (Psychology courses at Oak Valley are the tightly held preserve of a specialist teacher.) For still others the lines between specialist and generalist are blurred, as for the teacher who covers 'geography, rural culture, or maybe civics, but it's all, you know, related to government and history'.

These different assumptions, however, do not lead to different department policies; in each department the assignments are renegotiated each year. At Highlander, even after the schedule has been set by the chair and administrator, there is a round of individual negotiation among the teachers, where, one veteran explains, 'some of the other guys fight' or 'just trade within the department' so that a teacher can 'get a lower level class, but get one less prep'.

What does emerge as a dominant theme in these interviews is the difficulty of connecting this amorphous subject to the immediate needs of students. Repeatedly, across schools, Social Studies teachers talk about the problem:

> Generally kids don't care about it. They don't see a need for it. They can figure out why they're taking Math. They can figure out why they're taking English [and sometimes Science]. Social Studies, every time the semester starts 'how come I've got to take this class . . . what does Social Studies do for me?' (Highlander)

> They don't want to learn, terrible resistance. They want to do anything else but learn. [They ask] 'why do we have to do this stuff?' (Oak Valley)

> Most of the time the kids cannot, they don't see any reason for having to know about something that happened a hundred years ago. (Highlander)

An interview with a Rancho student confirms what these teachers fear: 'I do need to learn to write, you know. You know, that's why I take English' but 'I don't care about the past. I think history's a waste. They don't teach you about life; at least to me they haven't.'

Teachers in this subject thus strive to overcome a common problem, but, as might be expected, 'you know, we use different techniques.' As close studies of teaching in four Social Studies classrooms reveal, those 'different techniques' are likely to come from the varying disciplinary backgrounds of the teachers, who conceptualize and teach even the same unit of an American history course in markedly dissimilar — and disciplinary — ways (Wilson and Wineburg, 1988).

English

In contrast to Social Studies, English departments house only one discipline, and in contrast to their university colleagues, they are not subdivided by period or genre. Like the social sciences, however, this single 'academic tribe' is generally understood to have loose paradigms — multiple techniques and ways of knowing an imprecisely defined subject matter. Traditionally 'whereas science investigated materiality, sought universal laws, and produced "truth", literary study examined the human spirit, appreciated unique works, and produced civilizing effects' (Shumway and Messer-Davidow, 1991, p. 209). Activities such as these are hardly likely to produce standardized routines.

Yet in one sense English teachers are, as Joan Frances put it, 'all in agreement about certain things'. As she observed, they consistently stress interpersonal connection, and the need to fit the content to the individual needs of students: 'well, you see, you're dealing with individuals. As a whole, I think we're interested in that.' That interest in the individual, and on making individual, personal connections, surfaces not only in these three schools, but also in other studies. Pamela Grossman (1990), for example, quotes an English teacher who describes the subject as 'so personal. Say, more personal than Math' (p. 77). Mary Metz (1978) describes English (and Social Studies) as having 'a content that is vague, subject to change, and of personal relevance' (p. 76). A department head in Ball and Lacey's (1980) study explains that 'the espoused theory of the English department is to first of all treat the pupils as individuals on a personal level. That's a very strong part of their underlying philosophy' (p. 167). The recurrence of even the same word attached to the subject in these different studies, at different times, and in different countries, is remarkable, and suggests that this emphasis on the 'personal' may well be part of the underlying philosophy of contemporary English teachers more generally.

As a whole, the English teachers in this study are in agreement in their focus on interpersonal relationships. The expressive, the grammarian, and the literary themes which Ball and Lacey (1980) found as competing paradigms all exist in these departments, but have now been subsumed. Teachers talk of 'deriving personal meaning from literature', or a newly adopted focus on 'process writing', which appears, to at least one Oak Valley teacher, to have resolved the 'contest between creative writing and expository writing' by enfolding them both into 'personal expression'. English, as discussed earlier, is celebrated by one chair as 'a subject that allows us an opportunity to really get to know kids, sort of to allow them to express themselves personally and to react to literature and so forth'. To her, English is a subject which will 'allow' getting to know kids — but that knowledge of kids is valuable in that it 'allows' expressive writing and literary understanding to occur.

These teachers recognize the existence of competing paradigms in the field of English, but locate them outside their own departments or in the past. The Oak Valley chair, for example, reports difficulty coordinating with the other high school, since the departments 'have two very different philosophies', with the other 'grammar based' while her department is 'writing process curriculum, literature process, so to speak'. A Highlander teacher speaks of the dichotomy of traditional grammar and the more expressive process writing — but claims 'they're all important aspects', which he demonstrates in detailing his own classes. He will 'emphasize the classical essay form with a good introductory paragraph stating the thesis statement' but grade students' essays by 'whether they're able to put out some ideas that they have developed'. And at Oak Valley, after thirty-four years of teaching, another remembers what it was like to be a traditional grammarian:

> I was a traditional, stand-up, lecture behind the desk teacher, holding a textbook in hand, going page by page. And I hated it. I didn't know any better. I didn't know any other way . . . there was no personal contact with the students. It was boring. How could I be friends with the students, not realizing that I was putting all those obstacles in the way?

Now he talks of 'interactive process', of being a 'co-learner', and of faculty who 'share our poetry with each other; we share our stories with each other'. As he sees it, it is this interpersonal sharing, inside and outside the classroom, which makes his a 'great department' and keeps him from burn-out.

For many English teachers that sense of personal contact defines a 'good class': 'It would have to involve discussion, I've found, and probably literature based for me, where they've been really involved in something they've read.' To construct a good class, connections have to be established among the teachers and students and the texts — which requires individualizing curricula, for no class is quite like any other. Instead of pressure to match a timetable, or the pace of other teachers, English teachers feel pressed to choose content to fit a particular group: 'I don't believe that you have to take the student from where he is in order to get anywhere, and so I get a feel for the kinds of students that I have.'

Teachers operating under this assumption of teaching work to develop, as one elaborates,

> a general feel of the class, the make-up, the personality of the class as a whole; then I determine what I feel that I would best be able to get across to the students. Each class is different, even the two freshman English classes that I have.

Matching the content to the students takes time, and means that teachers are likely to prefer arrangements that give them the same students for longer periods. This is what makes the decision of the Oak Valley English teachers to continue their low-level classes make sense — the extra time and energy required to work with remedial students is offset by the extra time and energy required to get to know a new group of individuals. A Highlander teacher echoes the same idea: she 'would love to have all my students an entire year . . . it takes the teacher all over again a few weeks to learn the students.' And in English learning the students is essential to student learning.

This matching also requires flexibility in choosing texts, for not all books work equally well for all teachers, or with all students. While each department has certain guidelines about what should be taught when, these are deliberately defined broadly:

> There's all this freedom within the structure . . . The Literature 1 course is going to read at least four novels, so that's something that all the English teachers agree upon. And then, there might be twelve novels on that list that we could choose from.

This freedom within the general guidelines is seen as essential, even within Oak Valley's bonded department, to allow individual teachers to choose what will best suit them — and their students: 'there's enough choice in the literature to say "I'll never teach *The Great Gatsby*" and someone else will say "that's my favorite book." ' Across schools, English teachers place a high value on that choice, and have been the most resistant to attempts to standardize curricula or select textbooks at the district or state level.

English teachers' focus on interpersonal relationships shows up not only in the ways in which they relate to students and the right to individual authorship they require for curriculum, but also in their interactions with each other. And in English, unlike any of the other departments studied here, the persons involved in those relationships include a high percentage — and at Highlander (78 percent) and Rancho

(66 percent) a majority — of women. The high female presence in this subject is neither new, nor unique, for English has long been understood, as stated in one 1910 British policy report, as having 'greater appeal' to girls, and as offering 'the kind of advanced work best suited to their aptitudes' (cited in Ball, 1983, p. 76; see also Acker, 1983; Barzun, 1945; NEA 1972, 1987). What is interesting in this study is that the kinds of 'aptitudes' often associated with females, such as attention to connection, and emphasis on the personal, are here exhibited by entire departments.

For many English teachers, males as well as females, the importance of the department is described, as in this excerpt from Rancho, not in abstracted professional terms, but in the social terms of friendship:

> most of the time I spend with two other English teachers . . . and then outside of school I have a lot of friends, who are also English teachers, . . . with the teachers here I would say it's mostly social . . . although we do talk some about teaching, but the two I'm best friends with don't teach anything remotely like what I'm teaching . . . although [we] did at one time collaborate.

At Oak Valley the same personal theme appears in the stories of the former chair, a male, whose 'gregarious, sharing sort of nature' is credited with forging the closeness of that department, and in those of the current chair, also male, whose 'friendships' with one teacher in Science and another in history are building new interdisciplinary connections between departments. Across the interviews, these English teachers stress the personal relationships first, and the professional or pedagogical connections almost as afterthoughts — but it is the personal connection that allows the professional relationship to proceed.

School efforts to coordinate courses, or to form teams, have found as little success in these English departments as they have in Social Studies, but for different reasons. While these teachers value the relationships which occur around personal connections, and may collaborate with their 'friends', they resent the imposition of what Andy Hargreaves (1990a) has called 'contrived collegiality', the structured relationships which depend on official, rather than personal, connections. There is little imperative to formally coordinate courses, for if each course is unique and individual it makes no sense to hold them to the same schedule, and little sense to construct them sequentially. Formal teaming arrangements threaten their rights to individual discretion:

> we're a, I would say, a group of very talented individuals, and very dedicated individuals . . . we have people that like to do

> things differently. So we don't have common lesson plans. We
> share ideas quite a lot, but we don't say 'this is the way you
> do Comp. 1.' For instance, the Math department has a team
> approach to their courses; we [share] only informally.

This is a teacher from Oak Valley's English department, one where
informal sharing of ideas, materials, and strategies is an everyday oc-
currence, and where the ideals of a team approach are pervasive in
departmental interactions. But it is a department which has not retained
the formal team structure. Their willingness to share, like their assumptions about teaching and learning, proceeds from the value they
place on interpersonal relationships and connections.

Math

While English faculty, like the Highlander teacher cited above, may
not 'believe that you have to take the student from where he is in order
to get anywhere', that belief in ordered progression from place to place
through a sequence of steps is what fundamentally characterizes the
subject of Math. In the mature-paradigm discipline of mathematics
there is widespread agreement about what counts as knowledge, and
how it is organized and produced: 'one dominant feature is its relatively
steady cumulative growth, [where] new findings . . . are typically
generated by a linear development from the existing state of awareness'
(Becher, 1989, p. 13). While Becher was talking about mathematical
research, the same knowledge structure applies in its teaching, in what
David Hargreaves (1983) has called an 'incremental theory of
learning . . . a slow, systematic and progressive movement from the
simple to the complex' (p. 139). As a Highlander Math teacher explains,
'I think the thing that makes mathematics unique is that it's an area
that, as you go up the ladder, that each rung depends on all the previous ones.' An Oak Valley teacher uses only slightly different language: 'We're really concerned with the kid moving on to the next
level.'

Within this kind of knowledge model, Math teachers value testing, placement, and tracking as the means of assigning students to
the right rungs during their progress up the ladder. The conflict
over tracking at Rancho, analyzed in the last chapter in terms of its
political import, takes on new meaning when it is understood in terms
of the deeply, and widely, held assumptions of the discipline itself.
At Rancho, the Math teachers think 'there are three levels of kids in
this school below Algebra 1, and most people don't want to believe
that.' Eliminating tracking means dealing with students placed incor-
rectly, where 'they're just going to have a miserable year and fail, and
I'll have a miserable year, the kids that are ok will have a miserable

year; everything's miserable because . . . folks won't admit that they should be more attentive to where they put kids.' From outside the shared understanding of Math departments, the situation looks quite different. One teacher from another department described 'this convoluted little policy they had where there were nine thousand ways one got into mathematics. There was pre-algebra, pre-pre-algebra, pre-pre-pre-algebra, and things like that.'

Inside Math departments, across the schools, what outsiders see as 'convoluted' policies do make sense, and sound remarkably similar. 'Our progression' says an Oak Valley Math teacher,

> is foundations, is the very low kids who need help in basic skills. Then there's a general math class which is just before the pre-algebra class, which is like a basic math class. Then we have the next progression which would be to a pre-algebra class, algebra, geometry, 2nd year algebra and so on. If a kid comes in and starts in a general math class, it's not a foundation because his only option, right now, is to go on to pre-algebra . . . I'm ending up with some pre-algebra kids who have no intention of going on to algebra, but they've got nowhere else to go. And again, it is, to me that's a, I don't know if neglect is the right word, but that is a problem for those kids.

At Highlander, too, teachers are concerned that 'the scheduling is done for kids before the final grades are given. So you've got kids that are misplaced on that criteria, and that causes problems.' But because counselors and administrators can't understand this, Math teachers continually face what one characterizes as 'the inability to get kids into the right slots'. Their concerns are for their students, but their understanding of students' needs comes from the epistemological assumptions of their subject — and conflicts with those of other subjects.

Here again, the patterns which distinguish Math teachers' conceptions about tracking cross not only school but national boundaries — Stephen Ball (1987) reports a similar instance from his study of Beachside Comprehensive in England, where 'going mixed-ability' was the school policy at issue. Despite the geographical and cultural distance, the subject pattern is consistent: 'the advocacy of mixed-ability was spearheaded by the English department . . . the opposition was lead initially by the languages and mathematics departments' and the conflicting political positions could be traced to 'technical differences between the subjects' (p. 40). At Rancho, Oak Valley, Highlander, as at Beachside, pressures to eliminate tracking place Math teachers in a situation where the interests and expectations of the schools conflict with those of their subject, for, as Van Maanen and Barley (1984) explain, 'what is deviant organizationally may be occupationally correct' (p. 291).

The assumptions about progression and sequence apply to Math teachers' conceptions of the 'right slots' not only for students but for faculty as well. While Math, like English, is a single discipline in which one might expect that any teacher could teach any course, the logic of the ladder precludes that pattern. It is not just students who have to go up the ladder, but teachers too:

> for example, we had a teacher who transferred in from the Business department, I guess he had a Math minor, and was working his way up through the different courses. He taught algebra 1, and then geometry, and this year he's teaching an algebra 3/4 class. (Rancho teacher)

> I started teaching some pre-algebra and eventually it turned into algebra. (Oak Valley teacher)

That theme of hierarchical ascension up the ladder is common in Math departments, although not all teachers progress.

According to one chair there is a 'general rule' in Math that only those with a major can teach any course above geometry — and that major has to be in math itself rather than math education. The distinction between the pure subject and education courses is made repeatedly in Math departments, but not at all in any of the other departments. Occasionally there are problems — 'sometimes people request courses that they are not suited to teach' — but in general people seem to agree on what are the right slots, and the rules for determining them. A former chair, talking about the 'tension' of scheduling, explained that

> Not everybody's a Math major. You have to feel like there are certain limits. Some people recognize their own limitations. Like right now, Jim, because he's so involved in his coaching, he wants to teach algebra and pre-algebra. He does not want to teach anything higher.

This teacher, who does not have a major in Math, confirmed that he does not want anything higher: 'I feel real confident that I can do the job in those two areas. But I'm more of a follower at Math than I am a leader or a pioneer.' When he is 'so involved with his coaching', during his sport's active season, he can literally be a follower, relying on the lesson plans and worksheets that other teachers devise.

The practice of sitting in on other classes and following the example of a more advanced teacher, which was discussed as an example of social interaction in Chapter 5, is also a means of fitting into the 'slot' of a higher level course — an apprenticeship strategy which would be unthinkable in an English department. At Rancho, a teacher of advanced algebra had two teachers who wanted to move up to that level 'sit in on my classes, just to pick up on the curriculum'. Another teacher, who had been assigned a pre-algebra class she felt underprepared for, 'came in every day, she gave up her prep period . . . every day; she sat in on my pre-algebra class and would be two days behind me and just follow what I did. That seemed to help her.' The widespread agreement on content and sequence — the tight paradigm of mathematics — allows teachers to learn the routines, and encourages them to follow the same curriculum. It also tends to produce homogeneity across the subject. Even in elementary classrooms, Susan Stodolsky (1988) finds 'homogeneity in math instruction, whereas variety is characteristic of social studies instruction' (p. 31).

That agreement on what should be taught and when also leads to much closer coordination among Math courses — there are tight links between levels, since 'each rung depends on all the previous ones', and more formalized mechanisms for linking between sections at the same level, since each unit and worksheet can also be fit into its right place on the syllabus. Formal teaming arrangements are not only still in place in Oak Valley's Math department, they are now being fought for, since the school has abandoned the experiment. This teaming has allowed the links between courses to be exceptionally strong:

> We're basically making sure we are teaching the same material. We give the same tests. We give them all the same days . . . it's not really designed to take away from the teacher's individuality. You know, you are free to teach it in whichever manner you're going to teach the subject area. I think the main thing is just that we want to stay on this time table.

This conception of individuality stands in sharp contrast to the independence in Social Studies or the artisanship of English, but it makes sense if the goal is 'take the student from where he is in order to get somewhere', and if the 'somewhere' and the steps to reach it are known.

The metaphor of the ladder — with the dual emphasis on placing people on the right rungs, and arranging for an ordered progression up the levels — provides a useful image for how Math teachers address a number of issues; in what those who deal with fractal geometry would call self-similarity, the pattern recurs in various places, on larger and smaller scale. There are elaborate rules and concentrated attention devoted to arranging students on the right levels, and ensuring that there are enough rungs. The pattern recurs in the procedures for assigning teachers to the right courses, and providing mechanisms for them to climb to the next step. It repeats in curricular coordination devices to determine which units will have a place on the syllabus, and how to proceed, step by step, on the timetable. It even repeats within individual classrooms, as Hargreaves and MacMillan (1992) found in a Math teacher's cooperative learning experiment. Their fieldnotes reveal the

> hours of planning time in terms of the combinations of individuals who would be working in the different groups, and playing different roles (it took him five hours just to work out where the students would sit!!).

Even on this small scale, the observer sees 'the need to approach things in a "step-by-step", linear way, in the way that many Mathematics teachers do' (p. 16).

Science

Like Math, Science is characterized by linear ways of approaching things, step-by-step procedures, quantitative methods, and a mature paradigm. As one teacher puts it, 'Math and Science are twin brothers or sisters. You must understand one in order to be able to deal with the other.' But Science as a school subject, like Social Studies, brings together teachers from a variety of disciplines. These disciplines are not typically seen as in competition or conflict, although Oak Valley's split between the life and physical science teachers shows that this can happen. Science brings together not different ways of knowing the same content, but the same scientific method used to know different topics: 'the technique doesn't change, the material changes.' Courses match the disciplinary divisions, and teachers are hired as, and remain, disciplinary specialists: 'to an extent', explains a chemistry teacher, 'each person within the department has an area of expertise.' Another chemistry teacher provides the general principle:

> When we have a vacancy, generally people are hired to fill that subject, so unless something really fouls up in what you're doing, you tend to stay with the same subjects.

His own case, however, since he has a master's degree in biology but has taught 'primarily chemistry' for the fourteen years he has been at Oak Valley, suggests this may result from inertia as well as academic specialization: 'I just have never gone back into the biology, so it's more or less the slot they happen to get you into.'

There is a concern with placement in the right slots, but the slots are defined by discipline rather than level, and the boundaries around each specialty are taken quite seriously. A biology teacher explains that his schedule will consist exclusively of courses in that area, but at different levels: 'I teach micro-biology, advanced biology, and beginning biology', while another teacher has 'always taught chemistry'. Asked whether he might be assigned a biology course, a new physics teacher points out the naiveté of that question: 'I've had one biology class in my life. Ten weeks. I couldn't even tell you what a cell was. No clue.' And in talking about changes in the curriculum of chemistry, a specialist in that area provides 'one answer to your question about biochemistry, I have no background whatsoever in biology. That's one area where I am deficient. That's why, I think, we don't do more biochemistry.' At Oak Valley, a new course in oceanography has to be taught by two teachers: one semester a 'physical scientist' covers 'currents, plate tectonics and so on'; the other semester the 'zoology portion' is taught by a 'biologist'.

These disciplines are so clearly understood as different that a Rancho teacher can even sort incoming students by disciplinary orientation:

> we have the biology, zoology, and earth science, depending on whether the student is biologically oriented, or whether they're physical science oriented — [if physical] then we'll push them into the earth science. If they are heavy biology, then they'll do biology, and if they're not really sure where they want to be it's zoology, because they get the background on plants and animals and then the second part is more the ecology, environmental problems, weather and so on, so they get kind of a lens. They have a choice.

There are, as there are in Math, sequences of linked courses to take students through a progression, but they progress along different disciplinary routes.

With standardized method, established procedures, and sequenced courses, one might expect that these teachers would, like Math colleagues, form teams to coordinate curriculum as they do equipment. And teachers do try to coordinate: 'We emphasize certain things; we all try to stay within certain parameters, rather than overlap, we try to go side by side.' But because there are multiple disciplines and specialized teachers, they have few colleagues in their particular specialty. Team planning may occur, but only if there are enough sections of the same course: 'biologists normally team up.' External connections thus become particularly important for Science teachers — but they, too, are sorted by sub-specialty. A chemistry teacher tells of how he performs a regular

> reality check. What happens is, not officially, I know a few other chemistry teachers in the area, and I'll see them, so we all tend to talk and have dinner meetings . . . that way you know

> that what you're doing is probably running about the same
> speed as the other people in the area.

Another teacher says that he will 'go to all of [the] meetings' of the county 'chemistry teachers association' which meets monthly, but that 'all Science teachers very rarely ever meet.'

Science is also less abstract and more activist than its mathematical sibling. When Math teachers work on patterns of tiling, similar triangles, or golden rectangles those patterns are pulled out of their context, valued for their elegance, their consistency — for themselves. In the sciences teachers, such as a member of Oak Valley's department, tend to be concerned how to 'figure out the pattern' or 'underlying principle' of a variety of phenomena in 'everyday life' — outside the classroom as well as inside — and then do 'something with it'. At Rancho, for example, a physics teacher brings this orientation to his role as a union rep:

> Sometimes what happens is I'm down in the lunchroom and they're talking, and they don't even realize, but they're venting their frustrations, and sometimes I start to see a pattern in their frustrations.

For him, seeing the pattern is immediately and practically connected to taking action: send a memo, go to the principal, or 'rattle the cage with the complaint process'.

Inside the classroom an energetic new teacher at Oak Valley works to teach remedial students 'to see patterns, understand the patterns, I'm already trying to have them work through the pattern idea. For me that's what thinking means', but at the same time 'thinking implies that they did something with it.' He himself approaches the 'problem' of teaching these students with quintessentially scientific method. He lays out a 'complex matrix of variables', uses a 'certain empirical experimentation associated with all this', and attempts to 'discover the Law of' or 'the underlying principles' where 'we're back again to the predictive'. The fundamental drive behind this problem-solving effort is practical: 'what does that do for me, because all this theory garbage has to somehow play itself out at 1 o'clock; how does this theory get into practice?' This sense of being able to not only analyze but to effect change is also reflected in another Science teacher's goals for students: 'Some kids you can turn around, maybe not as great scientists but as people who can make a difference.'

The close link between understanding and making a difference has been a fundamental feature of modern Science, according to Evelyn Keller, since Francis Bacon proposed a 'marriage' between science and nature, with 'Nature herself who is to be the bride, who requires taming, shaping, and subduing by the scientific mind' (quoted in Keller, 1985, p. 36).

Also since Bacon, and as his metaphor illustrates, the dominant — and dominating — conception of Science has been 'bound up with masculinity' and the field marked by a long-standing absence of women (Keller, 1985). The Royal Society in England, for example, was founded in 1662, and Académie des Sciences in France in 1666, but they did not admit their first female members until 1945 and 1979, respectively (Shumway and Messer-Davidow, 1991). As in those professional societies, but on smaller scales, the pattern of absent females repeats itself in contemporary high schools through the distribution of faculty at the department, and the enrollment of students at the classroom, levels.

This absence of females in the sciences is a pattern that has recently become a national concern, and it is one that a number of the male teachers acknowledged. At Rancho, the chair explained, the department has

> . . . had all male teachers for quite a few years now; I can't remember how long it's been — seven or eight.
> [I:] Does that make a difference?
> [R:] It makes a difference. It's a little narrower out here as a result of that. We just don't have much female input, unless some other female faculty members come out and visit us.

Given the social networks of the school, the probability of female faculty members visiting is low. Another teacher explains the absence of women as a result of a 'society' where 'there wasn't a big push for women to go into science, and the last few years they've tried to correct that'. At Rancho what this corrective effort has meant is that they have had female student teachers, but none have been hired. At Oak Valley, too, the chair explains the imbalance of his department (twelve of the sixteen teachers are males) as a result of external conditions — the existing pool of applicants — but, interestingly, even the word 'women' is absent from his explanation:

> it's just that men keep applying. There appears to be more men applying for the jobs in physical science — I don't know why. I don't recall having but maybe one out of eleven interviews, they're almost all men.

In these three departments, as in Science teaching generally, 'they're almost all men', since women are not likely to hold teaching positions in Science, especially, as the chair observed, in physical science (Acker, 1983).

At the student level, Lynda Measor (1983) cites a headmaster's explanation for the absence of girls from advanced levels of science in his high school: 'There's no sexual discrimination here, but at the end of the second year, when it comes to option choosing, all the girls get out of science' (p. 189). Measor's study, however, finds that there is sexual discrimination going on here, in that girls have been largely absent from science teachers' thinking about pedagogical strategies, curricular choices, and the linking of content to student interests. At Oak Valley, this absence of girls is illustrated by one physical science teacher's response to a direct question about his 'visual and spatial' style of teaching. Asked whether he has seen a difference in how males and females respond, he replied:

> I don't think about those kinds of variables, girls versus boys, I'm not sure I can . . . In Science? No, I don't see any complications along those lines. It's funny — I'm not looking for it.

As soon as he does think about it, he translates that thought into possible action — 'I could build in further variables for girls being less spatial' — but it has apparently been absent from his thinking before this conversation.

Science is characterized not only by this absence, but overwhelmingly by the presence, in interview after interview, of teachers' references to their equipment, to the material tools of their trade. A Science chair, who was asked to describe how he would teach 'ideally, if you had everything, no barriers whatsoever', spoke for Science teachers generally when he responded succinctly, 'Give me more equipment.' If in universities 'science investigated materiality' (Shumway and Messer-Davidow, 1991, p. 209), in high schools Science teachers emphasize the materials students need to investigate science. The constant search for 'more equipment' and the demands of managing the equipment they have make teaching this subject quite distinct:

> this is a real intensive field to teach in in regard to materials, setting up labs and all that sort of thing. I try to do as much of that as I can in the morning . . . sometimes [I] have to come back in the evening.

This attention to materials that require constant attention means that Science teachers are more aware of, and more skilled at getting, scarce school resources such as time, money, and equipment. Time is a problem 'especially in Science, because you're always stuck with experiments and equipment. That alone can take a lot of time.' So, at Highlander, Science teachers have arranged for students to become classroom aides. Class size is also a special concern of Science, because lab stations and access to equipment are limited, and thus the maximum number of students is lowered for Science. Budgets are more of an issue, because not only are the lab materials expensive, they are consumable, the Oak Valley chair points out, and have to be reordered every year: 'In Math you don't have 700 students that need to dissect a fetal pig.' Not simply because of its status, but also because of these shared assumptions about its inherent needs as a subject, Science expects, and regularly receives, the 'lion's share' of the budget.

These Science teachers, with their activist orientation, have also devised a variety of means to procure or manufacture equipment outside of official channels. One physics teacher explains how he

> brought a pool table in to show momentum laws. You have to be opportunistic to be a Science teacher; you can't always afford the most expensive equipment, [you] have to use what's available . . . it's hard anywhere to keep up with the pace and the expense of the equipment. A lot of it you have to manufacture yourself. It's not difficult. Power packs, motion tables, I used to make, I don't have to do it now thank God, I used to make my own alcohol, scalpels, and dissecting things.

Science teachers tell of traveling to the beach to stock an aquarium with specimens, applying for federal block money to purchase computers, making linoleum, or working summers in industry to 'get in and learn how to run some of those sophisticated machines . . . and bring that back to our classrooms'. It's perhaps not surprising that Mr Wizard, the television educator who performed such wonderful experiments with household materials, is mentioned reverently by four different Science teachers.

The need to stay close to the materials of Science labs is used to explain why Science teachers 'pulled out of the unit format before anybody did' in the early days of Rancho's attempt to restructure faculty into advisory units, as was discussed earlier. This story of how the Science teachers 'pulled out' is one that appears several times in interviews, in almost the same words, enough to suggest that it functions as something of a ritual tale. At the risk of repetition, it is worth revisiting that story here, for is is not simply a tale of social cohesion, or political clout, but also of disciplinary difference. As one relates it,

> we didn't do it because we didn't want to socialize with the rest of the staff. It just wasn't feasible when you deal with some of the manipulatives that we deal with here in Science. We moved our desks. You see our desks out here? Our desks were in the unit office when the school opened. Everybody's was. And teachers spent their prep periods not in the classrooms but

in their unit office. So teachers, you would find all the teachers of the different disciplines in that office. Well, I did that for a year. Most of us did. The second year, we started waiting till dark and then sneaking our desks out of here . . . Because we didn't have the materials we need to manipulate or prepare in our unit offices . . . Here's where it's a great idea to have all the disciplines mix, but it just doesn't work out. Practically, it just doesn't work out when you have lab-oriented type subjects . . . So we started moving our stuff out here. And we were considered real bad people for that, we were considered real out in the fringes.

This is a tale in which several elements come together: the low value placed on having 'disciplines mix' (and the chemical understanding of which elements cannot), the orientation to action, the masculinity, and the emphasis on materials — which are all part of the subject culture of Science. Most of all, however, it is a story about asserting the boundaries of what these teachers see as their meaningful occupational community — their own subject colleagues.

Conclusion

By virtue of the subject they teach, these teachers bring the distinct perspectives, procedures, values, and discourses of their fields into the school — and sometimes into conflict. Intellectually and professionally, as well as socially, they inhabit quite different worlds. What is evident from examining the differences among these subject cultures is that in many ways teachers have more in common with geographically distant colleagues in the same subject than they may with colleagues in the same school but an intellectually distant department. As subject specialists, they share a sense of who they are, what they do, and what they need to do it — conceptions which may well be, in Van Maanen and Barley's (1984) words, 'organizationally deviant'. Conflicts arise around different issues — it is English teachers who are 'organizationally deviant' on centralized textbook selection, Math teachers on eliminating tracking, Science on bringing faculty out of their own classrooms, and Social Studies teachers, or at least some Social Studies teachers, on almost any issue.

The 'agreements' among these subject-specialists can vary markedly from each other, and sometimes from the school as a whole. Whether they are looking at pedagogical practice, at how courses should be arranged or students assigned to them, or what makes a useful professional development experience, these teachers bring the perspectives of their particular knowledge realms to bear on what they see. As one Rancho administrator puts it,

the department focus is fairly narrow, isn't it? It has been
. . . And you know, perhaps that's the way it should be. You
need to have some of that kind of an ethnocentric way of looking at it.

Whether it's the 'way it should be' or not is certainly open to question,
but each department does provide a distinctive focus to the ways in
which teachers tend to view their schools, their students, and their
own practice. Subject departments are not just smaller pieces of the
same social environment or bureaucratic labels, but worlds of their
own, with their own 'ethnocentric way of looking at' things. They are
sites where a distinct group of people come together, and together
share in and reinforce the distinctive agreements on perspectives, rules,
and norms which make up subject cultures and communities.

Notes

1   In their article laying out the theoretical base for occupational communi-
    ties, the authors briefly mention teachers, treated generically as teachers.
    By the terms of their own argument, however, the boundaries of high
    school teachers' occupational communities are more likely to be those of
    the subject area.
2   According to a staff member at the California Commission on Teacher
    Credentialing, the last general certificates were issued in 1963 or 1964;
    after that the state required at least a minor in the subject to be taught. By
    that time the assumption was that "if you wanted to be a good teacher,
    then what you needed was academic content, a lot of academic content."

Chapter 8

Underlining Differences

At a meeting at a city high school a cherubic-looking white-haired chemistry teacher kept nodding and agreeing with the argument I made in my presentation to the faculty that the number of students assigned to each teacher had to be radically reduced. She balked, however, at any compromise on her wish to teach nothing but chemistry, at least as she defined chemistry. I reasoned with her: this is too poor a school to more than double the teaching force. Couldn't she teach some mathematics to kids who were her chemistry students? *I'm not a mathematics teacher*, she replied. I countered, I'm not suggesting that you teach advanced math, just algebra. *I'm not a math teacher.* Can you teach chemistry to any standard without math? *That's different.* How? She broke into tears. *I would rather teach two hundred students chemistry than teach anything else.* But you can't know that many kids at all . . . *I know, I know, I know.* (Theodore Sizer, 1992)

Ridiculous — you can underline that three times . . . no policy level acknowledges that there is any difference between departments. (Department chair)

Over the last 100 years, gradually and quietly, departments have become a standard feature of high schools, creating internal divisions within the school, linking those divisions to particular subjects, and filling them with specialized teachers. Guided by research which has largely ignored the workings of these subunits, scholars and reformers have tended to treat departments as descriptive labels, as markers on an organizational chart. From that perspective, teachers who resist efforts to rearrange the chart or to implement effective — and standardized — standards of practice appear stubborn, recalcitrant, irrational.

But is the teacher in the first passage above, for example, simply exhibiting irrational resistance to change? Or do we need to attend more closely to how — repeatedly — she identifies herself, and to the meaning of that kind of identification? Both reformer and teacher agree that the typical high school teaching load of 150 students is impossible, that it has to be 'radically reduced'. He presents a seemingly simple equation: if the teacher would cover two classes — math as well as chemistry — with the same students, she could reduce her load by half. But while he 'reasoned', her reaction appears to be anything but reasonable: the 'cherubic-looking' teacher 'balked', and, under his persistent questioning, 'broke into tears'. What he persists in is thinking about subjects as labels that can be peeled off—there must be math under what she teaches as chemistry. For her, however, that is precisely what sticks; he treats as a label what she experiences as identity: 'that's different', she is 'not a math teacher'. As long as we don't acknowledge the differences, and the meaning of that identification for high school teachers, we can't see the reasoning that underlies her reaction.

If we look back at the stories from Highlander and Rancho,' and particularly from Oak Valley, where moving teachers between subjects is vividly recalled as a punitive device, we can begin to understand why a chemistry teacher might take on 200 students rather than a course in math. What the teachers there know is that such moves have had profound consequences, not only for individual teachers but for the department, and the profession, as a whole. They cut teachers off from their closest and most valued colleagues, and weaken the ability of the group to form a cohesive whole; they undermine the department's (and the faculty's) right to make decisions and ability to command resources; they confront teachers with new texts and unfamiliar ways of thinking, threatening their professional competence. What reverberates most clearly in the chemistry teacher's statements is that they violate teachers' subject-specific sense of who they are and what they do.

Departmental Differences

Subject departments create potent dividing lines within the high school, boundaries which teachers seldom step across. Where schools are large, where spatial arrangements segregate teachers by subject, where a full schedule leaves little time to travel far from the classroom, departments present formidable barriers to school-wide communication and community.

But what teachers know, and what this study has shown, is that departments are more than simply dividing lines — they play an active and complex role in the ways teachers think about and conduct their practice. Over the course of these interviews, teachers talked about their departments in three substantively different ways:

- **Social** — as 'we', the department represents the colleagues with whom they work most closely, whose individual efforts and group norms influence the ways teachers think about and conduct their practice;
- **Political** — as 'the department' it plays a primary role in acquiring and distributing resources and responsibilities among teachers; and
- **Subject** — as 'English' or 'Science' it is the subject matter central to who they are, what they do, and how they go about doing it.

In each of these roles departments can make a critical difference in the working conditions of teachers — and the way they work with students. Some develop social norms of inclusion, mutual support, and commitment to students, while others are fragmented and concerned with individual survival. One department may readily command and distribute the resources teachers need, while another in the same school cannot get them, or gives them only to a particular faction. One subject can demand curricular plans which are agreed upon and tightly sequenced, while another expects them to be fluid and adaptable to student needs.

In the preceding chapters these aspects have been treated as distinct, but in practice they are interactive and intertwined. Differences in the assumptions and languages of the subjects underlie the boundaries around departments, shape the interactions within them, and can lead to political conflicts between them. Social support and collaborative efforts can bring new levels of resources to an English department, and encourage a dissatisfied 'traditional, stand-up, lecture-behind-the-desk teacher' to rethink what his subject is all about.

These departmental differences matter to the outcomes that matter for education: to fostering collective commitment to students, to encouraging innovative techniques, to setting (and agreeing on) particular goals and standards — to the ways teaching and learning are understood and practiced.

As a result of living and working in these substantively different environments, teachers come to understand themselves, their work, and their students in quite different ways. To some degree, these can be understood as local and unique differences — a matter of the 'individuals involved' in one department, or the luck of having a 'gregarious' chair in another. But there are also patterns to the difference, patterns which can allow us to better understand the complexities of high school teaching, to anticipate where problems with a particular policy are likely to occur, and to design policies to fit particular needs.

What these teachers do have in common is a frustration with policies and routines which do not 'acknowledge the difference between departments'. Asking a chemistry teacher to teach a math course is one obvious — and exceptional — example. More commonly, throughout these interviews, teachers expressed their frustrations with what sound like uniform and equitable policies, but which have differential effects. Several times their comments were accompanied by their directives to carry that message to policy makers. The inequity of assigning English teachers, who have the added burden of students' writing to deal with, the 'standard' number of students is what the English chair cited above wanted me to 'underline . . . three times'. For Math teachers the issue was not numbers of students, but getting them in the right classes: 'write this down: placement of students.'

In the process of writing down, and underlining, these high school teachers' stories, the complex realities of departmental difference began to emerge. A centralized list of state-approved textbooks, for example, is a minor inconvenience for Math teachers, since one algebra book looks pretty much like another, but a major threat to English teachers. Even a small increase in class size is a particular concern for Science teachers, who face the physical limitations of a fixed number of lab stations, and who fear for the physical safety of their students.

Particularly salient, across departments and across schools, were two kinds of policies which touch most directly on teachers' conceptions of their professional practice: in-service and evaluation. Mandatory inservice offerings were repeatedly characterized as a 'waste of time'. What these teachers object to is not that such sessions take time, but that faculty time is not put to good use: 'It's something coming down from administration that we have to talk about; we can never really talk about the things we want to talk about.' It is important to note here that these teachers are not simply balking at efforts to improve practice — in fact a number of the ones cited here are most active in that area; rather they are challenging the substance, and the control, of those efforts. What they want to talk about is what's going on in their field, or how new strategies, such as cooperative learning, can be tailored to fit a math class. Instead most offerings are based on a conception of teaching as a generic occupation, one that does not match what high school teachers understand as their work, or what they need to do it.

One teacher, for example, complained of a district-mandated inservice program in mastery teaching, where they

> just ran everybody through it. I would have much preferred to see them say 'Ok, we'll let you, as a physics teacher, we'll sponsor you, give you some time to go to one of the major

science conventions and participate in the physics programs and so on.'

He contrasts that experience with a national science conference where he 'wanted to participate' enough to pay his own way; since it was 'a worthwhile opportunity I spent as much time in both physics and chemistry sessions as I could'. For him, that conference was much more worthwhile as an opportunity for professional development than the in-service program, since it fit what he does professionally — work with physics and chemistry.

Four English teachers at Oak Valley have competed to get into, and traveled to attend, summer institutes focused specifically on writing, again demonstrating a marked willingness to invest their own time, energy, and money in professional growth. Yet repeatedly teachers expressed their reluctance to spend even compensated time at required in-service such as 'clinical teaching workshops'. That kind of offering might be 'good for certain things', and teachers are 'not opposed to it, but it's too limiting'. By itself, it does not offer the kind of professional development they see as most important.

What drives these teachers to attend meetings and programs across the country — even at their own expense — is that there they meet with and learn from the 'scattered' members of their own occupational community — people who understand the difficulty of teaching the concept of a limit in calculus, or the stress of assigning weekly compositions you then have to grade.

Teachers are frustrated, too, with evaluation policies which fail to acknowledge this fundamental feature of their work — teaching specific subjects in subject-specific ways. One of the defining characteristics of an occupational community, as with a profession, is this sense that only 'the membership possesses the proper knowledge, skills, and orientations necessary to make decisions as to how the work is to be performed and evaluated' (Van Maanen and Barley, 1984, p. 309). Teachers argue that generic standards of teaching are inadequate, and that people who do not know their subject are ill-equipped to understand, let alone judge, what is going on in their classrooms.

A Science teacher worries that no outsider would understand what would be obvious to a Science specialist, 'especially if I was doing some aspect of physics and the administrator didn't have any background in physics'. He provided an example of an experience he had had watching another physics teacher's class:

> . . . the kids were out there on the sidewalk on skateboards and whipping up and down. Well, if you walked in as an outsider, you'd figure the person running this had gone screw-loose. Well, I realized right then what they were doing; it was a

section on mechanics and they were studying velocities and momentum, light person and heavy person and so on, and it was a legitimate lesson.

Taking action, using equipment, deriving general principles, and playing a male sport — this scene has all the elements legitimate in Science, but it might well appear 'screw-loose' to an 'outsider'.

In the same vein, a Social Studies teacher complained that his administrator 'didn't fit the bill at all, you know, I could ask him questions about Social Science skills and he asked me what I meant, and things like that'. Generic models of teaching skills simply do not satisfy specialist teachers who want to talk about the immediate and concrete needs of teaching particular subjects. They may be adequate to check for minimal classroom management skills, but for teachers, such as this one, who want help reaching higher standards, they don't 'fit the bill' at all.

In some instances the problem with administrators performing evaluations is not simply what they don't know, it's what they do know:

> it's the five-step lesson plan. Well, that works ok in Math on a daily basis, but it sure doesn't work in Social Studies on a daily basis. And [the administrators] expected to walk in here and see a five-step lesson plan . . . but you just can't do it in Social Studies on a daily basis, and that's what they were expecting.

Under such a model teachers are being expected, as they see it, to do something organizationally correct, but occupationally deviant.

Stanton, the school studied in the pilot for this project, provides an example of one organization whose evaluation policy has taken the somewhat 'unusual' step of acknowledging the difference between departments and the subject-specific nature of high school teaching. There, regular classroom evaluations are done by department chairs rather than building administrators. The English chair described her responsibility as often 'uncomfortable for me', but one which the teachers prefer: 'From what I've heard them say they'd rather have me do it than someone who doesn't know the discipline.' The Math chair echoed the same thoughts:

> it's extremely unusual . . . most of the time fine, but sometimes awkward . . . The teachers would rather be evaluated by someone who knows what he's watching. I remember having an ex-coach who became a vice-principal be the one who was

supposed to evaluate my math class; he was simply incompetent
to do it.

Competence to understand and evaluate performance is tightly and
repeatedly linked to 'someone who know's what he's watching',
someone who will 'know the discipline'. What these teachers suggest
is that the model, derived from studies of effective elementary schools,
of the principal as constructive evaluator and instructional leader is
simply impossible, or implausible, in a high school staffed by teachers
who see themselves as subject-specialists.

Conclusion

To see them as they see themselves is to begin to recognize the importance of subject departments to the professional identities and practice
of high school teachers. In doing so, we need not accept that such
divisions are the best way to organize the lives of teachers and students;
we need only to acknowledge that any efforts to improve high schools,
or even to understand them, can not ignore the power of departments.
Subject departments fill a variety of needs for teachers and schools;
they are deeply embedded in the social, political, and intellectual structures of high schools as institutions and teaching as an occupation.
These realms of knowledge are the territory in which secondary school
teaching now takes place. With teachers as guides, this study has attempted to explore that terrain, so that — before attempting to go
anywhere else — we can better understand first where we are right
now.

Primary Interviews

On the following pages are the list of the primary interviews, arranged by school, which were used in this study. As participants in the larger research project of the Center for Research on the Context of Secondary School Teaching (CRC), each **Site** was given a two letter code, and each person a three digit identifying number, listed under **ID**. Thus the principal at Highlander is identified as 'HI098' and can be located by this code in Center files. While the primary interviews listed on the following pages all come from Oak Valley, Rancho, and Highlander, I have also used interviews which come from other sites — district administrators, for example, or a former Rancho teacher who now works at another school in the CRC study.

Each person has a unique identifying code, and so does each interview, for a number of people spoke with us on more than one occasion. In the column **format** appear the codes indicating the type of interview: 01 is a first-year interview, while 02 took place in the second year. Those are 'core' interviews, which covered a wide range of topics (including departments), and were then fed into the collective Center data base. Other format codes represent more focused, special study interviews: 'tra', for example, is one from the special tracer substudy, which followed classroom observations with extensive debriefing sessions; 'U' denotes an interview centered on unions. Interviews conducted exclusively for the purpose of this study are marked with the format code 'D'.

In the following lists of interviews, additional identifying information is also provided, to reflect department, position, and personal characteristics of those who participated in this study.

The column **dep** identifies the department to which the teacher is assigned. 'M' stands for Math, 'E' for English — but 'H' is for Social Studies to avoid confusion with 'Sc' for Science. While most of the primary interviews are with teachers in the four academic departments, administrators and teachers from other departments provided useful, and different, perspectives on how these departments worked.

The **Position** refers to the respondent's official position within the organization: T for teacher, CH for department chair, P for principal. One Detention officer (Det), one Site Improvement Coordinator (Sip), and three counselors (Couns) are also included.

Race and **sex**, are also included for each person, where available.

Oak Valley Interviews

School	ID	format	dep	position	race	sex
OV	137	01	–	VP	w	m
OV	155	01	–	P	w	m
OV	141	01	–	Det	w	m
OV	155	D2	–	P	w	m
OV	067	U	ChildDev	CH	w	f
OV	058	01	E	CH	w	f
OV	056	U	E	T	w	f
OV	043	01	E	T	w	m
OV	077	01	E	T	w	m
OV	106	01	E	T	w	m
OV	077	D2	E	CH	w	m
OV	005	01	E	T	w	m
OV	077	D1	E	CH	w	m
OV	063	01	FL	T	w	f
OV	008	01	H	CH	w	f
OV	008	D	H	CH	w	f
OV	008	02	H	CH	w	f
OV	007	01	H	T	w	m
OV	013	01	H	T	w	m
OV	060	U	H	T	w	m
OV	061	01	HomeEc	CH	w	f
OV	074	01	M	CH	w	m
OV	049	01	M	T	w	m
OV	019	01	M	T	w	f
OV	074	D	M	CH	w	m
OV	036	01	M	T	w	m
OV	130	D	M	T	w	f
OV	084	D	S	CH	w	m
OV	006	U	S	T	w	f
OV	084	01	S	CH	w	m
OV	084	02	S	CH	w	m
OV	039	01	S	T	w	m
OV	072	01	S	T	w	m
OV	156	tra	S	T	w	m
OV	156	D	S	T	w	m
OV	112	U	SpEd	CH	w	f
OV	031	U	SpEd	T	w	f
OV	046	01	Voc	CH	w	m

Rancho Interviews

school	ID	format	dep	position	race	sex
RA	080	01	–	P	W	m
RA	080	01B	–	P	W	m
RA	087	01	–	SIP	W	f
RA	090	D	–	VP instr	W	f
RA	033	01	Art	CH	W	m
RA	033	U	Art	CH	W	m
RA	070	01	E	T	W	f
RA	003	01	E	T	W	f
RA	029	01	E	CH	W	f
RA	003	U	E	T	W	f
RA	038	U	E	T	W	f
RA	031	01	E	T	A	m
RA	071	01	H	T	W	m
RA	039	01	H	CH	W	m
RA	039	tra	H	CH	W	m
RA	036	St	H	T	W	f
RA	040	01	H	T	W	m
RA	058	U1	IA	T	W	m
RA	064	01	M	T	W	m
RA	035	tra	M	T	A	f
RA	046	D	M	CH	W	m
RA	022	01	M	T	W	m
RA	016	01	PE	T	W	f
RA	030	01	PE	CH	W	m
RA	021	01	Sc	T	W	m
RA	065	U	Sc	T	W	m
RA	021	U	Sc	T	W	m
RA	021	Ub	Sc	T	W	m
RA	076	01	Sc	T	A	m
RA	057	D	Sc	T	W	m

Highlander Interviews

school	ID	format	dep	position	race	sex
HI	098	01	–	P	B	m
HI	099	D	–	VP	B	f
HI	036	01	–	couns	B	f
HI	005	02	–	couns	W	f
HI	019	01	–	couns	W	m
HI	077	02	Art	T	W	f
HI	047	02	Bus	CH	W	m
HI	053	01	E	T	B	f
HI	028	D	E	T	W	m
HI	084	01	E	T	B	f
HI	039	02	E	T	B	f
HI	040	02	E	T	B	f
HI	075	02	E	T	B	m
HI	018	02	E	CH	W	f
HI	067	02	E	T	B	f
HI	056	02	E	T	W	f
HI	001	01	H	T	B	m
HI	082	01	H	T	W	f
HI	071	01	H	CH	W	m
HI	071	02	H	CH	W	m
HI	090	01	H	T	W	m
HI	007	01	H	T	W	m
HI	029	01	H	T	W	m
HI	033	01	M	T	B	f
HI	066	01	M	T	W	m
HI	063	02	M	CH	B	m
HI	011	01	M	T	W	m
HI	078	02	M	T	W	m
HI	002	02	M	T	B	f
HI	061	02	M	T	B	m
HI	012	02	M	T	W	f
HI	066	01	M	T	W	m
HI	049	02	PE	T	W	m
HI	060	02	Sci	T	B	m
HI	083	02	Sci	CH	W	m
HI	016	02	Sci	T	W	m
HI	070	D	Sci	T	W	m
HI	023	01	Sci	T	B	m
HI	020	02	SpEd	CH	B	f
HI	043	01	SpEd	T	W	f

Appendix B

Survey Questions

In each of the three fieldwork years, the Center for Research on the Context of Secondary School Teaching conducted a survey of all staff members in all of the sixteen CRC schools. The data sets from the first two years (1989 and 1990) were used for this study, and served four primary purposes:

- to identify people with particular demographic characteristics or organizational experience;
- to confirm patterns emerging from the interviews;
- to provide comparative measures of school or department characteristics; and
- to analyze networks of communication cliques.

Examples of survey questions for each category are listed below, labeled according to the year and the item number in the CRC questionnaires. Some questions — such as those under collegiality — replicated items used in the 1984 High School and Beyond study, allowing for further comparison with that larger national sample of high schools.

Identification

89–1 Including this year, how many years have you been a teacher at this school?
89–7 In addition to your classroom teaching, do you perform any of the following roles in your school? (selected items)
    coach for athletic team
    department head or chair
    coordinator of special program

teacher association/union representative
other
89–18 What is your gender?   1   Male   2   Female
90–1 Please indicate the number of classes you currently teach in the
following subject areas. (If you teach 5 English classes, write 5 on the
line next to English; if you teach in more than one subject area, write
in the number of classes you are teaching in each subject.)

Pattern Confirmation

89–2 Please list all the courses that you are teaching this school year.
Then write in the number of separate classes of each course you will
have taught during the 88/89 school year. In addition, indicate how
many years you have taught the course.
89–10 To what extent has each of the following helped you improve
your teaching or solve an instructional or class management problem
since you have been at this school (1–6)

> principal or school head
> department chair
> other school administrators
> department colleagues
> school colleagues outside department
> district specialist
> professional workshop or meeting
> school or district inservice

89–13 If you had to choose among the 8 goals for students listed below, how would you rank them according to their importance for
your teaching?

> basic literacy skills
> academic excellence
> citizenship
> specific occupational skills
> good work habits and self discipline
> personal growth and fulfillment
> human relations skills
> moral or religious values

89–15 I am familiar with the content and specific goals of the courses
taught by other teachers in my department. (scale 1–6)

Survey Measures

Departmental Identification (scale 1–6; range 2–12)

89–15 Using the scale provided, please indicate the extent to which you agree or disagree with each of the following statements.

    o. My closest colleagues are members of my department.
    z. Teachers in this school identify more with their department than with the school as a whole.

Collegiality: (scale 1–6; Range 1–30)

90–12 Using the scale provided, please indicate the extent to which you agree or disagree with each of the following statements.

    a.   You can count on most staff members to help out anywhere, anytime — even though it may not be part of their official assignment.
    u.   Teachers in this school are continually learning and seeking new ideas.
    y.   There is a great deal of cooperative effort among staff members.
    z.   Staff members maintain high standards.
    bb: This school seems like a big family; everyone is so close and cordial.

Network Analysis

90–5 Please list up to five colleagues in this school (teachers or other staff members) with whom you talk regularly about your teaching. Note: Names will be tabulated by code number and used only for quantitative analysis.

References

AAAS (1989) *Science for all Americans: A project 2061 report on literacy goals in science, mathematics, and technology*, American Association for the Advancement of Science.

ABBOTT, A. (1988) *The system of professions: An Essay on the division of expert labor*, Chicago, IL, University of Chicago Press.

ACKER, S. (1983) 'Women and teaching: A semi-detached sociology of a semi-profession', in WALKER, S. and BARTON, L. (Eds), *Gender, class and education* (pp. 123–39), Lewes, The Falmer Press.

ADDUCI, L.L., WOODS-HOUSTON, M.A. and WEBB, A.W. (1990) 'The department chair: Role ambiguity and role strain', Paper presented at the annual meeting of the American Educational Research Association, April, 1990, Boston, MA.

ATKIN, J.M. and ATKIN, A. (1989) *Improving science education through local alliances*, Santa Cruz, CA, Carnegie Corporation, Network Publications.

BALL, S.J. (1983) 'A subject of privilege: English and the school curriculum 1906–35', in HAMMERSLEY, M. and HARGREAVES, A. (Eds), *Curriculum practice: Some sociological case studies*, London, The Falmer Press.

BALL, S.J. (1987) *The micro-politics of the school*, London, Methuen.

BALL, S.J. and GOODSON, I.F. (1984) *Defining the curriculum*, London, The Falmer Press.

BALL, S.J. and LACEY, C. (1980) 'Subject disciplines as the opportunity, for group action: A measured critique of subject subcultures', in WOODS, P. (Ed), *Teacher Strategies*, London, Croom Helm.

BALLOU, F.W. (1914) *High school organization*, New York, World Book.

BARZUN, J. (1945) *Teacher in America*, Boston, MA, Little, Brown and Co.

BASCIA, N. (in press) *The role of unions in teachers' professional lives: Practical, intellectual, and social concerns*, New York, Teachers College Press.

BECHER, T. (1989) *Academic tribes and territories*, Milton Keyes, UK, The Society for Research into Higher Education and Open University Press.

BELL, L.A., PENNINGTON, R.C. and BURRIDGE, J.B. (1979) 'Going mixed ability: Some observations on one school's experience', *Forum*, 21, 3, pp. 14–17.

BERGER, P. and LUCKMAN, T. (1966) *The social construction of reality*, Garden City, NJ, Doubleday.

BERNSTEIN, B. (1971) 'On the classification and framing of educational knowledge', in YOUNG, M.F.D. (Ed), *Knowledge and control*, London, Collier-Macmillan.

BERNSTEIN, B. (1973) *Class, codes, and control: Towards a theory of educational transmissions*, Vol. 3, London, Routledge and Kegan Paul.

BIGLAN, A. (1973) 'Relationship between subject matter characteristics and the structure and output of university departments', *Journal of Applied Psychology*, 57, 3, pp. 204–13.

BLAU, P.M. (1980) *The organization of academic work*, New York, John Wiley and Sons.

BOYER, E.L. (1983) *High school: A report on secondary education in America*, New York, Harper and Row.

BRANDT, R. (1992) 'On research on teaching: A conversation with Lee Shulman', *Educational Leadership*, 49, 7, pp. 14–19.

BRESSER, R.K. (1984) 'The context of university departments', *Research in Higher Education*, 20, 1, pp. 3–15.

BROOKS, S.D. (1905) 'The extension of the high school influence', *Educational Review*, pp. 433–49.

BROPHY, J.E. and GOOD, T.L. (1986) 'Teacher behavior and student achievement', in WITTROCK, M.C. (Eds) *Handbook of research on teaching* (pp. 328–375), New York, Macmillan.

BROWN, J.F. (1926) *The American high school*, New York, The Macmillan Company.

BRUCKERHOFF (1991) *Between classes: Faculty life at Truman High*, New York, Teachers College Press.

BRYK, A.S., LEE, V. and SMITH, J.B. (1989) 'High school organization and its effects on teachers and students: An interpretive summary of the research', Paper presented at Choice and Control in Public Education conference, University of Wisconsin-Madison.

BURKS, M.P. (1988) *Requirements for certification* (53rd ed.) Chicago, IL, University of Chicago Press.

CAMPBELL, D.T. (1969) 'Ethnocentrism of disciplines and the fish-scale model of omniscience', in SHERIF, M. and SHERIF, C. (Eds) *Interdisciplinary relationships in the social sciences*, Chicago, IL, Aldine, pp. 328–48.

CAPLOW, T. and MCGEE, R.J. (1958) *The academic marketplace*, New York, Basic Books.

CARTER, B.B. (1990) 'The limits of control: Case studies of high school science teachers' responses to state curriculum reform, 1981–1987', Unpublished doctoral dissertation, Stanford, CA, Stanford University.

CHARTERS, W.W. (1969) 'Stability and change in the communication structure of school faculties', *Educational Administration Quarterly*, 5, 3, pp. 15–38.

CLARK, B.R. (1987) *The academic life: Small worlds, different worlds*, Princeton, NJ, The Carnegie Foundation for the Advancement of Teaching.

COHEN, M.D. and MARCH, J.G. (1974) *Leadership and ambiguity: The American college president*, New York, McGraw-Hill.

COLEMAN, J.S. (1988) *Educational research*, New York, *New York Times*, 13 November.

COURT, F.E. (1988) 'The social and historical significance of the first English literature professorship in England', *PMLA*, pp. 796–807.

CRANE, D. (1988) *Invisible colleges*, Chicago, IL, University of Chicago Press.

CREMIN, L.A. (1964) *The transformation of the school: Progressivism in American education 1876–1957*, New York, Vintage Books.

CUBAN, L. (1984) *How teachers taught*, New York, Longman.

CUBAN, L. (1988) *The managerial imperative and the practice of leadership in the schools*, Albany, SUNY Press.

CULLER, J. (1988) 'GRIP's grasp: A comment', *Poetics Today*, 9, 4, pp. 783–9.

CUSICK, P.A. (1973) *Inside high school*, New York, Holt, Rinehart and Winston.

CUSICK, P.A. (1983) *The egalitarian ideal and the American high school*, New York, Longman.

CYERT, R.M. and MARCH, J.G. (1963) *A behavioral theory of the firm*, Englewood Cliffs, NJ, Prentice Hall.

DARLING-HAMMOND, L. (1990) 'Teacher professionalism: Why and how', in LIEBERMAN, A. (Ed) *Schools as collaborative cultures*, New York, The Falmer Press, pp. 25–50.

DEATRICK, M. (1988) *Departments in colleges*, Center for Research on the Context of Secondary School Teaching.

DEMERATH, N. (1967) *Power, presidents and professors*, New York, Basic Books.

DOUGLASS, H.R. (1945) *Organization and administration of secondary schools*, Boston, MA, Ginn and Co.

DOWNING, L. (1950) 'Teaching in the little red schoolhouse: A sketch', in HOFFMAN, N. (Ed) *Woman's 'true' profession*, New York, The Feminist Press, McGraw-Hill.

DREEBEN, R. (1973) 'The school as a workplace', in TRAVER, R. (Ed) *Second handbook of research on teaching*, pp. 450–73.

DURKHEIM, E. (1894) *The division of labor in society*, New York, The Free Press.

EATON, M. (1991) 'Communication networks in four high schools', Paper presented at the American Educational Research Association, Chicago, IL.

EDMONDS, R. (1979) 'Effective schools for the urban poor', *Educational Leadership*, October, pp. 15–23.

ELMORE, R.F. and MCLAUGHLIN, M.W. (1988) *Steady work: Policy, practice, and the reform of American education* (R-3574-NIE/RC), The RAND Corporation.

ELSBREE, W.S. (1939) *The American teacher* (1st ed.), New York, American Book Company.

ERICKSON, G. (1987) 'Teacher perspectives and educational innovation', Unpublished Ph.D. dissertation, University of California, Berkeley.

ESLAND, G. (1972) 'Innovation in the school', in YOUNG, M.F.D. (Ed) *Knowledge and control*, London, Collier-Macmillan.

ETZIONI, A. and LEHMAN, E.W. (1980) *A sociological reader on complex organizations* (3rd ed.), New York, Holt, Rinehart and Winston.

FIRESTONE, W.A. and HERRIOTT, R.E. (1982) 'Two images of schools as organizations: An explication and illustrative empirical test', *Educational Administration Quarterly*, 18, 2, pp. 39–59.

FIRESTONE, W.A., HERRIOTT, R.E. and WILSON, B.L. (1984) *Explaining differences between elementary and secondary schools: Individual, organizational and institutional perspectives*, Philadelphia, Research for Better Schools Inc.

FOUCAULT, M. (1972) *The archaeology of knowledge and the discourse on language*, New York, Pantheon Books.

FREIDSON, E. (1986) *Professional powers: A study of the institutionalization of formal knowledge*, Chicago, IL, University of Chicago Press.

FULLAN, M. (1991) *The new meaning of educational change*, New York, Teachers College Press.

GEERTZ, C. (1983) 'The way we think now: Toward an ethnography of modern thought', in GEERTZ, C. (Ed), *Local knowledge*, New York, Basic Books, pp. 147–63.

GOODLAD, J. (1984) *A place called school*, New York, McGraw Hill.

GOODSON, I.F. (1987) *School subjects and curriculum change* (2nd ed.) London, The Falmer Press.

GOODSON, I.F. (1988a) 'Beyond the subject monolith: Subject traditions and sub-cultures', in WESTOBY, A. (Ed) *Culture and power in educational organizations* Philadelphia, Open University Press, pp. 181–97.

GOODSON, I.F. (1988b) *The making of curriculum*, London, The Falmer Press.

GOULDNER, A.W. (1957) 'Cosmopolitans and locals: Toward an analysis of latent social roles—I', *Administrative Science Quarterly*, 2, 3, pp. 281–306.

GRAFF, G. (1987) *Professing literature: An institutional history*, Chicago, IL, University of Chicago Press.

GROSSMAN, P. (1990) *The making of a teacher*, New York, Teachers College Press.

GUMPORT, P.J. (1989) *E pluribus unum? Cultural conflict in academic organization*, Paper presented at AERA, San Francisco, CA.

HAMPEL, R. (1986) *The last little citadel: American high schools since 1940*, Boston, MA, Houghton Mifflin.

HARGREAVES, A. (1990a) 'Contrived collegiality: The micro-politics of teacher collaboration', in BLASE, J. (Ed) *The politics of life in schools*, New York, Sage Publications, pp. 46–72.

HARGREAVES, A. (1990b) 'Teachers' work and the politics of time and space', *Qualitative Studies in Education*, 3, 4, pp. 303–20.

HARGREAVES, A. and MACMILLAN, R. (1992) *Balkanized secondary schools and the malaise of modernity*, Paper presented at the Annual Conference of the American Educational Research Association, San Francisco, CA.

HARGREAVES, A. (1993) 'Individualism and individuality', in LITTLE, J.W. and MCLAUGHLIN, M.W. (Eds) *Teachers' work*, New York, Teachers College Press, pp. 51–76.

HARGREAVES, D. (1983) 'The teaching of art and the art of teaching', in MAMMERSLEY, M. and HARGREAVES, A. (Eds), *Curriculum practice: Some sociological case studies*, Lewes, The Falmer Press, pp. 127–47.

HARGREAVES, D. (1980) 'The occupational culture of teachers', in WOODS, P. (Ed) *Teacher Strategies*, London, Croom Helm.

HERBST, J. (1989) 'Teacher preparation in the nineteenth century', in WARREN, D. (Eds) *American teachers: Histories of a profession at work*, New York, Macmillan, pp. 213–35.

HERRIOTT, R.E. and FIRESTONE, W.A. (1984) 'Two images of schools as organizations: A refinement and elaboration', *Educational Administration Quarterly*, 20, 4, pp. 41–57.

HILL, D. and BUSSEY, B. (1993) *Building a learning community* (Paper No. P93–149), Center for Research on the Context of Secondary School Teaching, Stanford, CA.

HOYLE, E. (1982) 'Micropolitics of educational organizations', *Educational Management and Administration*, 10, 2, pp. 87–98.

HUBERMAN, M. (1990) 'The model of the independent artisan in teachers' professional relations', Paper presented at the Annual Conference of the American Educational Research Association, Boston, MA. (Revised in LITTLE, J.W. and MCLAUGHLIN, M.W. (Eds) *Teachers' work*, New York, Teachers College Press, pp. 11–50.

JACOBY, R. (1987) *The last intellectuals: American culture in the age of academe*, New York, Basic Books.

JOHNSON, S.M. (1990a) 'The primacy and potential of high and school departments', in MCLAUGHLIN, M.W. TALBERT, J.E. and BASCIA, N. (Eds) *The contexts of teaching in secondary schools: Teachers' realities*, New York, Teachers College Press, pp. 167–84.

JOHNSON, S.M. (1990b) *Teachers at work: Achieving success in our schools*, USA, Basic Books.

JONES, K. and WILLIAMSON, K. (1979) 'The birth of a schoolroom', *Ideology and Consciousness*, 1, 6, pp. 58–110.

KELLER, E.F. (1985) *Reflections on gender and science*, New Haven, CT, Yale University Press.

KILPATRICK, V.E. (1905) 'Departmental teaching in the elementary schools', *Educational Review*, pp. 468–85.

KILPATRICK, V.E. (1907) 'The adaptation of departmental teaching to elementary schools', *Educational Review*, April, pp. 356–67.

KRUG, E.A. (1960) *The secondary school curriculum*, New York, Harper and Row.

KRUG, E.A. (1964) *The shaping of the American high school*, New York, Harper and Row.

KRUG, E.A. (1972) *The shaping of the American high school, Volume 2: 1920–1941*, Madison, WI, University of Wisconsin Press.

KUHN, T.S. (1970) *The structure of scientific revolutions* (2nd ed.), Chicago, IL, University of Chicago Press.

LABAREE, D.F. (1988) *The making of an American high school*, New Haven, CT, Yale University Press.

LABAREE, D.F. (1989) 'Career ladders and the early public high-school teacher', in WARREN, D. (Ed), *American teachers: Histories of a profession at work*, New York, Macmillan, pp. 157–89.

LARSON, M.S. (1977) *The rise of professionalism*, Berkeley, CA University of California Press.

LAWRENCE, P.R. and LORSCH, J.W. (1967) *Organization and environment: Managing differentiation and integration*, Boston, MA, Harvard University.

LEINHARDT, G. (1992) 'What research on learning tells us about teaching', *Educational Leadership*, 49, 7, pp. 20–5.

LEVITT, B. and NASS, C. (1989) 'The lid on the garbage can: Institutional constraints on decision making in the technical core of college-text publishers', *Administrative Science Quarterly*, 34, 2, pp. 190–207.

LIEBERMAN, A. and MILLER, L. (1984) *Teachers, their world, and their work*, Alexandria VA, Association for Supervision and Curriculum Development.

LIEBERMAN, A. and MILLER, L. (1990) 'The social realities of teaching', in LIEBERMAN, A. (Ed), *Schools as collaborative cultures*, London, The Falmer Press.

LIGHTFOOT, S.L. (1983) *The good high school: Portraits of character and culture*, New York, Basic Books.

LIGHTFOOT, S.L. (1985) 'Rosemont High', in PERRONE, V. (Ed) *Portraits of high schools*, Princeton, NJ, Carnegie Foundation for the Advancement of Teaching.

LINCOLN, Y.S. (1986) 'Toward a future-oriented comment on the state of the professions', *The Review of Higher Education*, 10, 2, pp. 135–42.

LITTLE, J.W. (1982) 'Norms of collegiality and experimentation: Workplace conditions of school success', *American Educational Research Journal*, 19, pp. 325–40.

LITTLE, J.W. (1987) 'Teachers as colleagues', in RICHARDSON-KOEHLER, V. (Ed) *Educators' handbook: A research perspective*, New York, Longman, pp. 491–518.

LITTLE, J.W. (1990a) 'Conditions of professional development in secondary schools', in MCLAUGHLIN, M.W., TALBERT, J.E. and BASCIA, N. (Eds) *The contexts of teaching in secondary schools: Teachers' realities*, New York, Teachers College Press, pp. 187–223.

LITTLE, J.W. (1990b) 'The persistence of privacy: autonomy and initiative in teachers' professional relations', *Teachers College Record*, 91, 4, pp. 509–36.

LITTLE, J.W. (1990c) 'Recovering the story: Narrative perspectives in the study of teachers' professional identity and community', Unpublished manuscript.

LITTLE, J.W. (1991) 'What do you mean "we?" The social construction of professional identity and community among secondary school teachers', Unpublished manuscript.

LITTLE, J.W. (1993) 'Professional community in comprehensive high schools: The two worlds of academic and vocational teachers', in LITTLE, J.W. and MCLAUGHLIN, M.W. (Eds) *Teachers' work*, New York, Teachers College Press, pp. 137–63.

LITTLE, J.W. and MCLAUGHLIN, M.W. (1991) *As teachers tell it: The urban math collaborative*, Center for Research on the Context of Teaching in Secondary Schools, Stanford, CA, Stanford University.

LITTLE, J.W. and THREATT, S.M. (1991) *Work on the margins: The experience of vocational teachers in comprehensive high schools*, National Center for Research on Vocational Education, Berkeley, CA, University of California Press.

LODAHL, J. and GORDON, G. (1972) 'The structure of scientific fields and the functioning of university graduate departments', *American Sociological Review*, 37, pp. 57–72.

LODAHL, J. and GORDON, G. (1973) 'Differences between physical and social sciences in university graduate departments', *Research in Higher Education*, 1, pp. 191–213.

LORTIE, D. (1975) *Schoolteacher*, Chicago, IL, University of Chicago Press.

LOUIS, K.S. and MILES, M.B. (1990) *Improving the urban high school: What works and why*, New York, Teachers College Press.

MARCH, J.G. (1965) *Handbook of organizations*, Chicago, IL, Rand McNally.

MARCH, J.G. (1988) *Decisions and organizations*, Oxford, Basil Blackwell.

MARCH, J.G. and OLSEN, J.P. (1976) *Ambiguity and choice in organizations*, Bergen, Norway, Universitetsforlaget.

MCLAUGHLIN, M.W. (1987) 'Learning from experience: Lessons from policy implementation', *Educational Evaluation and Policy Analysis*, 9, 2, pp. 171–78.

MCLAUGHLIN, M.W. (1993) 'What matters most in teachers workplace context?', in LITTLE, J.W. and MCLAUGHLIN, M.W. (Eds) *Teachers' Work*, New York, Teachers College Press, pp. 79–103.

MCLAUGHLIN, M.W., PFEIFER, R.S. and YEE, S.M. (1986) 'Why teachers won't teach', *Phi Delta Kappan*, 67 (February), pp. 420–26.

MCLAUGHLIN, M.W. and TALBERT, J.E. (1993) *Contexts that matter for teaching and learning*, Stanford, CA, Center for Research on the Context of Secondary School Teaching.

MCLAUGHLIN, M.W., TALBERT, J.E. and BASCIA, N. (Eds) (1990) *The contexts of teaching in secondary schools: Teachers' realities*, New York, Teachers College Press.

MCLAUGHLIN, M.W., TALBERT, J.E. and PHELAN, P. (1990) *1990 Report to field sites*, Stanford, CA, Center for Research on the Context of Secondary School Teaching.

MEASOR, L. (1983) 'Gender and the sciences: Pupil's gender-based conceptions of school subjects', in HAMMERSLEY, M. and HARGREAVES, A. (Eds) *Curriculum practice: Some sociological case studies*, London, The Falmer Press, pp. 171–91.

MERTON, R.K. (1975) 'Structional analysis in sociology', in PLAU, P. (Ed) *Approaches to the study of social structure*, New York, The Free Press.

METZ, M.H. (1978) *Classrooms and corridors: The crisis of authority in desegregated secondary schools*, Berkeley; CA, University of California Press.

METZ, M.H. (1990) 'How social class differences shape teachers' work', in MCLAUGHLIN, M., TALBERT, J. and BASCIA, N. (Eds) *The contexts of teaching in secondary schools*, New York, Teachers College Press, pp. 40–107.

MEYER, J.W. and ROWAN, B. (1978) 'The structure of educational organizations', in MEYER, M. *et al.* (Ed) *Environments and Organizations*, San Francisco, CA, Jossey-Bass, pp. 78–109.

MEYER, J.W. and SCOTT, R.W. (1983) *Organizational environments*, Beverly Hills, CA, Sage Publications.

MEYER, J.W., SCOTT, R.W., STRANG, D. and CREIGHTON, A. (1986) 'Bureaucratization without centralization: Changes in the organizational system of American public education 1940–1980', in ZUCKER, L. (Ed) *Institutional patterns and organizations*, Boston, MA, Pitman.

MEYER, M.W. and BROWN, M.C. (1980) 'The process of bureaucratization', in ETZIONI, A. and LEHMAN, E.W. (Ed) *A Socological Reader on Complex Organizations*, New York, Holt, Rinehart and Winston, pp. 441–60.

MILES, M.B. and HUBERMAN, A.M. (1984) *Qualitative data analysis*, Beverly Hills, CA, Sage Publications.

MORSS, C.H. (1905) 'The practicability of the extension of high school influence', *Educational Review*, pp. 441–9.

MUSGROVE, F. (1968) 'The contribution of sociology to the study of curriculum', in KERR, J.F. (Ed) *Changing the Curriculum*, London, University of London Press.

MYERS, J.E. (1964) The educational work of Andrew Jackson Moulder in the development of public education in California, 1850–1895, Unpublished doctoral dissertation, University of California.

NBPTS (1989) *Recommended standards*, National Board of Professional Teaching Standards.

NEA (1972) *Status of the American public school teacher* (1972–R3), Washington, DC, National Education Association.

NEA (1987) *Status of the American public school teacher 1985–86*. Washington DC, National Education Association.

NEUFELD, B. (1984) 'Inside organizations: High school teachers' efforts to influence their work', Unpublished Doctoral Dissertation, Cambridge, MA, Harvard University.

NIAS, J. (1989) *Primary teachers talking: A study of teaching as work*, London, Routledge.

NIAS, J., SOUTHWORTH, G. and YEOMANS, R. (1989) *Staff relationships in the primary school*, London, Cassells.

OLSEN, J.P. (1979) 'University governance: Non-participation as exclusion or choice', in MARCH, J.G. and OLSEN, J.P. (Eds) *Ambiguity and choice in organizations*, Bergen, Norway, Universitetsforlaget, pp. 277–313.

PERKIN, H. (1984) 'The historical perspective', in CLARK, B.R. (Ed) *Perspectives on higher education*, Berkeley, CA, University of California Press, pp. 17–55.

PERRONE, V. (1985) *Portraits of high schools*, Princeton, NJ, Carnegie Foundation for the Advancement of Teaching.

PERROW, C. (1970) 'Departmental power and perspective in industrial firms', in ZALD, M.N. (Ed) *Power in organizations*, Nashville, TN, Vanderbilt University Press.

PFEFFER, J. (1977) 'Power and resource allocation in organizations', in STAW, B. and SALANCIK, G. (Ed) *New directions in organizational behavior*, Chicago, IL, St. Clair Press.

PFEFFER, J. (1981) *Power in Organizations*, Marshfield, MA, Pitman Publishing Co.

PFEFFER, J. and SALANCIK, G.R. (1980) 'Organizational decision making, as a political process: The case of a university budget', in KATZ, D., KAHN, R. and ADAMS, J.S. (Eds) *The study of organizations*, San Francisco, CA, Jossey Bass, pp. 397–413.

PFEFFER, J., SALANCIK, G.R. and LEBLEBICI, H. (1976) 'The effect of uncertainty on the use of social influence in organizational decision making', *Administrative Science Quarterly*, 21 (June), pp. 227–45.

PFEIL, D.S. (1989) *Footsteps*, Albany, NY, Albany Academy for Girls.

POPKEWITZ, T.S. (1987) *The struggle for creating an American institution*, New York, The Falmer Press.

POWELL, A.G. (1980) *The uncertain profession*, Cambridge, MA, Harvard University Press.

POWELL, A.G., FARRAR, E. and COHEN, D.C. (1985) *The shopping mall high school*, Boston, MA, Houghton Mifflin.

PURKEY, S.C. and SMITH, M.S. (1983) 'Effective schools: A Review', *Elementary School Journal*, 83, 4, pp. 427–52.

REYES, P. (Ed) (1990) *Teachers and their workplace*, Beverly Hills, CA, Sage Publications.

RISEBOROUGH, G. (1981) 'Teachers' careers and comprehensive schooling: An empirical study', *Sociology*, 15, 3, pp. 352–81.

ROETHLISBERGER, F. and DICKSON, W.J. (1939) *Management and the worker*, Cambridge, MA, Harvard University Press.

ROGERS, E.M. and KINCAID, D.L. (1981) *Communication networks: Toward a new paradigm for research*, New York, The Free Press.

ROSENHOLZ, S.J. (1989) *Teachers' workplace: The social organization of schools*, New York, Longman.

ROWAN, B., RAUDENBUSH, S.W. and KANG, S.J. (1989) *School climate in secondary schools: Towards a multilevel model* (88–1300), Center for Research on the Context of Secondary Teaching, Stanford, CA, Stanford University.

RURY, J.L. (1989) 'Who became teachers?: The social characteristics of teachers in American history', in WARREN, D. (Ed) *American teachers: Histories of a profession at work*, New York, Macmillan, pp. 9–48.

RUTTER, M., MAUGHAN, B., MORTIMORE, P. and OUSTON, J. (1979) *Fifteen thousand hours*, Cambridge, MA, Harvard University Press.

ST. JOHN-BROOKS, C. (1983) 'English: A curriculum for personal development', in HAMMERSLEY, M. and HARGREAVES, A. (Eds)

Curriculum practice: Some sociological case studies, Lewes, The Falmer Press.

SARASON, S.B., LEVINE, M., GOLDENBERG, I., CHERLIN, D. and BENNETT, E. (1966) *Psychology in community settings*, New York, John Wiley and Sons.

SCHEIN, E.H. (1985) *Organizational culture and leadership*, San Francisco, CA, Jossey-Bass.

SCOTT, J.W. (1988) *Gender and the politics of history*, New York, Columbia University Press.

SCOTT, W.R. (1987) *Organizations: Rational, natural, and open systems* (2nd ed.), Englewood Cliffs, NJ, Prentice-Hall.

SCOTT, W.R. (1989) *Work-units in organizations: Ransacking the literature*, Center for Research on the Context of Secondary School Teaching, Stanford CA.

SEDLAK, M.W. and SCHLOSSMAN, S. (1986) *Who will teach* (R-3472-CSTP), The RAND Corporation.

SEDLAK, M.W. (1988) 'Let us go and buy a schoolmaster: Historical perspectives on the hiring of teachers in the United States, 1750–1980', Unpublished manuscript.

SERGIOVANNI, T.J. (1984) *Handbook for effective department leadership* (2nd ed.), Boston, MA, Alleyn and Bacon.

SHIBUTANI, T. (1955) 'Reference groups as perspectives', *American Journal of Sociology*, 60, pp. 522–9.

SHIBUTANI, T. (1977) 'Reference groups and social control', in ROSE, A.M. (Ed) *Human behavior and social processes*, London, Routledge and Kegan Paul.

SHULMAN, L.S. (1986) 'Paradigms and research programs in the study of teaching: A contemporary perspective', in WITTROCK, M.C. (Ed) *Handbook of research on teaching*, New York, Macmillan Publishing Co, pp. 3–36.

SHULMAN, L.S. (1987) 'Knowledge and teaching: Foundations of the new reform', *Harvard Education Review*, 57, 1, pp. 1–22.

SHUMWAY, D.R. and MESSER-DAVIDOW, E. (1991) 'Disciplinarity: An introduction', *Poetics Today*, 12, 2, pp. 201–25.

SIROTNIK, K.A. (1983) 'What you see is what you get: Consistency, persistency, and mediocrity in classrooms', *Harvard Educational Review*, 53, 1, pp. 16–31.

SISKIN, L.S. (1991) 'Departments as different worlds: Subject subcultures in secondary schools', *Educational Administration Quarterly*, 27, 2, pp. 134–60.

SISKIN, L.S. (1993) *Hermaphroditic roles: Teacher Leadership in Secondary Schools*, Paper presented at International Study Association on Teacher Thinking Conference, Gothenburg, Sweden.

SISKIN, L.S. (1994, in press) 'Is the school the unit of change? Internal and external contexts of restructuring', in GRIMMETT, P.P. and

NEUFELD, J.P. (Eds) *The struggle for authenticity: Teacher development in a changing educational context*, New York, Teachers College Press.

SIZER, T.R. (1964) *Secondary schools at the turn of the century*, New Haven, CT, Yale University Press.

SIZER, T.R. (1984) *Horace's compromise: The dilemma of the American high school*, Boston, MA, Houghton Mifflin.

SIZER, T. (1992) *Horace's school: Redesigning the American high school*, New York, Houghton Mifflin.

SMETHERHAM, D. (1979) 'Identifying teacher strategies', *CORE*, 3, 3.

SMITH, F.W. (1916) *The high school: A study of origins and tendencies*, New York, Sturgis and Walton.

SNOW, C.P. (1959 (reprint 1969)) *The two cultures and a second look* (2nd ed.), London, Cambridge University Press.

STINCHCOMBE, A.L. (1965) 'Social structure and organizations', in MARCH, J.G. (Ed) *Handbook of organizations*, Chicago, IL, Rand McNally, pp. 142–93.

STODOLSKY, S. (1988) *The subject matters: Classroom activity in math and social studies*, Chicago, IL, University of Chicago Press.

STRAUSS, A. (1978) 'A social world perspective', *Studies in Symbolic Interaction*, 1, pp. 119–28.

STROTHER, D.B. (1987) 'An interview with Michael Kirst: Bridging the gap between policy and research', *Phi Delta Kappan*, 69, 2, pp. 161–4.

SYKES, G. (1986) *The social consequences of standard setting in the professions*, Carnegie Forum on Education and the Economy.

TALBERT, J.E. (1980) *School Organization and Institutional Change: Exchange and Power in Loosely Coupled Systems*, IFG, Stanford, CA, Stanford University.

TALBERT, J.E. (1991) *Boundaries of teachers' professional communities in US high schools* (No. P91–130), Center for Research on the Context of Secondary School Teaching, Stanford, CA, Stanford University.

TAYLOR, F.W. (1911 (reprint 1967)) *The principles of scientific management*, New York, Norton.

THEOBALD, P. (1991) 'How to catch an elephant', *PC Report* (Boston Computer Society), 10, 7, pp. 46–7.

THORNDIKE, E.L. (1907) 'A neglected aspect of the American high school', *Educational Review*, March, pp. 245–55.

TRICAMO, T. (1984) 'Departmental decision-making: The relationship of prestige and paradigm development to control and consensus', Unpublished doctoral dissertation, Stanford, CA, Stanford University.

TROW, M. (1976) 'The American academic department as a context for learning', *Studies in Higher Education*, 1, 1, pp. 11–23.

TUCKER, M. (1986) 'Preface: Academic alliances', *American Association for Higher Education*, 1.

TYACK, D.B. (1967) *Turning points in American educational history*, Waltham, MA, Blaisdell Publishing Co.

TYACK, D.B. (1974) *The one best system*, Cambridge, MA, Harvard University Press.

TYACK, D.B. (1976) 'Ways of seeing: An essay on the history of compulsive schooling', *Harvard Educational Review*, 46, 3, pp. 355–89.

TYACK, D.B. (1991) 'Public school reform: Policy talk and institutional practice', Unpublished manuscript.

TYACK, D.B. and HANSOT, E. (1982) *Managers of Virtue*, New York, Basic Books.

TYLER, W.B. (1988) 'The organizational structure of the school', in WESTOBY, A. (Ed) *Culture and power in educational organizations*, Milton Keynes, Open University Press, pp. 15–40.

VAN MAANEN, J. and BARLEY, S. (1984) 'Occupational communities: Culture and control in organizations', *Research in Organizational Behavior*, 6, pp. 287–365.

WALLER, W. (1932/1967) *The sociology of teaching*, New York, John Wiley and Sons.

WEICK, K. (1976) 'Educational organizations as loosely coupled systems', *Administrative Science Quarterly*, 21 (March), pp. 1–19.

WILLOWER, D.J. and SMITH, J.P. (1986) *Organizational culture in schools: Myth and creation*, paper presented at AERA, San Francisco, CA.

WILSON, B. and CORCORAN, T. (1988) *Successful secondary schools*, New York, The Falmer Press.

WILSON, B.L. and HERRIOTT, R.E. (1990) *Formal subunits within American public schools: Their structure, power, and consequences*, Philadelphia, PA, Research for Better Schools.

WILSON, E. (1988) 'A short history of a border war: Social science, school reform, and the study of literature', *Poetics Today*, 9, 4, pp. 711–36.

WILSON, S.M. and WINEBURG, S.S. (1988) 'Peering at history: The role of disciplinary perspectives in the teaching of American history', *Teachers College Record*, 89, pp. 525–39.

WINEBURG, S.S. and WILSON, S.M. (1991) 'Subject-matter knowledge in the teaching of history', in BROPHY, J.E. (Ed) *Advances in Research on Teaching*, USA, JAI Press, pp. 305–47.

YEE, S.M.L. (1990) *Careers in the classroom*, New York, Teachers College Press.

YIN, R.K. (1984) *Case study research*, Beverly Hills, CA, Sage Publications.

YOUNG, M.F.D. (Ed) (1971) *Knowledge and control*, London, Collier-Macmillan.

Index